Over the Moon

Over the Moon

MY AUTOBIOGRAPHY

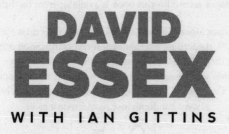

DAVID ESSEX

WITH IAN GITTINS

Virgin BOOKS

1 3 5 7 9 10 8 6 4 2

First published in the UK in 2012 by Virgin Books
This edition published in 2013 by Virgin Books, an imprint of Ebury Publishing
A Random House Group company

www.randomhouse.co.uk

Addresses for companies within the Random House Group can be found at:
www.randomhouse.co.uk

The Random House Group Limited Reg. No. 954009

A CIP catalogue record for this book is available from the British Library

The Random House Group Limited supports the Forest Stewardship
Council® (FSC®), the leading international forest-certification organisation. Our
books carrying the FSC label are printed on FSC®-certified paper. FSC is the only
forest-certification scheme supported by the leading environmental organisations,
including Greenpeace. Our paper procurement policy can be found at:
www.randomhouse.co.uk/environment

Printed and bound by CPI Group (UK) Ltd, Croydon, CR0 4YY

ISBN 9780753540343

To buy books by your favourite authors and register for offers visit:
www.randomhouse.co.uk

CONTENTS

INTRODUCTION

FROM JESUS TO
EDDIE MOON

The writer F Scott Fitzgerald said there are no second acts in American lives. I guess I must be lucky I'm British, then, as I reckon by now I have been through acts two, three, four and five and must be on the encore.

I recently spent five months on *EastEnders* playing that lovable rogue with a dark past, Eddie Moon. It was a privilege to be part of one of the biggest shows on British TV and I had a fantastic time making it. People seemed to take to Eddie, and I guess for a lot of people under thirty, that will be what they think when they see me now: Eddie Moon.

For people a little older than that, however, it is a different story entirely. They may well focus on one of my many incarnations in the past. Maybe they will remember me as Jesus, or at least his human form on earth, when I first emerged from obscurity in the musical *Godspell* all those years ago.

They might, however, prefer to think of David Essex the singer and songwriter, the pop star with the mop of gypsy curls who enjoyed a string of chart-topping hits and who for a while seemed to be on the front cover of *Jackie* magazine every week.

I know for some folk, I will forever be the smiling waif who sang 'Rock On' and 'Hold Me Close'.

Maybe others will always see me as Jim MacLaine, the angst-ridden anti-hero of the movies *That'll Be the Day* and *Stardust*, the working-class boy who longed to be a rock star and found fame and fortune only for them to destroy him. Jim seemed to leave a mark on a lot of people: he certainly left one on me.

I've been told by some people they will always think of me as the iconic revolutionary, Che Guevara, who had so much impact when I played him on stage in Tim Rice and Andrew Lloyd Webber's *Evita*. And for a few, I will always be the amiable lock-keeper with a dodgy past from TV show *The River*.

I think I have had quite a life – or quite a few lives – to date. I have written West End musicals, scored ballets and even (don't laugh) starred in a ninja action movie. And that's before we even mention the pantomimes, a novelty single and a *Carry On* film (yes, really) in my early years.

So a lot happened before I spent a while as Eddie Moon, and now feels like the time to reflect and tell my life story. I think it's a fairly extraordinary tale, and it began in a post-war East End district that was every bit as poor as Walford: a place called Canning Town.

1

YOU CAN TAKE THE BOY
OUT OF THE EAST END...

Over the years, people have made a lot of my relatively poor background and impoverished upbringing, but it never felt bad to me. As a kid, what you know is all you know, and my life always seemed fine and dandy. I could not have had two more loving parents, and when I think back, I remember a very happy childhood.

I wasn't quite a war baby but I wasn't far off. I made my first appearance on 23 July 1947, at a maternity hospital in West Ham in the heart of the East End. Forceps were involved. I was a bit on the light side, at six pounds four ounces, and was yellow with jaundice, so I can't have looked all that good.

I wasn't David Essex in those days, of course. I was born David Albert Cook, to my two loving parents, Albert and Olive – not that anybody ever called her that. My mum was a petite woman, very beautiful and full of life, who looked a bit like a doll and so went by the nickname Dolly, and that was what everyone knew her as.

The three of us were very lucky to be around. My parents had an eventful war. My dad, who worked on the docks when

London's Docklands really *was* docklands, had been conscripted into the Royal Artillery when hostilities broke out. He was stationed on the big guns in Dover, and got posted up to Sunderland for a while.

My dad had to get a twenty-four-hour pass to marry my mum and it was the luckiest thing he ever did, in more ways than one. He turned up at the church on the back of his brother George's motorbike as my mum waited for him in her BHS wedding dress. My dad's battalion set sail for Norway without him: they got blown out of the water, with no survivors.

This wasn't the only close call my dad experienced: the Germans scored a direct hit on his gun nest once, but he escaped with just a burn. As for my mum, living in the East End, she was exposed to the full horrors of the Blitz. One of the many times that the sirens sounded, she and her sister ran to a local school. They were turned away because the basement was full and fled to the tube station. The bombers scored a direct hit on the school.

Another time, Mum was walking in a country lane in Kent with her sister and niece when a Messerschmitt appeared in the sky and started machine-gunning them. They tried to escape down a manhole but couldn't get the cover off so ran to a nearby house and banged on the door, screaming, with the pilot still firing at them. How can a human being do that: try to blow up two women and a little girl? Luckily, he gave up and flew off.

Remarkably, Albert and Dolly came out of the war in one piece, except for a bit of damage to my mum's hearing, and set up home in a rented one-bedroom flat in Redriff Road, Plaistow. They were keen to start a family as soon as possible. Mum says she always knew she would have a boy and she was always going to call him David: maybe her gypsy roots gave her this inkling.

My mum was one of seven kids and her dad, Tom Kemp, was a gypsy. On her wedding certificate, it gave his job as 'Travelling Tinker'. When he first came over from Ireland, he moved around the country and made saucepans. Sadly, I never met him: he died before I was born.

Tom had been married before, to a gypsy woman. When she died and Tom married my nan, Olive, his first wife's mother came over from Ireland and stood outside Nan's house, cursing her. Dressed all in black, she waved a silver sovereign necklace at her door and said she would never have a penny in the world. Coincidence or not, that's just how Olive senior's life worked out.

From my parents' accounts, I was a happy baby and toddler and spent my time pouring my food over my head and falling over. The problem was that our Plaistow landlord didn't allow children in his flat, so Mum and Dad decided to move out and put our names down for one of the high-rise council flats that were replacing the bombed terraces of the East End.

This left us with nowhere to live in the short term, so we went to stay with my mum's sister, Aunt Ellen, her husband Uncle Bob and my cousin Rose in Canning Town. Their council house had a small garden and they were gracious hosts but it was cramped with all of us there, and even though I was only two years old, I think I sensed we were in the way.

My dad was back on the docks by now, and every day my mum would take me out in my second-hand pushchair to get us out from under Aunt Ellen's feet. We'd walk around Rathbone Street Market in Canning Town, a hubbub of stallholders and shoppers that felt like the most exciting place in the world, or take our ration book to the butcher's to get a few scrag-ends of meat.

This routine went on for a year, with the council showing no interest in offering us a home, so my parents tried to force their hand. After a brief family conference, it was agreed that Ellen and Bob would 'order' us to leave, and my dad would tell the authorities that we were homeless.

This plan backfired in a major way: the council put us into a workhouse.

I say workhouse, but a lot of people would call it a nuthouse. Forest House in James Lane, Whipps Cross was an institution for the homeless and the mentally ill. There was no room there for my dad, so he had to stay with his sister, Ivy, in Barking and pay the eighteen-bob-a-week rent for Mum and me to share a poky, curtained cubicle with a single bed and a cupboard.

Forest House was full of women and kids in the same desperate situation as us, crammed into tiny living units and all sharing one kitchen. Sixty years on, I can still picture the pink roses on the cubicle curtains, and remember the harsh smell of hospital antiseptic that lingered around its long cream corridors.

Forest House seemed massive to me, and as a wide-eyed kid I found it fascinating. It had a surreal, almost fairy-tale air. Troubled inmates trudged the corridors, singing to themselves. I got to know a few of them. One man asked me one morning if I would like some conkers, and returned that evening with a coal sack of them.

Another man asked Dad during one of his nightly evening visits if he would like him to fix his broken watch. He took it away and returned it in a hundred pieces, confessing that he 'didn't know how to fix them ones'. Yet Forest House had its dark side: I can remember one thrashing inmate being restrained as he had an epileptic fit.

My mum and I would have breakfast every morning at seven and clear out for the day. We'd walk around nearby Wanstead Flats or get the bus over to my nan in Stratford. These journeys could be a problem. As a toddler, I had blond ringlets, and Mum and I couldn't go anywhere without some old lady stopping us to coo over how 'sweet' I was. A shy kid, I hated this attention and normally reacted by bursting into tears.

Our six months in Forest House were an adventure for me, but I could sense sadness in my parents, and that period was awful for them. Once we had left, we never discussed it. The one time that we did, my mum confessed she had thought of jumping off the fire escape by our cubicle and ending it all. She said she would have done, if she hadn't had me.

It was just as bad for my dad. He was a proud man, and felt he had let us down. He came from an even bigger family than Mum as the youngest of thirteen. His father, a stern Victorian Scotsman from Glasgow, never called him by his real name, Albert: he called him 'One Too Many'. What a great ego boost that must have been!

Dad was a very smart man – if he hadn't come from such a poor family, I reckon he would have gone to university – and beneath his East End bravado and bluster, he was sensitive. His torment came to an end in the spring of 1951 when the council finally kept their word and gave us a prefab in Hooper Road, Custom House. It even had a garden.

Our new abode might have looked like a Nissan hut but to us it was paradise. Mum and Dad painted and decorated the inside, Dad turfed the garden, and at three years old I finally had my own bedroom. The docks were at the end of the street, and I loved gazing up at the ocean-going liners that towered over the terraced houses.

My dad vanished to that mysterious place every day. Now and then he'd take me along and his burly workmates would ruffle my hair and ask me, 'You all right, son? I can tell you're a little Cooky!' It made me feel ten feet tall. I watched them unloading cargoes of New Zealand lamb, smelled the oils and spices and gawped at the Indian and Chinese sailors walking around. It all felt so alien and exotic and I always assumed that I would work there one day.

Dad was my best friend and my hero and I couldn't have been happier in Hooper Road. The day's highlight was Dad coming home from work and, after we'd had tea, taking me out on the crossbar of his bike. We'd pedal for miles around the East End, soaking in the sights and sounds, me always urging him to go faster.

My world fell apart at Christmas 1951 when Dad contracted tuberculosis. He had been getting weaker for a while and had become less keen to take me out on the bike, telling me he was tired, but on New Year's Eve he gave in to my pleadings and we set off. We hadn't gone far when he had a violent coughing fit and turned back. By the time we got home, he was coughing up blood.

As the ambulance took my dad away, I felt as if my life was ending. He was twenty-eight and a doctor told him he was going to die. He didn't, but he spent three long months convalescing at the Victoria Chest Hospital in Hertfordshire. The house felt empty without him.

It used to take Mum and me a whole day to get to Hertfordshire and back to visit him, on the days she wasn't working as a pub cleaner. When we got there, we couldn't go near him because TB is so contagious. I can still picture the big photo of me that Dad had by his bed. I used to envy the photo, and wish that I were sitting there instead.

While Dad was still away I began my school career, at a nursery in Canning Town called Dockland Settlement nursery school. On my first day, as Mum let go of my hand and said goodbye, I felt nervous and intimidated. As an only child I hadn't been around other kids, and suddenly there were thirty of them chasing around, screaming and snatching toys off each other. I held back, stayed quiet and watched the chaos around me, but after a couple of weeks as an awkward outsider, I made a few friends.

The main distinguishing feature of Dockland Settlement was that its headmaster was the Reverend David Sheppard, the former England cricket captain who went on to be the Bishop of Liverpool. Reverend Sheppard was a lovely man who took an interest in me, mainly because he thought I might be decent at sport. He always told my mum he thought I was a bit special, which she obviously loved – but when he said I was good at football or cricket, I wished that Dad were there to hear it.

Dad finally came home from Hertfordshire and it was wonderful to have him back, although the tuberculosis had left its mark. He didn't have the strength and energy that he had before and he looked older. He wasn't well enough to go straight back to work so spent the first few weeks convalescing.

This change was hard on Mum. She was a vivacious, vibrant woman who loved dancing but now Dad couldn't join in and had to just sit and watch if they went out. The TB also put paid to any prospect of me having a brother or sister. I was OK with this, having never known anything different, but Mum would have liked more kids.

The good news was that we were about to go up in the world – literally. The council gave us a new flat on the third floor of a Canning Town low-rise, Avondale Court. Compared with the prefab, this was luxury. It had two bedrooms, a lounge and a kitchen, and a balcony that overlooked a playground. I would play football down there, and if I scored a goal, I could look up to the balcony for Dad's thumbs-up acknowledgement.

I lived in a lot of different places as a nipper but Avondale Court was the one that really felt like home. I used to love gazing out from the balcony and seeing the Docklands cranes – sadly, now all gone – and two massive milk-bottle-shaped chimneys on the horizon, belching out white smoke. Dad told me it was the local power station, but secretly, and poetically, I figured they were cloud-making machines.

Every Sunday my nan, Olive, would get the 69 bus over from Stratford to see us. I used to love her visits. She'd swear like a trooper and roll her own cigarettes and she always brought me sweets. I had to sing for my supper, though: she'd say, 'Come on Dave, do a show!' and I'd sing stuff like, 'What a mouth, what a mouth, what a north-and-south.'

Back in the world of education, I ended my innings at Reverend Sheppard's nursery and graduated to my first proper school – Star Lane Primary. If my arrival at Docklands Settlement had fazed me, Star Lane gave me no problems at all. On my first day, as terrified infants sobbed around me, I bade my mum a cheery farewell and marched straight in.

Maybe I sensed that I would be blissfully happy there. Star Lane was a typical massive old three-floor redbrick Victorian school, with two playgrounds and, importantly for me, a huge playing field for sports. I loved the place from the second I set eyes on it until the day I left.

I guess a school is only as good as its teachers and Star Lane had some excellent ones. The headmistress, Miss Hood, was an inspirational figure. All the kids loved her. She saw something in me and was always very supportive, and in turn I always wanted to do well to impress her.

I spent a blissful time at Star Lane playing and learning the three Rs. On summer afternoons, the staff would line up temporary beds under the playground trees for the kids to have a nap, and I would lie there daydreaming, watching the branches flutter in the breeze and hearing the lorries rumble past on their way to the docks.

I enjoyed my classwork too. We had a very charismatic English teacher, a Welshman called Mr Lloyd, who weaved spells in his rich, redolent accent and could control a class by force of personality rather than with a cane, unlike some teachers. His love for his subject permeated through to us.

Yet for all Mr Lloyd's noble efforts, English was not my first love. That was sport and, in particular, football. Star Lane had two PE teachers: an elderly gentleman called Mr Dunlop and another Welshman called Mr Morgan, who would bellow at us like a sergeant major as we ran laps of the rainy playing field. Most kids thought he was a psycho, but I never minded him.

Back at home, Dad was still recuperating from his illness and signing on for sickness benefit, which he hated. The TB had left him with only half of one lung fully functioning. He longed to get back to the docks, but knowing that he would no longer be able to heave heavy cargo off ships, he sat exams and became a tally clerk instead.

Mum carried on cleaning the pub and also sometimes played the piano there in the evenings – she was quite good, in a Winifred Atwell sort of way. They would have good old East End singsongs around the Joanna, and I remember a few balmy evenings sitting outside the pub, scoffing crisps and lemonade and hearing the music drift out of the door. This wasn't when I fell in love with music, though. That came later.

By the time I was seven, Mum was working full-time in a local electrical shop so I became a latchkey kid. Every day I would get home at 4 p.m. from Star Lane and stick my hand through the letterbox to grab the key dangling on a piece of string. I'd let myself in, munch down the bread and jam Mum had left for me, then head down to the playground to play football until my parents got in at seven. Far from feeling under-privileged, I loved it: it made me feel free, independent and grown up.

Admittedly, I might have taken this free-spirit thing a bit too far once or twice. Fireworks Night was big news around my way, with the post-Blitz wastelands of the East End being perfect for huge bonfires. Boys ran around hurling bangers at each other in firework fights. I got in bad trouble when I threw a sparkler at a girl, setting her hair alight. Secretly, I was proud of my aim: a direct hit from our top-floor balcony that would have impressed Reverend Sheppard. Well, maybe not.

But Sparklergate was not the worst of my fireworks-related atrocities. When I was about nine years old, I committed a crime for which I was never accused, convicted or punished, as a mild-mannered, easy-going East End schoolboy somehow became the dastardly Canning Town Arsonist.

The seeds of my misdemeanour were planted when I got hold of a box of coloured matches. Wandering around in my shorts and sandals one early evening, getting bored of lighting them and watching them fizzle out, I came to a piece of wasteland that doubled up as an overnight lorry park for truckers waiting to unload at the docks. There were about eight lorries there, with no drivers around.

With no particular purpose in mind, I walked around the lorries and clambered over a couple of them. I have no idea what made me suddenly remember the matches, or why I did what I did next, but at the time it made all the sense in the world for me to unscrew one of the truck's fuel cap and throw a lit match down into the tank.

Disappointingly, nothing happened, so I repeated the experiment a couple more times before having a brainwave. Why not light one of the matches, put it back into the box and drop the whole thing into the fuel cap? Half the box would be aflame by then – how could it possibly fail?

I expected a pretty flame to shoot out of the fuel pipe and then gently subside but my fiendish plan worked beyond my wildest dreams – or nightmares. As the matchbox hit the petrol tank, a twenty-foot flame shot out of the pipe – whoosh! The tarpaulin caught fire, and suddenly I was gawping at a towering inferno on wheels.

I turned tail and ran for my life, probably quite literally. Bang! The lorry exploded in a way I had only ever seen in Hollywood movies and the fireball consumed the lorry next to it ... and the one next to that. As I raced the quarter-mile home, the noises of explosion after explosion followed me, and clouds of black smoke filled the night sky. 'Are you all right?' asked Mum, as I tumbled, panting, through the doorway. 'Yeah,' I lied. 'We were just having a race.'

Jesus Christ, what had I done? For the next week I lived in terror of being exposed as the local schoolboy pyromaniac, but as days passed with no comeback I realised that I was going to get away with it. My heart missed a few beats when that week's *Stratford Express* led with THE CANNING TOWN ARSON ATTACK but thankfully the police didn't widen their search to include butter-wouldn't-melt-in-their-mouths little local boys.

It must have been thirty years before I finally dared to tell my mum the terrible truth. One day when I was visiting her, I asked her, 'Do you remember that big old lorry fire by Harry the Barber's when I was a boy?'

'Yes, it was terrible – imagine someone doing that!' she replied.

'Mum,' I told her, 'it was me.'

Understandably, she was horrified. 'Why did you do that, you bad boy?' she asked.

'I just wanted to see what happened,' I admitted.

'Yes,' she agreed. 'Yes, I suppose you did.'

2

GETTING IN TROUBLE
AND BLOWING BUBBLES

They say that childhood holidays are one of the best times of your life and you never forget them. I reckon I would agree with that. My parents and I didn't have many conventional, two-weeks-by-the-seaside, bucket-and-spade type holidays, but we did something that will live in my memory for ever: hop-picking trips to Kent.

In the mid-fifties, hop-picking trips were an institution for the women and children of the East End. They got you out of the Smoke for a few weeks, let you earn a little (very little) bit of money, and were a working holiday for people who couldn't afford to go away otherwise. My mum and nan loved them, and so did I.

Once when I was five, we had gone on a strawberry-picking holiday in Norfolk. For some reason there was a party of monks on our campsite who took a real shine to me. Weeks later, when we were back in London, two monks turned up on our doorstep and told my mum: 'We have seen something special in David. Would he like to follow the path that we have taken?' Mum was puzzled and impressed, but decided against packing me off to a monastery, rather to my relief.

The hop-picking trips were fantastic, though. Mum would pack our bare necessities and we would jump on the back of a lorry with a load of other families and head off for the depths of Kent. At that age, having hardly left east London, heading beyond the Blackwall Tunnel was an incredible adventure. Rolling through the villages and the acres of countryside, singing songs and waving to everyone we saw, was all too exciting for words.

Our destination was a village called Rolvenden, near Ashford. Once we arrived at the farm, with its motley collection of barns, huts and cowsheds, we would be given a hut – well, basically a shed – and a mattress, plus hay to stuff it with. Everyone shared a washhouse. Maybe Forest House had been good training for this.

The hop-picking jaunts may sound now like something from Victorian times, but they were amazing, enabling my naïve, impressionable young self to experience so many new things. I saw stars for the first time, in skies clear from the obscuring murk of the industrial East End. Cows were also new to me, as was falling asleep on a hay-smelling mattress under a gently flickering oil lamp as the adults sang around an open fire.

I say that I loved hop picking, but I must admit I didn't pull my weight when it came to the actual labour. I left my mum and nan to gather the bushels, much preferring to run around, climb trees and generally go wild in the country, including setting my new personal best for the high jump when I leapt a five-foot fence to avoid being gored by an irate bull.

The weekends in Kent were best because my dad and the other men would all come to visit, and we'd have impromptu football matches out in the fields, go fishing and sit outside pubs till late at night. Even at the time I knew these days were idyllic and now, nearly sixty years on, I can still recall how special they were.

Hop picking was also a chance to hang out with some of Mum's gypsy relatives, who would be doing seasonal work on the farms. Uncle Levi entranced me. He was a handsome and very charismatic swarthy man with jet-black hair, twinkling blue eyes and spellbinding stories. He told me that the most important things in life were being healthy and appreciating sunsets and nature. He seemed impossibly exotic and glamorous, and I guess he was a bit of a street philosopher.

Back in London, life in Avondale Court was pretty good. Mum and Dad gave me a fair amount of freedom, but I knew if I stepped out of line, they would come down on me. They rarely hit me, although one morning, when I let my hamster out of its cage instead of getting ready for school, my mum saw red and chased me around the flat trying to whack me with a cane from the clothes dryer.

There again, the hamster fared far better than another pet, a mouse named – and how original was this? – Mickey. Mickey had a bump on his tail so my mum told me to take him to the vet. The vet gave him one look, told me to hold him still, put a big needle into him and killed him. I was traumatised for days.

In the evenings I would chase around the neighbourhood with friends from school, playing in the ruins of houses destroyed in the Blitz or in old bomb craters. My real passion, though, was football. From the end of school to bedtime, I virtually lived in the playground beneath our flat, honing my skills in never-ending kickabouts.

By the age of ten, I lived and breathed football and nothing else mattered. I would have played 24/7. My dad rarely lost his rag with me, but he did one night when he called me in for my tea from our balcony. We were playing 'Next goal wins' but the next goal was proving elusive. Dad had run me a bath, and after tiring of waiting endlessly for me, he eventually marched down to the playground, picked me up, carried me upstairs and threw me in the bath fully clothed.

It was my obsession with football that led me to make a decision that impacted on my academic carer, and not in a good way. As I began my last year at Star Lane, the dreaded Eleven Plus exam loomed. Everyone knew what that meant: those who passed entered the hallowed portals of the local grammar school, the gateway to a bright and privileged future. Failures were doomed to become factory fodder in a bog-standard secondary modern.

I had been an A-class student throughout my time at Star Lane and so was viewed as a shoo-in to sail through the exam – but things weren't that straightforward. There was a major complicating factor. On the all-important sports side, the grammar school majored in rugby, while at the state secondary it was football all the way, meaning they had a far better team.

Now, 99 per cent of people would feel that education and the career it could lead to were way more important than getting a game in the school soccer team, but that wasn't how I saw it. By the age of eleven, I was sure that my future lay as a professional player with a local team – West Ham United or, at the very worst, Leyton Orient. I couldn't let this ambition be jeopardised by anything as daft as rugby. As I pondered my options, I hit on what Baldrick from *Blackadder* would doubtless characterise as a cunning plan.

My chance to put this plan into operation came in the Eleven Plus maths test. In the exam room, the maths teacher, Mr Milner, moved among us with the question paper then told us to turn it over and begin. I took a cursory glance at the detailed questions about long division and fractions, ignored them, and carefully drew a picture of that spinach-loving comic-book hero, Popeye. It wasn't even a good picture. In fact, it was crap.

My Eleven Plus failure thus came as no surprise to me but was a major shock to my parents, who had been proud of my decent academic record to that point. Loyally, they blamed it on my teachers and the failures of the state education system. I never had the bottle to tell them what I had done.

I was sad to leave Star Lane but not nearly as sad as I was when I realised what awaited me. Shipman County Secondary School, where I was to waste the next four years of my life, was to prove the archetypal dead-end, no-hope secondary modern. Forget about getting an education – you were happy just to get through the day in one piece.

Shipman County didn't have a uniform, unless you count the jeans, leather jackets and steel-toe-capped boots that all the boys wore. I was nervous on my first day, walking into school with an older lad, Mike Newell, who lived downstairs in Avondale Court. Mike abandoned me as soon as we got in the gate, to preserve his street cred. I can't say I blamed him.

The school had a local reputation as a violent, under-achieving hellhole, and gazing around the playground, the first thing I noticed was how huge a lot of the boys were. To a pocket-sized nipper like me, they looked like fully grown men. A lot of the girls looked pretty well developed too, but that was another matter entirely.

I survived my first week making new friends and trying to stay out of the way of the playground bullies and apprentice tasty geezers. Shipman County, and West Ham as a whole, had produced a stream of boxing champions, and I didn't fancy a future as a human punchbag. I also drew the short straw in the classroom seating plan, being stuck with a boy called Trevor who smelled of old biscuits and had a constant river of snot cascading from his nostrils.

After a few days, I was seriously questioning whether sketching Popeye was the best idea I had ever had, but at least one part of my plan worked out. We played football every Friday afternoon, and the sports teacher took note of my ball skills, honed night after night in the playground under Avondale Court. After our first kickabout he picked the team to represent the school. Number 6, the left half, was Dave Cook.

I couldn't have felt more proud, and my dad was just as chuffed when I got home and told him the news. The first game was the following morning, and I headed off to our home ground, the romantically named Beckton Dump, my red-and-white-squares shirt and black shorts tucked under my arm. I knew most of our opponents, Pretoria: they had been at Star Lane with me.

Pretoria's best player was Frank Lampard, who lived opposite Avondale Court and often joined in the after-school kickabout. Even at that age, Frank was special, and it was no surprise that he later went on to become an icon at West Ham, playing more than 550 games in an amazing eighteen-year career before becoming assistant manager to Harry Redknapp. (He is also, of course, the father of the Chelsea and England midfielder, Frank Lampard junior.)

Even with a future England international in the opposing team, Shipman still managed to edge the game 4–3, and thus began a period of my life when weekends were the be-all and end-all for me. I would play for the school every Saturday morning. Dad would be working overtime on the docks so could never come to watch, but he would get home the same time as me and I would furnish him with a full match report as he cooked us bangers and mash from Taylor's, a local butcher's that I knew for a fact made the best sausages in the world.

After lunch, on the weekends they were at home, I would head off to watch West Ham. Funnily enough, the Hammers weren't my first team. As a nipper, I was smitten with Wolverhampton Wanderers because I loved their nickname, Wolves, and their Old Gold shirts. I must have been the only little boy in the East End running around in a Wolves shirt. It got a lot of suspicious looks: quite right, too.

Yet Wolves was a passing fancy. West Ham was love. I would feel my heart beating faster as I jumped on the bus or walked the two miles from Canning Town to Upton Park and merged in with the crowds of people all thronging in the same direction.

By the time I got to the ground at 1.30 p.m., a full hour and a half before kick-off, there would be thousands of blokes, mostly dockers, in flat caps queuing to get in.

Football grounds were all-standing in those days, and once I'd got through the turnstile I would find myself stuck at the back, but the crowd took care of the kids and would pass us down over their heads until we were right at the front with a fantastic view. Everybody smoked, and I can still picture the hazy clouds of blue smoke that hung over the terraces. It was all part of the atmosphere of that magical place.

West Ham was a good team to watch in those days. Most of the players came from the East End. The great Bobby Moore, who went on to captain England to the World Cup in 1966, was just coming through from the academy team, as was Geoff Hurst. An Irish international, the gentleman Noel Cantwell, was a giant in defence alongside John Bond. The forwards were Vic Keeble and John Dick and our veteran goalkeeper, Ernie Gregory, looked about sixty years old to me.

It was my Saturday afternoon fix and I couldn't get enough of it. I remember walking home giddy with happiness one day after we beat Blackburn Rovers 8–1. It felt like our players were one of us: I would sometimes see them having a bacon sandwich and a fag in McCarey's café opposite Upton Park.

Back at school, Shipman County felt more like a Borstal than an educational establishment. The headmaster, Mr 'Ding-Dong' Bell, was a strange man with no inspirational qualities, and most of the teachers were just plain lousy. Nobody stuck around: an endless stream of temporary or supply teachers took one look at the place and headed for the hills, horrified.

After Star Lane, which I had loved, Shipman was a horror show. It can't have been easy for the teachers because I have to admit that we were a rebellious bunch, but in truth we had nothing to stimulate us. We didn't study art, music or anything creative, and a bleak mood of edgy indifference permeated the school.

We had science lessons, for a while, but even these stopped after the 'Gassing of the Bees' scandal. Our science teacher, Mr Dines, known to us for some reason as Daddy Dines, brought in some of his pet bees for us to see. He was proud of the way they would fly out through a small hole in their glass case, somehow locate some pollen in the urban sprawl of Custom House and return to the glass hive with their spoils.

Mr Dines showed us the queen bee and her workers and then made the mistake of turning his back. As he headed towards the blackboard, a couple of the boys inserted the rubber tube from a nearby Bunsen burner into the hole, fastened it in place with chewing gum, and turned on the gas. By the time Daddy Dines returned to the case, his precious bees were in a lifeless pile at the foot of the hive.

Mr Dines went completely crazy. Thinking back now, he may have been having a nervous breakdown, but at the time we could only laugh as this tall beanpole of a man, not unlike John Cleese as Basil Fawlty, leapt on a chair waving his cane and began yelling at us: 'Who gassed my bees?' He totally lost his mind, smashing desks and test tubes as the kids ran for cover. A few of the more sensitive ones were crying.

The classroom had descended into mayhem, but this doesn't explain why one of the boys then set fire to a broken chair (and can I make one thing clear: this was NOT a repeat performance by the Canning Town Arsonist). The fire alarm bells sprang into life and we all sprinted for the safety of the playground chased by a gabbling Mr Dines, who by now appeared to be verging on the certifiable.

This was an extreme incident but it reflected the mindset of Shipman County. Most kids felt that the teachers were all idiots who couldn't teach them anything. I was sorry for the teachers but I also had to consider my own self-preservation. Even if I could answer a question, I knew that if I put my hand up and did so, I'd simply draw attention to myself and most likely get my head kicked in later in the playground.

The playground was where your status in the school was decided. I was reasonably popular but I tended just to keep my head down as the bullies ran riot because there was nothing else you could do. I saw some awful scenes. One boy was duffed up for wearing brown winkle-pickers. Another lad, Peter, told his postman dad he was being bullied, and when his father turned up to confront the thugs, they kicked him to the ground and beat him up in front of his crying son. I found it all disgusting and very distressing.

My own key moment came in the first year when some older kids began picking on me. I stood up to them and was informed, 'We're going to have you after school!' Pre-arranged fights after school normally happened on a patch of wasteland at the appro-priately named Boot Hill nearby, but this was the first time that I would be a participant.

I was terrified but knew I had to go through with it or my school life would become a misery. When I got to Boot Hill with a handful of supporters, my opponent, Lenny, was waiting for me. He was an older boy with a big reputation for violence, swearing and spitting huge distances. A ring of boys gathered around us and their cry went up: 'Fight! Fight!'

Len tried to see me off quickly, with a haymaking punch that thankfully just missed my nose and a hefty boot to my right thigh. This was it! Driven by panic, I kicked him fair and square in the bollocks and, as he bent double, connected with a lucky punch that left my hand aching. Len looked astonished and backed off, and although the whole charade was pathetic, I knew that I would be able to walk tall in the playground from now on.

It was ironic that I had gone to Shipman County purely to play football because that was the only thing that made my life there bearable. I was still doing pretty well in the Saturday morning school-team matches, and at an away game when I was twelve, there was a breakthrough that made me think my whole Popeye-based plan for sports-related world domination might pay off, after all: I got scouted by West Ham.

Their scout approached me after the match and asked if I would be interested in a trial for the Hammers at nearby Cumberland Road the following Tuesday. This was kind of a silly question. It was all I had ever dreamed of, and I spent the next three days imagining myself at Upton Park putting pinpoint passes through for Vic Keeble or John Dick to finish off.

The fateful day arrived and I got to Cumberland Road to join the thirty or so other hopefuls, all kitted up and aiming to catch the eye of the three or four coaches. They divided us into groups, and after some ball work and a short match, Terry, the head coach, called a halt to proceedings. He read out a dozen names and called those boys to him. I wasn't one of them. So that was it. I was out!

I was sitting slumped and devastated on the grass with the other failures when to my amazement the kids that Terry had chosen all trooped off across the turf. He came back over to us, grinning. We were not the rejects: they were! Terry invited us back to train again the following week. It was official: I was now a West Ham United schoolboy player.

Over the next few weeks, I attended training faithfully and could not have found it more exciting. Some weeks, first-team players came to coach us so I found myself working with idols like Noel Cantwell, Phil Woosnam and John Bond. Mr Bond gloried in the bizarre nickname of Muffin and taught me how to send an opponent flying and then look totally innocent – a very useful skill.

My friend Frank Lampard was starting his illustrious West Ham career in the same schoolboy team as me and we became quite a decent double act. We were both left-footed, and combined well down that side of the pitch, switching and overlapping. I felt part of the club, especially as they gave us all free tickets to the first-team home games, meaning I no longer had to part with a shilling at the turnstiles.

We played our home games at Clapton FC's ground behind the Spotted Dog pub, and this illustrious venue was where I scored my solitary goal for the Hammers. We were playing Thurrock and as the ball reached me on the halfway line I swung a boot and hoofed it down the pitch to clear it. The opposing goalie misjudged the bounce and it just about trickled over the line. Naturally, I celebrated as if that had been my intention all along.

It's strange, though, how your priorities in life change. Playing for my beloved West Ham, being coached by my heroes and top international players, I was living the dream, and yet I had not played more than four or five games before everything shifted. A new interest entered my life and became just as all-consuming as my passion for football, which I now allowed to fall away.

As I turned thirteen, and became aware of those perennial adolescent fixations of girls and rock 'n' roll, I became obsessed with music, and specifically black-oriented blues music played by legendary American musicians. It was an interest that was to shape the rest of my life – and it was all sparked by an illicit trip to Soho.

3

SEX, DRUMS AND
ROCK 'N' ROLL

Life changes when you hit your teens. It's a cliché, but like most clichés it is true, that as you stand on the cusp between being a boy and becoming a man, you make a host of decisions that will most likely shape the rest of your existence. The biggest irony is that you make these decisions while you are a mass of raging hormones and often have no idea what you really want.

There is no doubt that I was in danger of taking a wrong path in life as I turned thirteen. The pernicious influence of Shipman County may have been warping my innocent soul, because outside of that sorry excuse for a school, I was getting involved in gangs – the Canning Town Boys, to be precise.

I hadn't suddenly become a bad boy, and largely my behaviour was down to peer group pressure, but slowly I was going off the rails. In the same way that I sometimes kept my head down and went along with the hooligan behaviour at Shipman, outside of school I was being swept along with the tribalism of fights with rival gangs from other parts of London.

The East End and south east London have never got on all that well – just look at the hatred between West Ham and

Millwall – and, true to type, the Canning Town Boys' worst enemies were from down Bermondsey way. They were mostly just fistfights, although the odd flick knife would sometimes get flashed about. Thankfully, I never saw one used.

We were no angels and we would head on to other gangs' turf and try to take their area. They would do the same: I was once in a youth club full of old snooker tables in Abbey Arms in West Ham when a mob from the Elephant and Castle came storming in. The resulting scrap, with snooker cues getting smashed over people's heads, was like a scene from a Wild West saloon.

Around this time I was also forming a love for motorbikes that has lasted until today. Once an unsmiling rocker named Rick offered me a ride down east London and Essex's very own Route 66, the A13, on the back of his BSA Gold Star. As we flew through the Blackwall Tunnel towards oncoming traffic at 100 m.p.h., I was in heaven. Needless to say, my parents didn't learn about this adventure.

I took another mini-walk on the wild side when I worked at a travelling fair that pitched up in a park near our flat. Maybe it appealed to my gypsy blood, because I loved its sense of community and danger, especially when I graduated from manning a tame stall where punters threw darts at balloons to collecting fares as I jumped between cars on the dodgems. When it came time for the fair to move on, I was all set to roll with them until my dad suggested it might actually be a better idea to go back to school.

It goes without saying that as well as my increasing delinquency I was forming an interest in girls and in sex, although I

was far too timid to do anything about it. I was also totally igno-
rant and naïve. When I was about eleven, some older boys had
told me that girls had one ball, and I half-believed that until I
was fourteen.

I was keen to learn, though. My favourite attraction at the
fair was a stall that invited men to hurl a wooden ball at a small
target next to a bed with two (real) women lying in it. If they
scored a direct hit, the girls were hurled out in a flurry of ciga-
rette ash, swearing and flying negligees. I would never have
dared to have a go myself but I observed closely and took some
stimulating memories home for later consideration.

Even so, a fleeting glimpse of thigh at a fairground was not
enough to satisfy my rising curiosity in the female form, and a
gang of mates hatched a plan to broaden our manly horizons.
We decided to undertake a trip to the West End, and specifically
to Soho's notorious red-light district.

Every undercover mission needs a cover story, so I duly lied
to my mum and dad that I was visiting a school friend in Custom
House and would be staying overnight. Instead, nine or ten
emboldened adolescents caught the bus into central London,
looking like a motley crew of pubescent gangsters in our Italian
suits, button-down shirts and chisel-toe shoes.

The two oldest boys, Tommy and Freddie, who fancied themselves relative men of the world at fifteen, led the way as we filed
through the sleazy streets of Soho, past the strip joints, peep
shows and dirty bookshops, trying to look sophisticated despite
our eyes being on stalks. It was pretty exciting and our hearts
were beating fast beneath those pinstripes.

Eventually we plucked up the courage to go into one of those alluring yet intimidating strip-club doors. For all of our false bravado, there was no way that we looked old enough for adult entertainment, but the Greek Cypriot bouncer on the door couldn't have cared less as he took our money and waved us up the stairs.

We found ourselves in a smoke-filled red-lit room. Three or four distinctly seedy-looking men sat in battered old cinema seats facing an empty stage as music played. For an awful moment I thought one man was the Shipman County headmaster, Mr 'Ding-Dong' Bell. I could not have been more relieved when I squinted through the semi-darkness and found I was wrong.

There was a tiny bar in the corner of the room, and after the hotpants-wearing waitress had finished a leisurely fag, we ordered drinks. I asked for a rum and black in a voice a few octaves below its everyday pitch, and as I took my first sip, a stripper took the stage. She was introduced as Lulu: she was the image of my friend Roger Foster's mum.

'Lulu' the erotic dancer went through the most mechanical and non-erotic dance routine you can imagine to the strains of Guy Mitchell's 'She Wears Red Feathers and a Huly-Huly Skirt'. I didn't know where to look. 'This is great!' whispered Kenny Palmer, but although the atmosphere in the club was exciting, I found watching the poor woman strip down to her G-string embarrassing, not arousing. As she shuffled off with a sigh, I could only think, 'I wonder if she likes doing this?'

It transpired that a handful of women spent their nights trudging between Soho's clubs doing the same routine in each dive, so I had another deep-voiced rum and black as we waited half an hour for the next girl to show up to entertain us. Without being rude, she was a poor man's Doris Day, but she at least threw herself into her performance more than listless Lulu had.

Despite this, as we endured another thirty-minute wait after she had gone, we felt that we were being fleeced, and we decided to do a runner without paying for the drinks. Ten besuited schoolboys bolted en masse down the stairs and into the street. I evaded the Cypriot bouncer's clutches by the skin of my teeth.

We were cockily congratulating ourselves on getting away with it when we turned a corner and a grey Jaguar pulled up alongside us and slowed down. Its windows were wound down so I could see clearly the man in the front passenger seat as he smiled at me, snarled, and then produced a tasty-looking butcher's hook from his lap.

'Run!' I yelled, as the man's mate in the back seat of the car unveiled a shotgun from under a cloth. Terrified, we scattered in every direction. Jimmy Anderson and I shot down a back alley, scaled a ten-foot wall as if we had a rocket up our arses and sprinted to safety through some market stalls.

We had now lost both the Jaguar and the rest of our mates, so Jimmy and I prowled nervously around Soho's back passages for a while before sneaking back down Wardour Street. As we crept along the pavement, nervously scrutinising each car that passed, we heard some killer music blasting out of the door of a club called the Flamingo. We joined the queue on the pavement and filed into the dark interior.

You get a few – very few – moments in your life when suddenly something happens and you know immediately that things will never be the same again. I believe they call them epiphanies and here was mine. What I found in the Flamingo altered everything I intuited, felt and knew about myself, and about my future. It rearranged my very DNA.

The Flamingo was an all-night rhythm and blues club – from the days when rhythm and blues meant Mose Allison, not Beyoncé – full of black American soldiers on leave. As they used to say in the movies, the joint was jumping. Georgie Fame and the Blue Flames were on stage, and while I didn't know much about Georgie before that night, his band blew me away.

The Flamingo felt alive. The atmosphere and the energy were incredible. This was the blues as it should be played: rich and strong and loud and powerful. Previously, I knew clubs as discos where a lame band or a DJ went through the motions as boys stood around drinking and girls shuffled from foot to foot, but here was something else entirely.

Everything in the bar was special. The fantastic musicianship; the vibrant, edgy ambience; the cool blues records they played between the bands. I would never have thought it possible, but suddenly I couldn't care less about the West Ham youth team or becoming a footballer. I had found my star over Bethlehem, my crescent over Mecca, the meaning of my life.

The Blue Flames transfixed me. I loved the propulsive, thrilling thrust of the guitar, the suggestive sexy throb of the bass, and most of all I loved the drums. They were the rock that the whole amazing musical edifice was built on, the foundation for this crazy, explosive racket. That was my future settled, then: I was going to be a rock 'n' roll drummer.

The Flamingo boogied and jived until 4.30 a.m. and Jimmy and I stayed glued to the music until the bitter end. We had spent all our money – those rum and blacks didn't come cheap – so as the lights came up, we picked up our jackets and started the long walk home. As we floated back to the East End, we made plans non-stop. We would form a band: I would drum, with Jimmy on the trumpet; we would play the Flamingo. This had to be.

By the time I got home and stumbled in the door of Avondale Court at 7.30 a.m., Dad was up and about in the kitchen, making his morning cup of tea. 'Hello, mate,' he greeted me. 'Did you enjoy yourself last night?'

I had to bite my tongue. I couldn't let Dad in on the secret of my strip-club misadventure or, more importantly, tell him about my life-changing Flamingo all-nighter, for the very good reason that he thought I'd been kipping at a mate's house in Custom House. 'Yeah, it was neat,' I said, but I knew we had to have a big conversation, and my mind was racing as we carried our cuppas through to the front room.

'You look tired, son,' Dad told me. 'Yeah, I didn't sleep much last night,' I replied. Too excited to hold back, I decided there was no time like the present: 'Dad, you know I wanted to be a footballer? I think I'd actually like to be a drummer.'

This bombshell could have triggered a very negative response – on a practical level, the thin walls of our council flat were not a fitting setting for a budding Buddy Rich – but to my relief, Dad reacted with his usual sangfroid. He didn't even quiz me about my bizarre change of heart: he said it sounded 'a good idea' and he'd have a word with Mum.

I had saved up a bit of money from a couple of part-time jobs I had been doing, selling evening newspapers and helping out on a weekend market stall, so I had enough for a basic snare drum, but I knew I could do nothing without Mum's say-so. She was understandably sceptical at first, thinking my newfound love for drumming was a passing fad, and would say only: 'We'll see.'

For the next few days, I made a detour after school each evening to gaze at a snare in the window of a second-hand music shop in Barking Road, then carried on home to bash along to the radio on a makeshift drum kit of biscuit tins, cushions and ash-trays as my football lay ignored in the hallway. Then came some progress: 'How much is this drum you want?' Dad asked me.

I told him it was only a fiver and he suggested we head down to have a look at it. Once in Barking Road, I pointed it out in the window and we went in to what seemed like an Aladdin's Cave to me: an intriguing, overwhelming mass of guitars, saxophones and drum kits.

The Johnny Cash-like cool-dude assistant fetched my desired snare from the window and gave me a pair of sticks to try it out. It sounded worse than Mum's biscuit tin, and even Dad looked disappointed: 'Is it supposed to sound like that?' Johnny told us we couldn't expect much for that money. When Dad asked him what else he had, he pointed us towards an impressive-looking snare and stand for £15: 'Try this one.'

I did, and it sounded great: like a real drum. 'Do you want that one instead?' asked Dad. I could hardly believe it, and was even more made up and gobsmacked when we headed home not just with the drum but also sticks, brushes and a rubber practice pad. He couldn't have made me any happier.

The little drummer boy had arrived, and now I finally had some kit, I threw myself into practising with a passion. Every day, as soon as I got home from school, I was banging away at the skins – within limits. Always fair-minded, my dad had no desire to piss off our neighbours, so decreed that I could only practise in my bedroom from 4.30 p.m. until six, and had to make maximum use of the rubber practice pads.

I loyally obeyed this dictum but even so my daily racket was too much for our downstairs neighbour, Mr Johnson, who was driven to distraction. He frequently banged on his ceiling as I crashed through my routines, threatened to ask the council to evict us, and one night decided to take direct action.

As usual, I was quietly honing my paradiddles in my bedroom when I heard shouting at the front door. Deciding to tackle the problem at source, Mr Johnson had come bounding upstairs to confront us, and had no time for my dad's reasonable argument that I only ever practised for ninety minutes, as quietly as possible.

It would have been no more than a noisy standoff if Mr Johnson had not decided to emphasise his point by poking my dad in the chest. Big mistake. The two men squared up, and I emerged from my bedroom in time to see Dad take down his opponent with two left jabs and a killer right hook.

Dad was so supportive – to a fault, Mr Johnson might say – because he could see my love for the drums was genuine. As I edged into my early teens, I threw myself into music. It was jazz drummers that really moved me, and I thrilled to the exquisite technique and consummate playing of the likes of Art Blakey, Joe Morello and Phil Seamen.

My musical Mecca was a specialist record shop called Dobells in the Charing Cross Road and I made regular pilgrimages. In addition to my jazz idols, I would head home with records by venerable blues men such as Muddy Waters, Howlin' Wolf and Memphis Slim. If it looked black and obscure, I would buy it.

The blues moved me far more than chart pop and the music on the radio such as the Beatles, which I looked down on in some snotty, intangible way: my thinking was that if girls screamed at it, it must be lightweight and worthless. But jazz and blues spoke to me, and despite my tender years, as often as I could I caught live gigs at the 100 Club, the Marquee, and back at the Flamingo.

Music and drumming had lent my life a new focus and direction but my parents were still concerned with my changes in attitude since going to Shipman County. They didn't know about the Canning Town Boys but I think they sensed an incipient delinquency in me that helped to shape their decision to move out of the East End.

When east Londoners want a quieter, better quality of life, they invariably turn to Essex, and in 1962 my parents started looking into council-house exchanges. We would tootle off in our grey Ford Popular, a new acquisition, to look at gaffs around Grays and Romford. If I were lucky, Dad would let his fourteen-year-old son take the wheel in a quiet country lane.

I didn't exactly repay Dad very well for this kind gesture. One fateful afternoon, taking a break from drumming, I 'borrowed'

– without asking – his James Captain motorbike and went for a ride around the block with Jimmy Anderson on the back. When we got to the A13 I couldn't resist its wide-open spaces and opened up the throttle. This felt amazing! I was probably doing 60 m.p.h. in a 40 m.p.h. zone when the police car pulled me over. A friendly cop asked me if I knew I was speeding.

'No,' I replied in my deepest rum-and-black voice, hoping that the white scarf wrapped around my face would conceal the fact that I was underage. It didn't. 'How old are you?' asked the policeman. 'Fourteen,' I admitted, and my breaking voice chose that moment to turn into a squeak, as if to emphasise my tender years. The policeman bundled Jimmy and me off the bike and into the squad car.

My dad was horrified and gave me a serious bollocking, not to mention a rare clip around the ear. Jimmy got even worse from his dad. I had to go to court, where I was fined £20 and given a six-month ban to come into effect from my sixteenth birthday, when I could legally hold a licence.

The incident probably cemented my parents' decision to get me out of the East End and away from trouble as soon as possible, and we quickly moved out of Canning Town to a ground-floor flat in the more genteel, countrified surroundings of Chadwell Heath. I missed my mates but had to admit it was nice to be in a clean, green environment rather than the usual fog and dirt.

The best aspect of the move was that living on the ground floor meant no more Mr Johnson, and greater freedom to practise the drums. Saving up money from my part-time jobs, I had added more drums and cymbals to my kit, and Dad recognised my dogged commitment and asked if I wanted drumming lessons.

My new teacher was a dedicated and very clean-cut gentleman named Eddie Freeborn, who spent his evenings drumming in a dance band at the Grosvenor House hotel. Eddie introduced me to big band jazz and also helped me to work through a textbook of exercises by the king of drummers, Buddy Rich. Instructing me patiently in the fine art of bossa nova in my bedroom, Eddie was a fine teacher and gave me an invaluable grounding.

Despite our move to Chadwell Heath, I still had one foot in the East End. As I was to leave school in a year's time, aged fifteen, we decided I would see out my non-education at Shipman County, rather than have the hassle of finding a new school. This meant two buses each morning and two each evening as I navigated the five-mile journey there and back.

Shipman hadn't got any better, and it was hard to imagine a way it could get any worse. In my last year, I was handed the poisoned chalice of being made a prefect. It didn't last long: when I tried to quieten down a kid on some stairs he hit me and I promptly thumped him back. Cue the end of my prefect badge.

The chances of a reprobate from Shipman County going on to have any kind of interesting or rewarding career were precisely nil, but nevertheless as my time at that rancid institution neared its end, the careers officer came calling. One by one we were called in to see this bored-looking individual to tell him what we would like to do with our lives.

I had no idea what to say to him. A few months ago the honest answer would have been a professional footballer, and now it would be an avant-garde jazz drummer, but I felt that either of those responses would evoke bafflement, contempt or outright derisive laughter. This did not look like a man disposed to urge idealistic youths to aim high and live their dreams.

So I told him I wanted to be an electrical engineer. I had no idea what this actually was, but my Uncle Alfie did it and I thought it sounded vaguely impressive. The careers adviser nodded and said he would arrange an entry exam for an apprenticeship in the summer holidays for me. Whatever. I thanked him, and left.

Yet it was still music that was firing my soul, and after a few months of Eddie Freeborn's diligent tuition, I felt ready to play in a band. Scanning the small ads in our local rag, the *Ilford Recorder*, one advert caught my eye:

DRUMMER WANTED FOR TRIO
Phone Reg

My dad told me to give it a go so I gave Reg a ring. He was friendly and up for a meeting, so even though I was privately harbouring doubts that his trio would be fluent in my preferred style of post-Art Blakey beatnik bebop, Dad and I piled my drums into the car and headed off to Romford.

My instincts were correct. Appearance-wise, Reg didn't suggest an Essex John Coltrane but a fifty-something cardigan-wearing accountant probably packing a pocket full of boiled sweets. As I set up my kit, he asked if I could play ballroom music such as waltzes and foxtrots.

The third trio member, clarinettist and saxophonist Eric, turned up in a flurry of finger jewellery and Old Spice and said 'Hi', a phrase I had only heard before in Hollywood films. Not to be fazed, I mumbled 'Hi' back. Eric produced his clarinet, which he preferred to call his 'liquorice stick', and off we went, Reg on piano and me swishing the skins with my brushes.

Reg and Eric liked what they were hearing, complimented me on my bossa nova, and told me I was in. The trio was complete. They showed me our upcoming gig schedule, which basically consisted of Thursday nights at a Conservative Club in Hackney and Saturdays at a Working Men's Club in Dagenham. I guess at least we were covering both ends of the political spectrum.

It was nice to be playing live music and Reg and Eric were good guys but the trio was not to my musical taste. As a precocious teen in love with jazz and Delta blues, tickling the drums with brushes as two middle-aged band mates eased through cha-chas and Paso Dobles was not where I wanted to be. At least I could give my sticks some welly during the Gay Gordon, to Reg and Eric's horror.

As I was making this deeply unpromising start to my musical career, almost as an afterthought I left Shipman County. I was fifteen years old, didn't have one qualification to my name and had learned precisely nothing in my four years there. On my last day, the local police turned up to protect the staff from any last acts of retribution by departing pupils. It felt like a fitting farewell.

Now I no longer had to commute to school each day, I began to take stock of Chadwell Heath. It lacked the life and soul of the East End but I slowly began to fit in, and when a new friend,

Ronnie, took me to a local youth-club night that descended into a mass brawl, it started to feel like home.

I had been out of Shipman County for less than a week when I learned that the careers officer had been true to his promise. A letter arrived from a company called Plessey's inviting me to sit an exam for an apprenticeship in, yep, electrical engineering. My heart didn't exactly leap with joy but I needed to earn some money, so I pitched up at their factory in Romford at the stipulated time the following week.

There were about thirty other teenage candidates, some of whom may even have actually known what an electrical engineer was. Turning over the paper, I managed not to sketch Olive Oyl or Bluto and instead set about tackling the fairly demanding maths, English and IQ questions. It helped that the boy next to me whispered his answers to himself as he wrote them down.

After the test, the supervisor took us on a tour of the factory that was one of the most bizarre and inexplicable experiences of my life. In recent weeks I had been having troubling dreams about being in a vast, cacophonous place full of pounding, monstrous machinery. We walked down to the shop floor and I froze. Here was the place I had been dreaming of: Plessey's!

To this day I don't understand that experience. Was it an omen? A coincidence? I had no idea, but made my way home to await the results of the exam, and meanwhile turned my mind to shifting my musical career up a notch from Reg and Eric.

Eileen, a cousin who has always been more like a sister to me, had heard of an audition. A Stratford-based rhythm and blues band, the Everons, were looking for a drummer, so I called the band's leader, John. He sounded keen and we arranged to meet for a jam at his father's pub in Leytonstone.

The Everons consisted of John on guitar and vocals, his friend Brian on rhythm guitar and Brian's sister – and John's girlfriend – Sandra on bass. This close inter-relationship meant they were also very tight musically, and I loved the audition and the fact that I could hammer away at my drums with sticks rather than the brushes favoured by dear old Reg and Eric. After an hour, I was in.

This felt like serious progress. I was delighted to be in a modern group that used amplifiers and were a lot nearer my age. We were playing mostly Chuck Berry covers and the occasional Beatles song rather than my beloved obscure Deep South blues, but as we set to rehearsing three nights a week in a church hall in Stratford, we quickly got pretty good and started picking up bookings. We even landed a residency, at the Bell pub in Ilford on Saturday and Sunday nights.

Life was good, and my parents were pleased I was doing OK and happy, but doubtless secretly also felt that playing drums in a pub wasn't A Proper Job. When Plessey's wrote to tell me I had passed their exam and offer me a five-year apprenticeship as an electrical engineer, Mum and Dad felt I should get a trade under my belt in case the music dream didn't work out. I was in two minds, but saw their point and agreed.

Two weeks later, I showed up for my first day at Plessey's in Ilford, makers of electronic parts for the telecommunications and aircraft industries. As a trainee electrical engineer – and I still wasn't sure what that involved – I would clock in at 7.25 each morning, clock out at 5.25 each evening, and be paid £3 19s 11d per week.

Plessey's was a huge sprawling complex and seemed pretty intimidating as two other new boys and I were led from the personnel department to the shop floor. Yet I quickly got used to the routine there and even though it never remotely felt like my vocation in life, I came to sort-of enjoy it.

The apprentices' main duties were setting up lathes and presses for the skilled workers to assemble the airplane parts. These workers were on piecework and had to make so many parts each hour to get a bonus payment, and if an apprentice made a mistake that slowed them down we would get a terrible bollocking – especially from the women.

Plessey's was not short of characters. One woman from Oldham would talk non-stop, only breaking off to demand a kiss and a cuddle, which thankfully she never got. We were also warned about a homosexual man in the stores who went by the rather unappealing name of Squeaker, who used to materialise beneath you looking for a quick grope if you were up a ladder getting parts off a shelf. He would be hauled before a tribunal today, but I guess things were different back in those days.

I quickly got used to the Plessey's routine. By now I had bought a Lambretta scooter and used it for the two-mile journey to work each morning. At lunchtime, we'd play football on some grass behind the factory. The job didn't even interfere with the Everons too much, apart from the early mornings after a late gig.

Yet a steady job and playing with the band were not enough to quieten some deeper stirrings. When you are a sixteen-year-old boy, girls are never far from your thoughts, and I was about to fall head-over-heels in the way sixteen-year-old boys do. The object of my infatuated devotion was a girl called Carol.

Carol was a face down the local youth club, a pretty brunette with a sunshine smile and sparkly green eyes, and, like me, she was a bit of a Mod. Probably I should have been a rocker, with my taste for blues and rock 'n' roll, but I liked the Mods' threads as I fancied myself as a bit of a natty dresser. Plus, of course, I had the Lambretta.

As a boy, I was painfully shy, and it's a condition that has never fully left me even half a century later. I had managed to make occasional eye contact with Carol and maybe even exchange a smile, but I was genetically incapable of swaggering over to her and trying to chat her up, as many boys would do so easily. I would just freeze, paralysed by nerves and self-doubt.

This all changed one night when Brian from the Everons invited me to go to a dance with him to check out another local band, the Falcons. Having arrived early, I was hanging around outside the hall aimlessly, watching people go in as I waited for Brian, when my heart suddenly missed a beat. It was her! Carol was in the middle of a group of girls making their way towards the door.

I could have turned away and pretended not to see her, or shrunk into the background as per usual, but somehow I made the superhuman effort to meet her gaze and say 'Hello'. Her mates giggled at this, but Carol nodded at me, said 'Hello, David' and smiled as she walked off. What an amazing development! I hadn't even been sure until that moment that she knew my name.

Brian arrived and we parted with 2/6 each and went into the gig. It was busy. In the traditional British disco scene, groups of girls danced round their handbags while the boys leaned against the wall, drinking. Brian wanted to go backstage to say hello to the Falcons but I always felt awkward doing that sort of thing, so it was a relief when the band appeared on stage.

A five-piece, they looked pretty nifty in their suits and Beatles-slash-Rolling Stones shaggy cuts. Like the Everons, they ran through a succession of old classics and chart hits, and I remember that I liked their version of Screaming Lord Sutch's 'Jack the Ripper'. Yet for once in my life, my mind wasn't on the music.

I could see Carol dancing near the stage – she was only a few feet away, but for a romantic coward like me, those few feet were a million miles. What would I say? What if she blanked me? I went through agonies as two or three braver souls than me asked her to dance, and was delighted when she turned them down. Then as the Falcons aped the blues boogie of Chuck Berry's 'Memphis Tennessee', she turned around, saw me, and smiled. I was rooted to the spot. Did that really happen?

The Falcons finished with a flourish and strode offstage and Brian scuttled back to congratulate them, leaving me alone. It was now or never. As the DJ started the sequence of records leading up to the slow dances that signified the end of the evening, I somehow willed my legs to lurch across the floor to her and my mouth to shape the timeless question: 'Do you want to dance?'

'Yes,' said Carol. It was that easy.

I have never been one of life's dancers, but luckily for both of us, Carol was seriously good. She started off doing the Bird as I moved awkwardly from foot to foot next to her, but then the ska records gave way to a classic old-school slowie. Would my nerve fail me? No: I took her hand, she put her arm around me and we swayed gently to the rhythm, her hand on my shoulder.

So this was what it felt like: the feel of being close to a girl you adored, inhaling her perfume, feeling the contours of her body and her gentle skin against yours. It felt amazing.

There was only one place to go from here: the bar. 'Would you like a drink?' I asked, and led her by the hand across the dance floor to a serving hatch, where I bought us two Cokes. After we chatted for a while, I posed the all-important question: 'Can I walk you home?' Certain of rejection, I could hardly believe my ears when Carol said, 'Yeah, all right.'

We wended our way through the throng and towards the door with me doing my best to ignore Brian's lairy 'Give her one from me!' thumbs-up and wink as he watched us go. Out in the night air, we did our best to make self-conscious conversation but the words faded awkwardly to nothingness, so we turned into an alleyway and kissed.

It was wonderful. There were no noses in the way, no banging of teeth, no slobbering tongues: just a warm, gentle kiss. We hardly said another word as we walked slowly, our arms around each other, back to Carol's door, where we shared another lingering goodnight kiss. I could hardly believe it. I had a girlfriend.

I floated back home on a cloud of happiness, even at one point jumping in the air and clicking my heels Charlie Chaplin-style. Mum and Dad were just going to bed. Dad asked me his usual question: 'Have a good night?' 'Brilliant!' I told him, went to bed and replayed my big romantic scene in my head, over and over again.

The next day was Saturday and my parents were coming to see the Everons play a gig in Bermondsey in the evening. I woke up early, greeted them in the kitchen with a smile and broke my big news: 'I've got a girlfriend. She's really nice. Can she come with us tonight?'

'That'll be all right, won't it, Albert?' asked Mum. 'OK by me,' said Dad, picking up his crash helmet and heading off for the docks. There we were, then. We had our first date.

Carol didn't know this yet, of course, so I donned my snazziest gear – I believe pink jeans were involved – and walked over to her house. On the way, nerves kicked in again. Maybe our kiss had been a one-off and meant nothing to her? Maybe she had a boyfriend already? I was reassured when her younger brother opened the door and called Carol, who greeted me with a kiss on the lips and invited me in to meet her parents.

It went OK. Carol's dad had a moustache and was fairly quiet. Her mum was pretty glamorous and looked like she wore the trousers. They gave me a cuppa and asked me a few questions about myself before agreeing that, yes, Carol could come with me to Bermondsey that night.

As I left in the late afternoon, Carol told me she was nervous about meeting my parents. 'They'll really like you,' I assured her. 'I do.' 'I really like you too,' she said. Her words rang in my ears like music.

That evening, Carol and I, Mum and Dad and my Slingerland drum kit headed off to Bermondsey in the Ford Popular. They seemed to get on fine, and I was delighted to see Carol up and dancing with my mum during the Everons' set. The band went down pretty well – as we always did in that particular pub as long as we stuck to chart hits and went nowhere near the blues.

My life now settled into a new, fairly satisfying routine. I was setting up the lathes and presses in Plessey's from Monday to Friday, rehearsing and playing gigs with the band and seeing a lot of Carol. We got on great, and I felt sure we would stay together for ever and eventually get married.

In fact, we followed the trajectory of almost every first teenage romance. Initially, we were inseparable, devoted young lovers keen to explore each other in every way. Our romantic fumbling and fondling got more intimate, and often my heart was beating not only with passion but also because her parents were sitting the other side of a council-house door.

Carol and I also had plenty of days out on the Lambretta that I had bought from a workmate at the factory, which proved to be a complete disaster. It virtually never made a bank holiday run to Brighton or Clacton without breaking down, leaving the two of us stranded in a lay-by. I spent way too many hours glumly pushing that bloody thing down the road in my Mod parka and beret.

Actually, the parka and beret were the least of it. As my interest in clothes and fashion grew, I took to sporting a mohair suit, tab collar shirts, knitted ties and chisel shoes. There was even a bizarre short-lived craze involving Pac-a-Macs and Hush Puppies, although I am glad to say I drew the line at blue hair, as sported by one of my more sartorially daring mates.

Apart from my recalcitrant Lambretta, there was nothing too wrong with my life in the summer of 1964 – though it maybe lacked a touch of glamour. Happily, this was to arrive courtesy of Ted, the father of Brian and Sandra from the Everons, who helped to get bookings for the band. We were gobsmacked when he told us that he had possibly secured us a new gig – in Cattolica, Italy!

The plan was for us to fly out on a package holiday, attend an audition at the club Ted had spoken to, and hopefully impress them enough to get a mini-residency. Mum and Dad didn't just give me permission to go: they said they'd come with me.

This was a huge deal. It would be my first time on an aeroplane – in fact the first time abroad for all three of us – so Mum started to make detailed inquiries about what we needed to pack. She asked important questions of the very few people we knew who had been as far as France, or even the Isle of Man: could you buy things like teabags, milk and soap, you know, *abroad*?

For Carol and me, it would be our first time apart. We had now been going steady for more than a year, and while things were essentially OK between us, the odd niggle and argument had crept in. Maybe I subconsciously felt that we were slipping into a bit of a cosy routine the night that I suggested to her that she should dye her black hair blonde.

My fortnight's break from Plessey's began. The Cooks and the Everons were flying to Cattolica on a Saturday morning, so after work on Friday I called for Carol and we sat outside a pub with a pint of brown and mild (my drink of choice at the time) and a Babycham. She was sorry I was going away. I figured I would miss her, but my main feeling was of rising excitement at the next day's big adventure.

There are some rite-of-passage moments that you never forget: your first day at school; your first kiss; driving your first car; losing your virginity. Your first trip abroad is definitely one of them, and I will always remember walking down the steps of the plane in Italy.

The very air was different. It felt warm, sultry and, well, *foreign*. The sun seemed somehow hotter, more intense, and the artfully dilapidated buildings appeared impossibly exotic, as did the whiff of coffee that pervaded the air. Cattolica is arguably the Italian equivalent of Blackpool, but to me it appeared the most glamorous place on earth.

Likewise, our bog-standard package hotel seemed like The Ritz to me, accustomed as I was to cramped council flats. Brian's dad, Ted, a more cosmopolitan soul who had seen a bit of the world, took it all in his stride. He wasn't even fazed by the bidet in the bathroom: the Arabs used them instead of loo roll, he informed us.

My parents hit the beach, although my normally easy-going dad was put out by what he perceived as the Continental racket of charging sunbathers for loungers and parasols. They wouldn't get away with *that* in Clacton, he would grumble, fiddling in his pocket for some spare lira.

Brian and I spent some time on the beach but more cruising around the town and soaking up the sights. We were surprised to find we were quite a hit with the local girls, who regarded us as dapper emissaries from swinging London. Brian loved the female attention, but I was far too gawky and awkward to do much with it – plus, of course, I had Carol waiting at home.

Even I couldn't deny the chemistry with one dark-haired signorina, though. One afternoon, a gorgeous brunette served me an ice cream in a bar. She spoke no English, and Italian had not been big on the curriculum at Shipman County, but there was a strong frisson as I held out my hand for her to take the money for the *gelato*. Our eyes met.

'David,' I told her.

'Margarita,' she replied.

We smiled at each other. Subconsciously, I thought: to be continued.

First, though, I had to kickstart my international music career. The Everons headed down to the audition that Brian's dad had arranged for us. The club consisted of a giant circus tent with a stage holding the resident band's gear, which luckily included a drum kit.

We set to tuning our borrowed equipment and hit the genial club manager with two of our best shots: the Motown hit 'Money' and the Isley Brothers/Beatles song 'Twist and Shout'. He seemed impressed, and we were hired to play a forty-five-minute set the following night, after a magician's turn but before the resident band's headline show.

It was hardly the Beatles in Hamburg but we were all elated at this success and, possibly getting ahead of ourselves, spent the hotel-buffet dinner discussing learning Italian and maybe even emigrating en masse to Italy. Yet a thought was distracting me: I wondered if Margarita would like to witness the Everons' triumph?

After eating, I slipped away from the rest of the party and went back to her café. She was frothing up cappuccinos and waiting tables and I ordered and worked my way through three Pepsis before gathering the courage to talk to her. Did she like music?

'*Si, molto!*' she said, smiling. It was a promising start, but my halting attempts to invite her to see the band foundered on the language barrier, and our 'conversation' was going nowhere fast until a waiter who spoke a bit of English interceded. It turned out he wasn't just a waiter: he was also Margarita's older brother.

The brother did a bit of rudimentary translation between us and then firmly informed me that Margarita was allowed neither to go to clubs nor to miss a night at work. Eventually, however, we reached a compromise: she could meet me after the bar closed at 11.30 the next night.

'Great!' I said.

'I come too,' added the brother. 'Chaperone.'

So there were to be three people in this relationship! Even so, I smiled my agreement and arranged to return the next night. Back at the hotel, I lay in bed full of anticipation but also wondering what I was playing at, and feeling guilty about Carol.

We spent the next day on the beach, where Dad continued to fume at the extortionate umbrella-rental system and I played football with the locals. I was delighted when my shaggy hair and ball skills led them to christen me George Best, but less so at ending the day with typical English-abroad lobster-red shoulders.

The evening brought our debut gig, with the Everons under strict instructions to start up once the magician had finished his plate-spinning trick. As the conjuror wandered off, the compère nodded at us: 'Ladeez and gentlemen, all the way from Enger-land – the Everons!'

Our opening shot, Chuck Berry's 'Johnny B. Goode', triggered some dancing but also some pained expressions, and the compère appeared behind my shoulder, ordering us to turn the volume down. Otherwise, the gig went well, and at the end the manager confirmed our booking for the rest of our holiday.

There were jubilant scenes backstage, but I once again made my excuses and left, heading off with a spring in my step – and butterflies in my stomach – for my bizarre three-way date. I had no idea how it would work, but we took a stroll along the beach and her brother allowed Margarita and I to go ahead as he kept a wary eye from a polite distance.

Margarita was shy and pretty and I was flushed and tongue-tied, and the lack of a shared language was a definite hindrance. But it was thrilling to be holding hands and walking by the crashing sea under the starry night sky, and I ended our enchanting evening with a kiss on the cheek for Margarita, a handshake for her brother, and a promise to do it all again the next evening.

What a night! I had played a cool rock 'n' roll gig and wooed a beautiful stranger in a glamorous land. As I wandered back to the hotel through Cattolica's dark and deserted streets, I felt like the star of my own private, dramatic European movie.

The holiday played out in the same vein. The days were fun, the gigs went well, and after our third date, Margarita's brother decided I could be trusted and abandoned his chaperone post. On our last night, she and I swapped kisses and addresses and I wondered if our holiday romance would survive any longer.

I had told Margarita I had a girlfriend in England but had not been sure she had understood: I think she might have thought I was saying I had a sister. On the plane home, I pondered the problem of her and Carol and quietly worried over what would happen next.

The answer was a development that I certainly hadn't predicted. Arriving home, I went straight round to Carol's to tell her most – but not all – of my holiday adventures. I knocked on her door, she opened it and I took an involuntary sharp intake of breath. Carol had a yellow head.

'Do you like it?' she asked me.

'Yes,' I lied. 'I think so.' It seemed that while I was away, Carol had resolved to follow my suggestion about dying her hair blonde, but I hadn't envisaged it turning out such a grisly shade of orangey-yellow. I decided to keep quiet and hope it would grow on me, or, better, grow out.

I gave Carol and her parents my judiciously edited version of the Italian holiday. Over the next few weeks, she and I looked to fall back into our set routine, but something had changed, and to me, her orange hair seemed to symbolise the problems that were besetting our relationship.

We started seeing less of each other, and arguing more. When she also got a job at Plessey's, it made our periodic bouts of not talking to each other decidedly awkward. Nevertheless, she was still my girlfriend, I wasn't trying to ditch her, and when I caught her on the factory roof, snogging the face off another of the apprentices, I was deeply hurt and upset. Although, in the circumstances, I suppose I had no right to be.

Margarita and I had become pen pals, but her letters – clearly written with the heavy assistance of an English/Italian dictionary – were difficult to decipher, and eventually the lira dropped for both of us that our holiday fling would go no further. As the months passed the letters dwindled, then stopped completely.

So both of my romantic interests had exited stage left and I was stuck ticking over in my dead-end job, desperate to forward my musical career without the first idea of how to do it. I was badly in need of some guidance. Luckily, it was just about to arrive.

4

THE SMASHING OF
THE CHINA PLATES

Some people in show business see artist managers as essentially exploitative figures. If things are going well, they are parasites creaming off 10 per cent of their earnings for doing very little; if they are going badly, they're the natural scapegoat. I don't doubt that rogues like that exist, but a good manager is worth his weight in gold, and I reckon I owe almost everything to the visionary who took the reins of my career – and life – in 1964.

Ted was doing his best, and to give credit to Brian and Sandra's dad, he had got the Everons a fair few bookings and even helped us to conquer Italy (!) but we were hitting the wall. If the band was ever to progress from weddings and pub residencies, we felt we needed a manager.

Brian had a day job as a cooper and his boss in the barrel world was a man called Stan Murray. Stan's son, Martin, had been in the original line-up of the Honeycombs, who had had a number-one hit earlier that year with 'Have I the Right?' and this tenuous connection was enough for Brian to ask Stan to manage us.

Stan freely admitted that he didn't know enough about the pop world to be of much help – but he knew a man who did.

He was friends with a show business writer and critic named Derek Bowman, and he agreed to bring him down to watch the Everons rehearse in a pub called the Eagle in Stratford.

Stan and Derek turned up the following Wednesday night. Stan was a small, friendly guy with a passing resemblance to Sid James, but Derek cut a more sophisticated figure, standing out a mile in the rough-edged East End boozer. Dapper in a grey mohair suit and smoking Peter Stuyvesant cigarettes, he looked every inch the part of a sharp, worldly-wise band manager.

Fondly imagining that this audition could be our passage to the big time, the band were all extremely nervous. After attempting some awkward small talk in the bar downstairs, we invited Derek and Stan up to hear us do our thing.

We had decided to play a mix of our usual covers and a song or two that I had written. This was a fairly new development, and although I didn't really know what I was doing, I figured it was important for the Everons that we developed our own identity rather than just rehashing more successful bands' stuff.

The first song I had written had been distinctly autobiographical and was called 'Carol-Anne'. It was basically a white East End teenager trying to write a heartbroken Mississippi blues classic: the chorus proclaimed, '*Oh Carol-Anne, the day that you leave me, girl, I'll be a dying man.*' It had been rather overtaken by recent events in my life that had proven it to be both misguided and, well, wrong.

The hall over the Eagle was poky and smelled of stale beer but we had carefully laid out a table and two chairs in front of the stage for Derek and Stan, and John made a short speech before we fired into a Memphis Slim song. The rock 'n' roll soon got rid of our nerves and by the third song we were even smiling (except for Sandra, who never smiled, but that was cool in itself).

Derek was scrutinising us very intently and clearly liked what he saw and heard, because after we had run through our set, he and Stan agreed to manage us. Stan would finance us, because he had a few bob, and Derek would make use of his knowledge of the entertainment scene to plot our masterplan for world domination. The Everons had managers and we could not have been more delighted.

There could be no doubt that Derek was well connected because over the next few weeks he brought a string of showbiz A-listers down to the Eagle to show them his new charges and try to get a word-of-mouth thing going. The saloon-bar regulars must have been utterly gobsmacked to see Peter O'Toole, Lionel Bart, Ian McShane, Vidal Sassoon and Susan Hampshire swanning through the pub and up the stairs.

They were a stellar crew, but our celebrity guests didn't mean a lot to me. A shy, typical teenager who found it hard to string a sentence together, I mostly hid behind my drums as Derek's famous friends came to have a butchers at us. I spoke to Mary Quant, who was very posh and wide-eyed and, well, quaint, but often I simply had no idea who our star visitors were. If Howlin' Wolf or Muddy Waters had come down, it would have been a different matter.

We were very grateful for Derek's efforts and had a lot of faith in him but a few of his ideas had us scratching our heads. He was keen to emphasise our East End roots and kept asking us to play an instrumental version of 'Limehouse Blues'. In a similar vein, he insisted we change our name from the Everons to the China Plates – Cockney rhyming slang for mates. I was fairly horrified by this but we went along with it.

After a trip to Carnaby Street, where Stan's cash kitted the China Plates out in matching white tab-collar shirts, sky-blue jackets and Cuban-heel boots, came a symbolic leap forward – our first recording session.

The venue was a fleapit studio in Leytonstone, run by a fat man with a beard who looked as if he slept under the production console. He was also the engineer, and painfully led us through the complexities of headphones and vocal booths. At first we found it intimidating, but we managed to commit two of my songs – 'Carol-Anne' and 'Got to Work' – to tape, as well as a Memphis Slim track. The China Plates had made their first recording.

This was heady stuff and I began to suspect that my dream of being a professional musician could even become a reality – but there was one major problem. I was still clocking on every day as an apprentice electrical engineer at Plessey's and, what was worse, I had signed a five-year contract. If I was really going to live the dream, I would have to escape this arrangement.

I met up with Derek at a Soho hangout called the Arts Theatre Club and told him my intention. He gave me a timely reality check, assuring me that he felt I was talented but also cautioning that only a tiny percentage of the people who tried to make it in show business actually succeeded. We agreed I should have a chat with my parents before taking the plunge.

Mum and Dad said the usual parental things about it being good to have 'a trade to fall back on' but were reliably supportive and ultimately left the decision to me. I was seventeen, and knew that if I saw my contract through at Plessey's I would be twenty-one by the time I left, which sounded ancient and far too old to crack the rock 'n' roll world.

Plessey's personnel manager was an avuncular soul named Mr Baker, who agreed to a meeting. I knew that he was entitled to hold me to my contract if he so wished, and I felt nervous as I explained that electrical engineering wasn't really for me and I wanted to be a musician. Mr Baker sat, listened and weighed me up through a cloud of pipe smoke.

'Well, son,' he eventually said, 'if you want to leave, there is not much point in staying, is there?' He sent me on my way with his best wishes, even saying I could always come back if things didn't go well. I was grateful for the kind words but suspected and hoped that I had set my last lathe.

I had made the break but initially it looked as if my decision had been about as inspired as my brainwave about drawing Popeye. It was becoming clear that things weren't really working out for the China Plates. Derek had taken our studio demo on a tour of record companies but nobody was biting and we remained distinctly unsigned.

Stan was getting tired of seeing no prospect of any return on his investment in the band and when Derek asked me to meet him at the Arts Theatre Club again as he had news, I was expecting the worst. It duly arrived: Derek informed me that Stan had given up and was withdrawing his financial backing.

Yet there was more. Derek went on to tell me that the reason he had agreed to manage the band when he first came to see us at the Eagle was that he had recognised potential in me. He added that a lot of the people he had brought down to see us had also singled me out as something special. I was flattered, but also nonplussed – what did this mean, exactly?

I soon found out. Derek went on to explain that he shared Stan's misgivings about the China Plates' future but he believed that I had the potential to make it big on my own. 'Would you like to be a solo singer?' he asked me.

The question totally threw me. It was something I had never even remotely considered, or had the slightest interest in: I didn't even like singing that much. I wanted to be a jazz drummer. Also, we were a close-knit group and I felt a fierce loyalty to the band. I didn't want to betray them or walk out on them. 'I don't know,' I told Derek honestly.

We went our separate ways and as I mooched through Soho, a suffocating melancholy descended on me. The Everons/China Plates had played great gigs, wowed Cattolica, got management backing, made a recording: it had seemed that the world was opening up for us. Was it really to be over so quickly?

Well, that was how it was looking. By the time we met for our next rehearsal, Derek had called John, Brian and Sandra and told them Stan had pulled out and he could not manage us without financial backing. The mood was sombre. We hardly played a note, and John even suggested breaking up the band.

Brian was still bullish about making the China Plates work but John and Sandra seemed already resigned to failure and

Derek's suggestion of a solo career began to play on my mind. I hung in there but gigs and rehearsals became few and far between as the band lost its direction, and after a few weeks the China Plates just fizzled out.

John and Sandra decided to get married and move to Australia. Talk about a clean break! Brian and I lost contact. I had no band and no job, and only one offer on the table. What had I got to lose? I reached a decision, and phoned Derek.

'If you are serious about me going solo,' I told him, 'I'm in.'

5

OH MY, THIGH HIGH, DIG DEM DIMPLES ON DEM KNEES

While Derek had been managing the China Plates, he had been a friendly and supportive but slightly distant figure, who tended mostly to deal with John because he was the leader of the band. Now that I was his solo charge, I started to learn exactly what he was about and what kind of man he was.

After my fateful phone call, the first thing he did was to arrange to visit my parents to discuss my future. He arrived carrying a management contract and our meeting went on for hours as we weighed up the pros and cons of me trying to make it on my own. He wasn't pushy, but left the contract for them to peruse.

Derek made a good impression on my mum and dad and it was easy to see why. Tall, handsome and about fifteen years older than me, he was an Oxford graduate and academic who spoke eight languages. As a critic, he had an encyclopaedic knowledge of film and theatre and, as I'd already learned, a bulging contacts book.

Looking back, it's hard to discern exactly what embryonic talent Derek had spotted in a shy, self-conscious seventeen-year-old pub-band drummer, but whatever it was he was determined to nurture it. He was hugely positive about what I could go on to do, and it was his fervent, profound belief in me that impressed Mum and Dad most of all.

Over the years, people have occasionally asked me about my relationship with Derek and whether he might have been a Brian Epstein-like figure infatuated with his young charge, but there was never any hint of that kind of tension between us. In fact I never knew him to have a partner and had no idea about his sexuality. He was more than merely my manager and mentor, though: he gradually became the older brother that I never had.

Derek's personal circumstances were difficult. His mother and his sister were both schizophrenic and he was heavily involved in their care, spending all the time that he wasn't looking after me looking after them. It was clear he was one of life's caring people and he just wanted the best for me.

My parents could sense that, and after he had left, the three of us sat up into the early hours worrying over exactly what I should do, before going to bed with no decisions reached. The next day, however, I had another of those invaluable epiphanies that help to write your life's script, and everything became clearer.

One drawback with Derek's plan was that I was not even sure I wanted to be a singer, but alone in the flat the next morning, I put a blues album on as usual. Instead of concentrating on the drums, as was my habit, I focused on the singers. Immediately a whole new world opened up.

It was Buddy Guy who got me. I played 'The First Time I Met the Blues' and suddenly there he was, at the heart of this vivid, incredible music, singing as if his voice was a wound and his passions an open book. He was singing of the inescapable pull of the blues and their hold over him: *'Blues, you know you've done me all the harm that you could.'*

Yet it also sounded more universal than that: like all great blues singers, Buddy was lamenting life's agonies, and cheating women, and good loving gone bad. It was powerful and human, and it moved me. Would I ever be able to convey a fraction of that emotion? Suddenly I knew that I wanted to try. I knew that I wanted to be a singer.

When Mum and Dad came home from work that night, I told them as we ate tea that I had made my decision and wanted to throw in my lot with Derek. Despite their misgivings, they didn't even quibble, but signed the contract there and then. The die had been cast.

Derek was delighted that I had acquiesced to being his grand project and he was determined to hit the ground running. Over the next few weeks and months, he began honing my talents via a steep learning curve that didn't have much to do with Mississippi blues but instead gave me an old-fashioned grounding in all aspects of light entertainment and show business.

My first port of call was a church hall in Marylebone where an elderly black American named Buddy Bradley schooled me two evenings a week in the mysteries of – wait for it – tap dancing. It wasn't something that I could imagine Lead Belly doing but it was fun and Buddy was the coolest guy I had ever met. He even declared that I was a natural. Maybe it was my drummer's sense of rhythm.

Derek would come to watch, as he did when I started singing lessons in Soho with a very correct chap named Eric Gilder who looked like a wise old owl. Before that, I had only sung into a microphone doing backing vocals with the Everons, using what I supposed was a generic blues voice that I had copycatted from American records.

This was very different. Eric would play the piano while I sang standards and show tunes such as 'Fly Me to the Moon' and 'Who Can I Turn To?' He taught me classic techniques such as singing from the stomach and breath control and helped me to find my voice. We even ventured into opera, and some of the huge, resounding noises that I summoned up amazed me, not to mention Derek.

Not content with turning me into a tap-dancing opera singer, Derek decided that the next discipline required in my all-round entertainment crash-course was acting. He packed me off to see an acting and voice coach called Robbie Ray, who gave me dramatic thespian speeches to read and worked at rubbing the rough edges off the harsh vowels and glottal stops of my East End accent.

The climax of this acting training was a two-week course at the Royal Academy of the Dramatic Arts (RADA), where I had to declaim a Shakespearean soliloquy. I felt pretty sure I was the first ever Shipman County alumnus to do *that*. In truth, a lot of these new artistic endeavours felt pretty weird to me, but they were an adventure, and I trusted Derek, so I ploughed on with them.

Derek's aesthetic training for his new East End protégé also encompassed inviting me to the theatre as his guest when he wrote newspaper reviews. The first play he took me to was Sean O'Casey's *Juno and the Paycock*, a classic drama about a ne'er-do-well Irish family, but the plot made less of an impact on me than how polite and attentive the audience were. Unlike at the Everons' gigs, nobody was chucking bottles at the cast or lurching drunkenly on to the stage. Maybe the theatre was OK after all.

With my training complete, Derek started looking for work for me. I was pretty keen on this idea as well, as the money from both Plessey's and the band had now obviously dried up and I was broke all the time. I wouldn't get any acting jobs without being a member of the actors' union, Equity, so Derek applied for me to join. Back came a message that they had a David Cook registered already. If I wanted to act, I needed a new name.

You would think that a decision about what name you would be known by for your entire professional life would be traumatic and require much agonising over, but in actual fact it took less than a minute. Derek phoned me and suggested David Essex, as I was living there. I had no better ideas, so I said 'OK'. David Essex it was. I always tell people now that I'm just grateful I wasn't living in Middlesex. Or Northumberland.

Although I was a willing pupil in the rigours of showbiz, Derek knew I was still hankering to make music and hadn't neglected that side of things. He announced that he had found a record producer who might be interested in working with me, and we headed off to a flat in Knightsbridge to meet him.

Bunny Lewis had produced four number-one singles and written songs for Helen Shapiro but was not at all the rock 'n' roll figure I was expecting. A middle-aged, very English gent with a demeanour that was so stiff-upper-lip that it verged on the military, he had very pronounced front teeth, which I suspect had earned him his nickname.

He was a lovely man, though, and had dug out a song he figured would be just right for me. An overwrought Walker Brothers-style big ballad called 'And the Tears Came Tumbling Down', it was a classic boy-meets-girl, girl-leaves-boy number.

An arranger taught me the song as we crowded around Bunny's piano. Bunny had the idea that I could pretend to cry as I sang it, which seemed pretty corny to me, but I belted it out, and Bunny was so enraptured that he presented us with a recording contract and a studio booking on the spot. Derek and I left delighted. This seemed like serious progress.

I practised the song at home non-stop over the next few days so that even poor Mum and Dad knew it inside out, but this didn't remotely prepare me for walking into Olympic Studios in Barnes. I was already nervous enough without finding a thirty-piece orchestra and professional backing singers waiting for me!

Sensing my terror, Bunny hopped down from the production desk in the control room to give me some manly reassurance, and as I stood by the conductor on his podium and heard the orchestra run through the song, my nerves dissipated. I had never heard anything so powerful at close quarters and suddenly I wanted to be part of it.

Bunny packed me off to the vocal booth where I emoted my way through 'And the Tears Came Tumbling Down', trying to sound both heartbroken and in tune. After three takes Bunny was satisfied, and with trepidation I headed to the control room to hear the results.

My voice sounded thin and reedy to me but Bunny and Derek were delighted – although Bunny had more pressing things on his mind. 'I told you that you could do it!' he snapped. 'Now do the other song – we lose the musicians in half an hour.'

In those days the Musicians' Union ruled the roost and their members played for the time they were booked for and not a minute more. I sang the B-side, 'You Can't Stop Me From Loving You', in no time then repeated the playback experience – I was still dissatisfied with my vocal, but Bunny seemed chuffed.

Despite my misgivings, I was incredibly excited when a box of advance promo singles arrived at home, with my new name on the label next to the famous blue and silver Fontana logo. Mum and Dad could not have been more proud; I could not believe it was actually my voice coming out of the gramophone at 45 r.p.m.

Yet 'And the Tears Came Tumbling Down' sank without trace. I did a few promo press interviews and sang the song at a pirate radio-sponsored roadshow at the Lyceum, which I hated, but its only radio play was a couple of spins on crackly old Radio Luxembourg 208. I heard one of them, and honestly had no idea whether to run into the street waving my transistor radio or hide under the bed until it had finished.

However, Bunny was not a man to give up easily and his next selection of song for me was a Solomon Burke blues track, 'Can't Nobody Love You'. This was more like it. I enjoyed recording it and it picked up a smidgeon more radio play and even managed to hit the dizzy heights of number seventeen in the pirate-radio charts. *Record Mirror* praised 'a big-voiced newcomer who punches lyrics like a heavyweight'.

This was still small beer, though, and I didn't really feel like an all-singing, all-dancing entertainer. I was missing the life and camaraderie of being in a proper rock 'n' roll band. Unknown to Derek, I started scanning the musicians-wanted pages in *Melody Maker*, and when I saw an ad for a vocalist, asking anybody interested to call Pete, I did exactly that.

Pete, who had a voice like he regularly gargled with gravel, told me he was a member of a five-piece rhythm-and-blues band named Mood Indigo who were based in Stevenage. He had vaguely heard of me and invited me to audition at a rehearsal at a warehouse in Hertfordshire in a couple of days' time.

Derek was initially disapproving when I confessed to this freelance activity but came round to the idea. On the appointed night, a friend called Frank Fairchild drove me to Stevenage. Frank, who liked to go as Fairs, was a good mate, a Georgie Fame lookalike and a bit of a wide boy I had met at a club he ran in Ilford called El Grotto, and over the years we had had a few misadventures together.

Mood Indigo were a pretty hirsute bunch and looked the part of a jazzy R&B band. They had two saxophone players, an organist, a bass player and a drummer but no guitarist – an odd line-up, but it seemed to work. I was particularly impressed with the black baritone sax player, Paddy.

We got on from the start and I loved their dextrous, powerful musicianship as we fired through a couple of songs, including Wilson Pickett's 'In the Midnight Hour'. I realised how much I'd missed being in a band. They were just as keen, and by the end of the audition, I was in Mood Indigo.

To my delight, they were a proper gigging band, and once I had joined the ranks, I decided to pitch in and help out with life on the road. Mood Indigo had been renting vans for tours and I had passed my driving test as soon as my ban was lifted and was set to buy a car. I suggested that I buy a van instead and the band pay a small fee to use it, and they loved the idea.

The second-hand Ford Transit that I finished up with was slightly more roadworthy than the Lambretta (although that's not saying much) but it still had its moments. I was happily driving the band down the North Circular one day when a wheel went shooting past the van and smashed through a garden wall. A second later the Transit dropped on one side: it was our wheel. The woman whose wall I had to retrieve it from was not best pleased.

Yet it usually got us from A to B, and we were doing plenty of that. David Essex and Mood Indigo would often play three gigs in one night. We roamed up and down the country and I also got to play the iconic London venues where I had devoured gigs as a kid: the Marquee, Eel Pie Island and, yes, the Flamingo.

At this stage I still wasn't that confident as a front man, but after weeks of tap-dancing and acting lessons, it felt great to be back in the game and paying my dues with a band. As a fixture on the pub and club circuit, we also bumped into plenty of other young tyros striving for the big time.

David Bowie hadn't yet changed his name, painted his face or invented Ziggy Stardust back then. He was just the polite young singer in Davy Jones and the Locker, who were playing R&B and copying American stars the same as we were. We also shared bills with Bluesology, and their quiet, non-singing keyboardist, Elton John.

Steampacket clearly had something, with three vocalists in Long John Baldry, Julie Driscoll and a really impressive young singer with a fantastic voice named Rod Stewart. Yet normally we'd be turning up just as these bands were leaving, or vice versa, so we never got a chance to do much more than nod a quick hello.

I was now young, free and single and singing in a rock 'n' roll band so theoretically my love life ought to have been decidedly lively but it never seemed to work out like that. For our treks out of London, Mood Indigo had a band rule that everybody slept in the van unless they pulled a girl, in which case they could dip into the communal kitty for a B&B for the night.

Very occasionally I got lucky, but normally my natural shyness and reticence meant that I ended the night helping to pack away the gear before bunking down in the back of the van in a pool of petrol for the night, listening to Pete or Paddy's axle-rattling snoring. I wonder if Rod Stewart was doing the same?

Around this time I did have a chance encounter that was to have rather more significance for my romantic life, although I didn't know it at the time. On a night off from the band, I headed down to meet my mate Frank at his club in Ilford: it may well have been the night that I pulled up outside El Grotto in time to see Frank bashing a troublesome punter with a temporary bus stop.

Frank and I sat at the bar chatting about our beloved Hammers and clocked two pretty girls who came in wearing mini-skirts. I thought one of them was gorgeous: Frank told me that her name was Maureen Neal, her mate was Kath, and they had been in before.

A local Lothario called Phil the Greek joined them at their table but Frank didn't think either of them was involved with him. We chatted on, but later that evening, as I decided to head home, Maureen caught my eye and gave me a wave. I gave her a wave back. Again: to be continued.

Derek had no objection to me singing with Mood Indigo but the band was going nowhere fast and I was getting tired of the long drives to Stevenage to rehearse. My manager suggested that we reconvene with dear old Bunny to make another attempt to get my solo career moving.

Bunny had had a brainwave and it was one I was very excited about. For my next single, he decided to hook me up with a new producer – J J Jackson, a larger-than-life soul and R&B singer and songwriter. J J was black and American, which ticked a lot of boxes for me.

A massive man dripping with jewellery, J J had written his own hits in the States but decided that I should cover a Ray Charles song, an upbeat jazz-blues number called 'This Little Girl of Mine'. J J was very charismatic and persuasive and I loved the tune, but the record-buying public didn't share my enthusiasm and I had another flop single under my belt.

Mood Indigo didn't seem to be playing so many gigs and I was getting tired of bumping around in the Ford Transit van (it was hardly a girl magnet) so I decided to upgrade to a car. My love for all things American saw me plump for a Nash Metropolitan, a small Yank car introduced to Britain in the late fifties by American servicemen stationed over here. Without getting all

Top Gear on you, it was two-tone blue with white-wall tyres, a bench seat and column gear-change, and I loved it.

The Nash was my transport when I went to the 100 Club in Oxford Street one night after my eighteenth birthday to see a mate play a blues gig. Getting to the venue early, I fell into conversation with a Swedish girl named Beth, pronounced Bet. In the sixties, Swedish girls had a reputation for free love that I desperately hoped was true, but Beth wasn't the stereotypical six-foot-tall Scandinavian stunner: she was an elfin tomboy with short brown hair and a very masculine dress sense.

Beth was the daughter of a university professor, spoke perfect English and was working as an au pair for an American family living in posh Highgate in north London. After the gig I gave her a lift back to their sprawling mansion and for the next six months we became inseparable, even if our idea of a hot date was Wimpy's or the Golden Egg.

It was good that Beth had given my personal life a boost as work-wise things looked somewhat bleak. Mood Indigo were winding down, Bunny had gone incommunicado and, skint again, I had no choice but to work my way through a motley selection of part-time jobs.

If you want to see all aspects of humanity – but mainly the darker ones – then you should try driving a taxi. As I waited for Derek to get things moving again, I spent a few months as part of a team of drivers working for a very eccentric owner of a small mini-cab company.

The guy was basically a complete chancer but inadvertently extremely entertaining. He was a bald man who kept a wig on his desk, which he would whip on to his head whenever a punter walked in the door. He'd also try to fabricate an air of busy-ness by constantly being on the radio at the base, despite the fact that only one of the cars actually had a radio in it.

'Where are you, Rod?' he would ask, seeking to impress a credulous customer.

'I'm just around the corner.'

'Where are you now?' he'd ask him, five seconds later.

'I'm still around the f****** corner!'

It went on all night. Poor Rod must have been tempted to rip the radio out.

I got put on the nightmare shift from around 11 p.m. to 5 a.m. the next morning. No two evenings were the same and they were usually dreadful. The start of the shift would coincide with the pubs chucking out, which meant drunks fighting over, or in, your cab, trying to avoid paying the fare, threatening you and now and then, just for good measure, throwing up down the back of your neck.

The early hours were mellower and were when the freaks and weirdoes came out to play. One regular customer, who was a nice guy, was a hopeless insomniac who would pay me just to drive him around aimlessly in his pyjamas for an hour.

Another time, a very drunk middle-aged woman asked me to take her south of the river. We pulled up at the destination, I asked her for the fare, and she pulled down her knickers and invited me to 'take it out of that'. I was absolutely horrified, as well as having no idea what she would give me for a tip.

Even more disturbing was the night that I picked up a man named Michael in Hornchurch, who asked to be taken to a place called Warley Hospital. As we drove through the dark country lanes of Essex, I figured there was something amiss as Michael suddenly tried to scramble from the back of the car into the front seat, using my head as a lever.

I managed to push Michael back into the rear of the car and all became clear as we swung into the grounds of the Warley: it was a mental hospital. Michael was a patient on weekend leave. Locking him in the car, I walked up to the towering Gothic building, silhouetted in the moonlight, to announce his arrival.

Ringing the bell, I was greeted by a man in a white coat who snapped that Michael was 'Very late!' and accompanied me back to the car. Michael was by now in the front passenger seat and attempting to climb through a tiny crack in the window, and looked alarmed when he saw my escort.

Back inside the hospital, I asked Michael for my fare. The poor guy opened a sad little tobacco tin and offered me the sixpence that lay inside. I saw his terrified eyes and told him, 'It's OK. Forget it,' but the orderly was less forgiving and began yelling at him and berating him. I slunk back to the car, leaving sorry, wretched Michael to his nightmare of a life. The mini-cab driving came to an end soon afterwards, when Wiggy's office was petrol-bombed and burned to the ground by a competitor.

After this, window cleaning was straightforward. I worked as part of a small team under a wide-boy Cockney foreman called Tommy. In theory, we cleaned office buildings under contract, but Tommy had perfected a system whereby we identified the office of the bloke who signed the payment dockets, did a great job on his window and ignored the rest of the building. This opportunistic labour-saving device meant we were often done for the day by lunchtime and could bunk off for the afternoon.

I was more conscientious in a job painting factories, although a lunchtime pint one day was nearly the death of me. Returning to the roof from the pub, I put my foot on the wrong piece of scaffolding and crashed through the roof to the concrete floor twenty feet below.

As I fell through the air head first, I managed to twist my body around to land on my side but still smashed my head fairly hard on the floor. A trip to the A&E department followed, where they kept me in for a few hours for concussion.

My already varied CV also expanded to include a fortnight in a hardware shop working for one of the most unpleasant men I have ever met. A severe sergeant-major type, he regarded my fashionably shoulder-length hair with huge disapproval and took great pleasure in barking orders at me, and doling out physically impossible tasks for me to perform.

The worst job he gave me was helping to unload our deliveries of gas canisters, which meant standing beneath the lorries as two burly workmen dropped ridiculously heavy metal bottles down for me to catch. My hands would be bleeding by the end, and next to this torture, my spell peeling spuds in a fish and chip shop and my week in a factory making tent parts were a doddle.

It was a relief when Bunny reappeared on the radar and hooked Derek and me up with J J again, but J J's next decision was an unmitigated disaster. He had written a song especially for me to sing, which was flattering, but my heart sank when I heard it: it was a tribute to every man's favourite female garment, the mini-skirt, called 'Thigh High'.

The chorus, to be sung in a lecherous growl, ran: '*Oh my, thigh high, dig dem dimples on dem knees!*' With hindsight, I should never have recorded it but I was slightly in awe of J J and so I went along with the fiasco. The single died a death ('Ugh!' said the *Daily Mirror* review, correctly), which at least stopped J J from turning me into some kind of novelty-act precursor of Black Lace.

Everything seemed to be coming to an end. Bunny had lost a few thousand pounds trying to kickstart my career, and decided to cut his losses. I also parted ways with Mood Indigo, after our final tour, arranged by a berserk booking agent – we would be in Sunderland one night, Bournemouth the next – ended with me poleaxed with pneumonia in Manchester. The band had been great fun, but it felt like it was over.

Even worse, Beth's six-month spell in London finished and she had to return to university in Sweden. This really upset me and I missed her a lot, but a trip to Scandinavia to attempt to rekindle things didn't work out: I arrived out-of-sorts after an exhausting journey, Beth was a bit aloof, and her university-professor father gave the distinct impression that he didn't feel I was worthy of his daughter.

When love affairs come to an end, it helps to be able to throw yourself into your work, but the way my music career was going down the plughole, I didn't have any work to throw myself into. Undeterred, the eternal optimist Derek decided to switch to plan B. It was time for me to tread the boards.

6

LUVVIES, GANGSTERS AND SNOGGING BROWN BEARS

With his academic career and newspaper critic connections, Derek was really more steeped in the world of theatre than in music, and with my pop career resolutely refusing to take off, he began to point me more towards the acting side of things. I still had my reservations but, as usual, I went along with it.

He secured me an audition with a touring repertory company run by a husband-and-wife couple, Zack Matalon and Elizabeth Searle. Zack was a very outgoing, larger-than-life American, while the quieter Elizabeth was a successful musical actress who had starred in *The Pyjama Game*.

I felt fairly clueless at the audition – I remember trying to appear cool and suave, which I really wasn't, by rather preposterously sprawling all over a church spire that was part of the scenery – but to my amazement, I got the job. The money was rubbish but Mum and Dad, who had been understandably worried about me, were very proud, and as rehearsals neared I looked forward to becoming a stage actor.

The rehearsals were to be held in a church hall in Bayswater, west London, and on the first day the booming, very thespian

Zack introduced me to the rest of the company. It took me no time to realise that they were all notably more upper crust and well spoken than I was. It seemed a fairly safe bet that none of them had been to Canning Town in their life.

In quick succession, I met a classical actor type named Roy who had a bald head, glasses and an immaculate speaking voice; a posh, miserable young actress called Susanne; two nice, friendly character actors; a female musical director; a black-clad, ginger-haired female stage manager and a very white girl who looked as if she lived under a toadstool. Only one cast member really stood out: a huge, imposing Zulu called Dambuza.

The company tended to learn three or four productions and take them out on tour, and Zack ran us through our schedule. Over the next three weeks we were to rehearse the first show, a long-running Broadway musical called *The Fantasticks*, to performance levels before learning two other offerings on the road.

The musical director, a petite American girl in her thirties with glasses and a lot of hair, played us the score to *The Fantasticks*, in which I was to play the juvenile lead, Matt. There were elements of *West Side Story* in its plot of two star-crossed young lovers from warring families and it had some good songs, with 'Soon It's Gonna Rain' and 'Try to Remember' standing out.

Oh, Kay! was also a musical, a George and Ira Gershwin offering that in truth I thought was a load of bollocks, and in which I was hopelessly miscast as a duke. The repertoire was completed by a drama, *To Dorothy a Son*, in which I was to have the happily non-onerous role of an off-stage phone voice.

I crammed my part in *The Fantasticks* at home and on the long tube journeys from Newbury Park to Bayswater, and was pleased to discover that learning lines came pretty easily to me. Zack even gave me some drumming to do when he learned of my musical background. We began our tour in Paignton in Devon and on the first night I didn't feel at all nervous until I heard the audience applaud the overture.

That was when the adrenaline kicked in. There was a slight out-of-body air to my stage debut, with my mind racing and the action appearing at times to be in slow motion. Was this really happening? Was it going well? Happily, the audience appeared to think so, giving us a generous ovation at the final curtain. Derek, who had travelled down for the opening night, seemed very pleased and also gave me a few useful tips.

We quickly settled into a routine of seaside digs and end-of-the-pier theatre shows, learning the other plays as we went along. I even got to make use of my tap dancing in *Oh, Kay!*, although for obvious reasons I didn't feel terribly convincing as a blue-blooded aristocrat.

I normally roomed with Dambuza, who was a fascinating man. He had fled South Africa during the apartheid regime, playing the lead role of a boxer in a West End show named *King Kong* and then securing asylum to stay in Britain. We would talk for hours into the night and I would sit transfixed as Dambuza regaled me in his rich baritone with tales of Africa and his fight for freedom.

The company was fairly closely knit but while it was a bit more civilised than sleeping in a pool of petrol in Mood Indigo's van, there were similarities. The same attitude prevailed of what happens on the road stays on the road, and I had flings with both the ginger-haired stage manager (I wore her down) and the American musical director (she wore me down). Zack, for his part, tried his luck with any female around.

As Derek had predicted, I learned a lot from my first repertory tour, but as it drew to an end I was hankering to return to music, as usual. Fortunately Derek had been busy on that score, securing the interest of Mike Leander, an upcoming record producer who had been working with a singer called Paul Raven (who, incidentally, was later to become Gary Glitter).

We met up and Mike suggested that I should record a cover of 'She's Leaving Home', a song that he had arranged on the album of the moment, the Beatles' *Sgt. Pepper's Lonely Hearts Club Band*. Due to a deal that Mike had with a label called Uni Records, an offshoot of Universal Pictures, my version would be released in America only.

I was impressed with Mike, a confident and flamboyant figure who, unlike Bunny, seemed music industry through and through and was the epitome of a top record producer. In the studio, I was taken with his foppish air, his meticulous professionalism and, most of all, his orange suit as we tackled 'She's Leaving Home' and a song that Mike had written for the B-side, 'He's a Better Man Than Me'.

Mike told me to sing the latter song in a very English accent, as the Beatles and the British invasion meant that Americans could not get enough of swinging London. His idea was vindicated. When the single was released in the States in summer 1967,

DJs flipped it over and played 'He's a Better Man Than Me'. It even squeezed into the Billboard chart at number seventy-eight.

In truth, I was underwhelmed by this chart placing but Derek and Mike were delighted and Mike volunteered to produce a follow-up, to be released on both sides of the Atlantic. We settled on a song by US songwriter Randy Newman, which suited me: I liked his sarcastic slant on everything, and the fact that he can hardly sing.

Newman's 'Love Story' was a typically quirky little number and one of the first times I felt as if I was singing in my own voice, rather than trying to impersonate a black American blues belter. Released in May 1968, it failed to chart but had the distinction of being the first and last record of mine to be played by the BBC's arbiter-of-hip DJ, John Peel. But Mike Leander expected success, so that was the end of our relationship.

Another experiment saw me twinned with a black girl called Rozaa by a three-man songwriting team called Arnold, Martin and Morrow. We recorded a duet with the catchy title of 'You Are the Spark that Lights the Flame', but while Rozaa was a nice girl, our flame remained resolutely unlit and I had another non-hit under my belt.

Derek also put me in touch with a composer and producer called Tony Macaulay and we recorded a number called 'Just for Tonight', which didn't do anything. Tony then asked me to sing another tune he had written, 'Build Me Up Buttercup', but I turned it down out of hand, without even hearing the song. 'It's a stupid title,' I told Derek. 'It sounds like something you might sing to a cow.' Undeterred by my rejection, Tony recorded it with the Foundations, who took it to number two in Britain and number three in America. Thinking back, that wasn't my best snap decision.

Derek was still arranging a few live appearances and showcase gigs to get my name around and earn a bit of money. I did a couple of jazz-club gigs, singing standards with the Dudley Moore Trio. Dudley was friendly enough: he was working with Peter Cook, but wasn't yet the huge name he later became.

I also sang a residency at the Valbonne Club, a painfully hip venue in the West End with an inside swimming pool and a vast fish tank by the bandstand. It didn't work out. The loud music killed off the poor fish and when the band messed up the filter system by leaping into the pool fully clothed, our residency was terminated.

Somewhat more foreboding was a show at the El Morocco club in Soho owned by the legendary East End twins and villains, Reggie and Ronnie Kray. I was apprehensive but the show went well, and Derek and I were relaxing afterwards when the summons came back: 'Ronnie Would Like a Word.'

The stocky, impassive figure awaiting me certainly had an aura about him. Ignoring Derek standing next to me, he cut straight to the chase: 'Do you want a manager?'

'I've got one, thanks,' I told him.

'Is he any good?' Ronnie asked me.

'Yeah, he's great.'

'Well, if you need any help, son, you know where to come,' he concluded, indicating that the conversation was over. Derek suggested that it might be a good time to leave.

Even if the offer of being managed by a legendary gangster had appealed to me – which it didn't – I wouldn't have jettisoned Derek. His belief in me remained immense and passionate and even when things were going badly, like now, I was still grateful for his efforts.

My faith in him could easily have been slightly shaken by my next booking, though. After an audition during which I sang a Mood Indigo song that I had written, 'Any Day Now', I secured the juvenile lead of Prince Zelim in a Christmas show – to all intents and purposes, a pantomime – called *The Magic Carpet* in Guildford.

This was a bizarre experience. *The Magic Carpet* cast were a bunch of overwrought thespians and the director was a luvvie determined to eradicate any trace of an East End accent from his Prince Zelim. As his withering admonishment 'Vowel sounds, David!' echoed around the rehearsal studio for the fiftieth time, I knew how Eliza Doolittle must have felt.

My time on stage was mostly spent wearing a turban and acting opposite a thirty-foot dragon. It was a bit of a slog, although I did enjoy the night that the principal dancer, reacting against the boredom and banality of it all, danced his big solo with a paper bag over his head.

Socially, I was seeing a lot of Frank. We went on holiday with a couple of other mates to a chalet in Leysdown in Kent. It was a typical English holiday in that it rained all week. The sole high-light was Frank, trying to impress a girl, tearing around the campsite in his souped-up Mini with go-faster stripes, losing control and demolishing the front wall of our chalet, coming to rest by the sink, where I was washing up. 'Cup of tea, Frank?' I asked him.

Frank was still running El Grotto, and on a night off from my Prince Zelim turban I went down and spotted Maureen, the girl who had caught my eye on a previous visit, and her friend Kath. I commented on them to Frank. 'I'm sure they're lesbians,' he assured me. 'They never dance with blokes – only each other.'

Thankfully, Frank's instincts were as off-target as his sexual politics (but give him a break, it was the sixties). Maureen and Kath came over to the bar next to me to buy a drink, and Kath greeted me: 'Haven't seen you for ages.'

'No, I've been working,' I said. 'Let me buy you a drink.' I was chatting away to Kath, but it was Maureen that I was really interested in. She quickly joined in the conversation and was just as outgoing as Kath: beautiful, vivacious and with a winning line in funny banter. They were quite the double act.

We began to hang out and slowly but surely Maureen and I began a proper old-fashioned courtship. At first I was still very focused on my career, or lack of it, but Maureen was fantastic fun and great company. She was also very switched on and with it, which I liked, and ahead of all the latest trends from working in boutiques on the King's Road and in Carnaby Street.

She was the daughter of an East End car dealer, Alfie, and I got on well with him, her Irish mother, Rita, and her brother Ronnie. I was puzzled by an early trip to a Wimpy Bar where Maureen refused to eat anything and just sipped at a frothy coffee. She later confessed she was too embarrassed to eat in front of me in case she got messy. We were having a great time, and after a few weeks I realised this was something special.

Despite this, our relationship was a bit of a slow-burner at first, partly because we were both still living with our parents. They had always been great but I felt ready to move out, and began renting a bedsit in Earl's Court. I was a child of my time: the décor was all Che Guevara and Jimi Hendrix posters and joss sticks. Well, it made sense back then.

With my music career enduring another hiatus, Derek wanted to skew things back towards the acting side and decided that I needed an agent. We started at the very top when Derek secured a meeting with Leslie Grade, who together with his brothers Lew Grade and Bernard Delfont seemed to run British showbiz at the time.

The Grades' empire covered variety, film and theatre, and in between puffs on his giant cigar, the elderly, larger-than-life Leslie magnanimously agreed to represent me for 10 per cent of my earnings. He dispatched me to audition to be an understudy for an American musical called *Your Own Thing* that was due to open at the Comedy Theatre. I got the job, but the show closed before I got a chance to appear.

I auditioned for hippy musical *Hair* at the Shaftesbury Theatre and the producers wanted to use me but Leslie had other ideas. 'Taking your clothes off and running around in the nude? You don't want to do that!' he advised me. In truth, I also had reservations about that aspect, so that was that.

Derek also secured me a few very minor film roles. This was a new experience and I enjoyed the filming but I think my fleeting appearances were too short even to count as cameos. I wore a brown suit and had a couple of lines in a film called *Smashing Time*. It was fun, but to this day I haven't seen the film.

In a movie called *Assault*, I played a young man who goes into a chemist's shop that is promptly blown up. The star was Frank Finlay, who took an avuncular interest in me and brought me a cup of tea in the canteen. Our paths were to cross again years later.

I spent a long boring day hanging around a wedding in a suit as an extra on *All Coppers Are*, whose title was changed to *In the Devil's Garden* for America. I even dipped my toe into the saucy, uniquely British milieu of the *Carry On* films, although sadly my contribution was never to see the light of day.

Set in the court of Henry VIII, *Carry On Henry* was a typical lewd romp starring the *Carry On* A-team of Sid James, Kenneth Williams, Barbara Windsor, Charles Hawtrey, Joan Sims and Kenneth Connor. As a lowly extra, I had no dealings with these luminaries, and in fact was existing on a different plane entirely: I was so broke that I had to return a pile of empty bottles to afford the petrol to get to the set.

After hanging around for a couple of days in Tudor dress, my big moment came during a serfs' meeting addressed by Kenneth Connor, when I had to shout: 'What about the workers?' I was pleased with how it went, but this cinematic landmark was destined to hit the cutting-room floor. Like the failure of 'Thigh High', maybe it was for the best.

My backroom team had a bit of a reshuffle, with Leslie Grade delegating his son, Michael, to be my agent. Michael Grade, of course, was to go on to become chairman of the BBC thirty years later, but as my agent at the dog-end of the sixties he was – as he freely admits himself – bloody useless.

Michael only ever secured me two jobs and the first was to be the walk-on understudy for Tommy Steele, the veteran British singer and light entertainer, in the London Palladium's 1969 Christmas panto, *Dick Whittington*. Prior to this, I had never heard the phrase 'walk-on understudy', but it transpired to mean that I would learn the role but only play it if Steele were ill or indisposed.

The upside to this was that I would have regular money coming in for the three months that the production ran. The downside was that it was monumentally, insufferably boring. I realised I would prefer to have the most minor, inconsequential extra role imaginable in a drama, and actually have something to do, than this sorry, shadowy existence of interminably waiting around for … nothing.

The understudies would rehearse two mornings each week and then vanish back into the void. Tommy Steele appeared in rude health, yet every day I had to go through the meaningless ritual of turning up at the stage door thirty-five minutes before curtain to report to the stage manager just in case of any mishap.

I tried to fill the dead time constructively: watching and re-watching the show, intensely observing Tommy's part, hanging out in the Palladium dressing room with a couple of old lag actors who regaled me with tales of music hall, variety and days gone by. I even took judo lessons at a polytechnic over the road. But lethargy set in, and eventually I wasn't even bothering to shave before I ambled into the theatre.

This all changed on 19 March 1970. Sauntering down Oxford Street before the matinee performance ten minutes late

Mum aged 15, hop picking
in Kent.

Dad looks on as
I meet Santa.

Me and Mum on
a day out by the
sea in Clacton.

Me and some
friends in the
playground in
Canning Town.

At a holiday camp in Leysdown with Mum, Dad and some cousins.

Pouring a pint for Dad.

Window cleaning.

The China Plates in residence at The Bell pub in Ilford.

Me and the dragon in my first theatre appearance as Prince Zelim in *The Magic Carpet*, at the Yvonne Arnaud Theatre in Guildford.

Jesus in *Godspell*, 1972.

The Crucifixion.

Maureen, me and
baby Verity.

Godspell at The Roundhouse,
London, with (left to right)
Jeremy Irons, Deryk Parkin,
Neil Fitzwilliam and Tom
Saffrey.

Me and Ringo playing crazy golf in *That'll Be the Day.*

Lots of fun filming with Ringo.

Silver Dream Racer at Silverstone.

Twiggy and I on TV in my own BBC series.

James Hunt, the champion F1 driver, but a nervous pillion passenger.

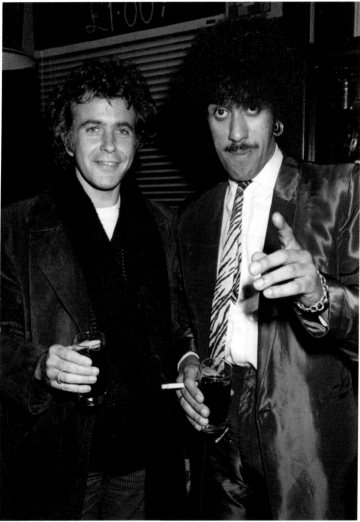

With Phil Lynott of Thin Lizzy out on the town.

Playing Byron at
the Young Vic.

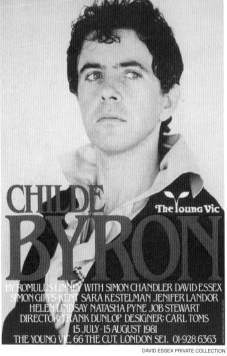

CHILDE
BYRON
The Young Vic

BY ROMULUS LINNEY WITH SIMON CHANDLER DAVID ESSEX
SIMON GIPPS-KENT SARA KESTELMAN JENIFER LANDOR
HELEN LINDSAY NATASHA PYNE JOB STEWART
DIRECTOR: FRANK DUNLOP DESIGNER: CARL TOMS
15 JULY - 15 AUGUST 1981
THE YOUNG VIC, 66 THE CUT, LONDON SE1. 01-928 6363

The brilliant Frank Finlay
as Captain Bligh and me as
Fletcher Christian in *Mutiny*.

Doing valuable research
for *Mutiny* in Tahiti.

Recording the *Mutiny* concept album, with me conducting the Royal Philharmonic Orchestra …

… and me singing, with John Cameron conducting.

Banging the drum with RPO percussionists.

Mike Batt, myself and Tim Rice at the recording of 'A Winter's Tale'.

Art Garfunkel and I meet the Queen after the Royal Variety Performance.

In TV show *The River*.

and turning into Argyll Street, the home of the Palladium, I saw a gaggle of wardrobe and production people frantically waving at me. 'Tommy Steele is sick!' said the stage manager as he shoved me into the theatre and through to dressing room number one. So this was it! My moment had come.

It was hard to catch my thoughts as people swarmed around me, dressing me in Dick Whittington's costume and microphones, and co-stars such as Kenneth Connor put their heads around the door to wish me luck. But it was not exactly confidence building to hear a Tannoy announcement – 'Due to Tommy Steele being unwell, the part of Dick Whittington will be played by David Essex' – being followed by a huge groan of disappointment in the auditorium.

The dressing room emptied and I had a few precious moments to stare at myself in the mirror surrounded by light bulbs. 'You can do this,' I told myself. 'This is why you've been wasting your time here every day for weeks.' Yet I felt as if I couldn't remember a single thing about the part, until the sound of the overture jolted me into action.

The half-hearted understudy rehearsals to rows of empty seats suddenly seemed hopelessly inadequate as I took the stage to a begrudging round of applause. The spotlights beaming down on me felt as bright as the sun, the orchestra blasted from the monitors and everything was overwhelming. My knees knocked and my mind froze. Could I do this?

Somehow I got my first line out, and grew in confidence as the opening scene unfolded perfectly. This is all going to be fine, I thought, as I exited and headed back to my dressing room for a costume change – en route passing three giant brown bears that were crashing their way to the stage through a specially built tunnel cage, their German trainers prodding them along.

Now, I knew that Dick kissed one of the bears before going into a song, but the bruins had not attended understudy rehearsal so I had no idea how this worked. What was their motivation in the scene? I soon found out. As I returned to the stage, one of the Germans slipped a Polo mint into my mouth just as the largest of the bears waddled towards me.

The trick, apparently, was to grip the mint firmly at the front of your mouth between your teeth so the bear could easily remove it, but nobody had told me. The Polo was right at the back of my throat, so as the bear slipped the longest tongue I had ever seen through its muzzle and deep into my mouth, I endured the most obnoxious French kiss imaginable in front of 2,000 people in a sold-out Palladium.

The reek of the bear's breath was revolting, and with its saliva plastered all over my face, I was sure I was about to throw up as it lumbered off with its prized mint. Meanwhile the orchestra struck up 'There's Gotta Be Something Better Than This'. You could say that again! The only plus point to this ordeal was that after that, anything else the performance could throw at me was a doddle.

By the interval I was enjoying myself, and the matinee audience seemed to appreciate me belting out Tommy Steele hits such as 'Little White Bull', 'Flash Bang Wallop' and 'What a Mouth' (which I first sang to my nan, aged five). By the curtain call, I was delighted to find that their disappointed groans had been replaced by enthusiastic cheering, and shouts of 'Bravo!'

After this triumph, I felt elated. It had made up for the weeks of kicking my heels that had preceded it. The next three days' performances went from strength to strength, partly because I knew to grasp the Polo between my teeth, and Tommy Steele rose from his sick bed to return earlier than his doctor advised, possibly because he heard I was going down rather well.

Michael Grade then produced his sole other booking for me as my agent: another pantomime, in Manchester. I was less than thrilled, and it reflects well on Michael that forty years on, when I occasionally bump into him, he still apologises and tells me: 'I'm so glad you left me. I would have ruined your career.'

However, Derek talked me into taking the part by telling me the Manchester producer had seen my Dick Whittington and been impressed, and at least I wasn't an understudy this time: I was to play Dandini in *Cinderella*, alongside music-hall legend Arthur Askey and singers Lonnie Donegan and Mary Hopkin.

I decamped to Manchester for a few weeks, renting a bedsit just outside the city. It was a rudimentary, student-digs sort of place, and so cold that when I took a bath, the steam in the bathroom was so thick that I couldn't see myself in the mirror.

Cinderella was a bit of a bore. Dandini was a wet character who didn't do a fat lot except carry round a glass slipper and sing the occasional duet with the prince, Tony Adams, a friendly guy who later went on to play Adam Chance in *Crossroads*.

I might not have been going to the ball on stage but I had a good time in Manchester. I befriended two fellow cast members and northern comics, Dailey and Wayne, who both had super-human capacities for alcohol, and our nights off frequently seemed to descend into a drunken stupor.

One evening they invited me with them to watch the opening night on tour of legendary British rocker Billy Fury. The nightclub was pretty packed but we had places reserved at a table with one of their mates, a livewire that I had not met before called Freddie Starr.

Freddie seemed fairly manic but Dailey and Wayne were more interested in pointing out the people sitting at the table in front of us, who they said were feared local gangsters known as the Quality Street Gang. As a man who had hobnobbed with the Krays, I was hardly likely to be impressed by hoodlums named after a box of chocolates, but I kept an eye on them as the lights dimmed and Billy Fury appeared.

Billy was doing fine until his third song when a familiar-looking figure materialised uninvited on stage next to him, a cushion rammed up the back of his jumper like Quasimodo, and began a very decent impression of the perplexed singer. Bored of sitting at our table, Freddie Starr had decided to make himself part of the entertainment.

Freddie's appearance intrigued the Quality Street Gang and a couple of them jumped up to take a closer look, obstructing their boss's view. Grunting 'I can't bloody see!', he grabbed a candle from their table and set fire to his sidekick's Afro hairdo. It was quite an inferno, and his mates all started smacking him around the head to try to put it out.

A proper trouper, Billy Fury soldiered on through 'Halfway to Paradise', but with Freddie Starr capering alongside him and gangsters knocking hell out of each other in the audience, he was forced to beat a tactical retreat. Watching him go, I got flashbacks to Shipman County, Daddy Dines and his massacred bees.

On a similar note, as *Cinderella* limped to the end of its run, I also decided to liven up proceedings. The highlight of my role as Dandini was the panto's final scene, when I marched onstage with the glass slipper, slipped it on the delicate foot of Cinders, played by Mary Hopkin, and uttered the immortal words: 'It fits!'

Mary was taken aback one night to see me appear bearing not the slipper but a Wellington boot, which I gently eased on to her foot. The audience roared with laughter as Cinderella and her handsome prince sang their love duet with Cinders clumping around the stage in a huge welly.

Mary Hopkin, who was a good laugh, took the jape in her (Wellington-booted) stride and even thanked me afterwards for livening up the evening's finale, but Big-Hearted Arthur Askey was disapproving. I guess that I shouldn't have been surprised. As I had learned from Tommy Steele, sometimes the biggest stars like to keep all the laughs for themselves.

7

'DON'T YOU MEAN *GOSPEL*?'

Dandini might have been a bit of a drip but at least he helped to put a roof over my head. Despite my alcoholic excursions with Dailey and Wayne, I had managed to save some money from my stint in *Cinderella* in Manchester, and when the panto ended and I got back down south, Maureen and I decided to buy a house.

It was a big decision, but also an easy one to make. Maureen and I were in love and getting on great. We had been together for nearly two years, and our relationship had survived all of my absences in shows or on tour. It felt like the real deal.

It was March 1971. Like most parents, my mum and dad and Maureen's would have preferred us to get married before we moved in together, but they approved of us as a couple and agreed it made better economic sense for us to buy a place than to rent. Maureen's dad, Alfie, was doing well with his car dealership and chipped in towards the deposit.

We settled on a Victorian terrace house in Vicarage Lane, Seven Kings, near Ilford in Essex. It cost £3,950, it had three bedrooms and a small garden, and we loved it. Figuring we needed some help with the mortgage, we invited Maureen's inseparable mate Kath and her boyfriend, Mike, to live with us.

We all got on well and the arrangement worked nicely, although the house got a lot smaller when Mike made the decision to get an enormous Pyrenean mountain dog, Hector. Mike thought it hilarious occasionally to give Hector a saucer of brandy and milk, after which his mutt would slobber all over us and carouse and crash around the house.

Domestically everything was hunky-dory but my career remained a serious worry. Derek had now been guiding my solo fortunes for five years and the big breakthrough simply hadn't come. All we had to show for our efforts were a string of flop or near-miss singles, a handful of film cameos, theatre understudy roles and provincial pantos.

After *Cinderella* finished, I had been forced to sign on, and was still unemployed as we moved into Seven Kings. Derek was still trying to find auditions and would lend me a fiver so I could get into town to attend them, but he was feeling the pressure too and began suggesting things I didn't fancy, like cheesy cabaret club gigs.

He could not have tried harder to make things happen for me but failure was driving a wedge between us and my relationship with Derek began to cool. I never asked to be this 'David Essex' character, I reflected daily as I kicked my heels waiting for Maureen to come home from her latest job, delivering flowers. It wasn't my idea. It had been a mistake. I just wanted to be a jazz drummer.

Which was when Maureen told me that she was pregnant.

It came as quite a shock. Maureen and I had not been trying for a baby but I guess, thinking back, we had not been trying

97

not to have one, either. The news was a bolt from the blue and made me decide two things: I had to get a steady, proper job, and we should get married.

Maureen and I had never really discussed marriage before then but we were young and in love with a baby on the way so it was clearly the thing to do: we didn't want our son or daughter being called a bastard in the school playground. But we had no money so we decided to keep the day as simple as possible.

Maureen can have been no more than ten weeks pregnant when we tied the knot at Seven Kings Registry Office. The day's sole extravagance was that Alfie was determined to lend us a white Rolls-Royce so he borrowed one from one of his car-dealer mates. It turned up outside our gaff and my blushing bride headed off in it, followed by Frank, my best man, and me in Frank's Mini.

After the ceremony, our handful of guests followed the skint but happy couple in their Roller back to our place for sandwiches and a cuppa. There was no reception, no speeches and, it goes without saying, no honeymoon. It was a lovely day but could hardly have been more low-key.

So suddenly I was married, a father-to-be … and unemployed! Full of resolve and driven by panic, I began to scour the local rag's small ads for options. My gypsy soul has always rebelled against the idea of a nine-to-five, but I figured there must be plenty of jobs that would allow me to earn a living while also giving me some freedom: long-distance lorry driving? Back to mini cabs?

In the meantime, I threw myself into doing up the house, which I painted and decorated from top to bottom ready for the baby's arrival. I even replaced the windows, which is what I was doing the afternoon that the phone rang. It was Derek. Again.

My manner was curt and brusque as he explained that he had an audition he wanted me to go to. Psychologically, I had given up on the whole process, but I decided to hear Derek out even as I thought, 'This is the very last time.'

'What show is it?' I asked him.

'It's called *Godspell*.'

'Don't you mean *Gospel*?' I snapped back, sarcastically.

'No, David: *Godspell*.'

He explained. *Godspell*, a musical, told the story of Christ as related in the Book of Matthew. It had already opened off-Broadway in New York, and now its producers were keen to bring it to London, with a British cast. Reluctantly, I agreed to attend the audition.

Even though I auditioned a lot back then, I never enjoyed them. Beforehand, I would get ferociously nervous; afterwards, if it had gone badly, the rejection would be hard to take. I was deeply unenthusiastic about *Godspell*, and my mood wasn't helped when I turned up at the Globe Theatre at 11 a.m. the following Thursday to find literally hundreds of other hopefuls milling around.

It was early afternoon before I was called on stage and greeted by the play's co-writer and producer John-Michael Tebelak, a soft-spoken, bearded American hippy in overalls. Accompanied by a pianist, I sang 'Going Out of my Head'. When he wanted to hear something a bit more music hall, I followed up with my old stand-by, Tommy Steele's 'What a Mouth', which he seemed to enjoy.

John-Michael took my number. Thank you, we'll let you know. Next!

How had the audition gone? I didn't know, and I didn't care. I was done with showbiz. The following Tuesday I fixed up an appointment for an interview for a job as a van driver. Maureen was at home, and as I painted what would be the baby's room, lost in my thoughts, she answered the phone and called me.

Was it the *Godspell* people? I half-wondered as I made my way downstairs. No: it was the van depot confirming my interview. Then the phone rang again. *Godspell* wanted to recall me for a second audition.

When I arrived at the Prince of Wales Theatre, the situation was very different from the crowd scene at the Globe. No more than twenty of us had made the cut, and the producers soon had us singing, dancing, miming and impersonating trees and animals. I didn't terribly enjoy jumping around being a monkey.

During a long and wearying afternoon, John-Michael Tebelak also guided us through some hippy-dippy, very American 'trust-enhancing' exercises. We took it in turns to fall off tables and not try to break our fall, trusting our fellow actors to catch us. We even walked hand-in-hand through London's traffic, one person with their eyes firmly closed, the other leading the way.

This stuff didn't come naturally to me but I stayed with it and my perseverance paid off. I got home to Seven Kings to a phone call from a very excited Derek. The producers had called him already, saying they were thinking of casting me as John the Baptist, who became Judas Iscariot in the second act. An actor named Murray Head was lined up to play the lead role of Jesus.

It transpired this wasn't the whole story. There was a split in the producers' camp between Tebelak, who favoured Murray Head to be Jesus, and his *Godspell* co-writer Stephen Schwartz, who liked my stage presence. The standoff was only resolved a few days later when Murray Head was offered – and accepted – a big movie role, in *Sunday Bloody Sunday*. So it was decided. I was to be Jesus.

The money wasn't great but it was a lead role in an interesting-sounding production and the timing was wonderful. At least it allowed me to cancel the van-driving interview. Even so, I was wary about getting too excited about *Godspell*, especially when John-Michael and Stephen called me in for my first meeting and gave me their vision for my role: 'We play Jesus as a red-nosed clown.'

Godspell was originally based on John-Michael's university masters thesis and his interest in a book by a Harvard professor, Harvey Cox, called *Feast of Fools*, led him to decide that the cast would all wear clown costumes and/or hippy robes. At our first rehearsal, I met my fellow hippy clowns.

We were mainly young and unknown but it was still a fairly formidable cast. An upcoming actor and part-time busker called Jeremy Irons had taken the dual John the Baptist/Judas role that had originally been marked for me, while the male cast was completed by Neil Fitzwilliam, Deryk Parkin and Tom Saffrey.

Of the female cast, Marti Webb had already starred as Nancy in the first touring production of *Oliver!* Julie Covington would also become a household name in years to come, while Verity Anne Meldrum, Gay Soper and Jacquie-Ann Carr were all ferociously talented. I quickly realised that I would have to be on top of my game to carry this one off.

When rehearsals began, we soon developed into a very tightly knit ensemble, largely because it soon became very clear we would be essentially directing ourselves. *Godspell* was Jean-Michael Tebelak's concept and he had written the script, but as a director this subdued, complex hippy in overalls, no older than the cast, was so laissez-faire that he verged on the comatose.

I wanted to respect Jean-Michael but it wasn't easy. He gave us so little guidance. Whenever we suggested script or acting ideas, his answer was invariably a mumbled, 'Yeah, sure.' A positive side effect of this was that the cast began to feel as if this really was our own production, especially as we were all on stage for the entire duration of the play.

Our set was basically some big wire fences enclosing a space not unlike a schoolyard. There were planks, and two sawhorses. I had to play a ukulele at one point: at another, I brandished a ventriloquist's dummy. This was not Jesus as Hollywood or Cecil B DeMille had ever envisaged.

The rehearsals were going well but outside a storm was brewing around us. It is bizarre to reflect that until 1970 it was illegal to portray Jesus on stage in the West End. When the media learned of the leftfield, arty spin *Godspell* was to put upon the story of Christ, they quickly scented a story.

Like most scandals confected by the tabloids in order to sell newspapers, it was disingenuous but highly effective. Papers screamed that the production would be blasphemous, while the *Evening Standard*'s headline implied that their sense of outrage was partly predicated on my own humble roots: 'DOCKER'S SON TO PLAY JESUS AS RED-NOSED CLOWN'.

A few weeks earlier, I had been anonymous, signing on the dole and applying for van-drivers' jobs: now I was at the centre of a media firestorm. I didn't like it at all. The *Standard*'s comment seemed gratuitously offensive towards my parents and the overall coverage was deliberately misleading about *Godspell*'s intentions.

I had never been a churchgoer or interested in organised religion but nor was I an atheist. I guess you would call me an agnostic, and from that non-partisan standpoint it seemed to me *Godspell* illustrated some sensible Biblical teachings very cleverly. The play didn't dress Jesus as a clown to mock him: it did it to strip away the High Church's rituals and pomposity and reconnect people with the simplicity of the message.

In any case, we couldn't do anything but keep our heads down and carry on rehearsing. The tabloid furore probably brought people in to the show in the long run, but in the short term it had a major drawback. *Godspell* was due to open at the West End's Prince of Wales Theatre, but scared by the ongoing controversy, the theatre owners pulled the venue.

So now we had a show, but nowhere to play it. The rehearsals dragged on slightly aimlessly until one of the producers came up with the lifeline of an alternative. Banished from the West End, *Godspell* would instead open on 17 November 1971 at the Roundhouse, an old railway building turned arty theatre and gig venue in Chalk Farm, north London.

One or two of the more showbizzy cast members such as Marti Webb felt we were slumming it outside of W1 but most of us were just relieved finally to have a date for an opening night. I personally felt the rough-and-ready Roundhouse was ideal for our play, with its rudimentary set and four-piece rock band in towers above the stage.

Stephen Schwartz flew in from New York for the last couple of weeks' rehearsals and provided a welcome dose of energy and creativity after John-Michael's insipid direction. We had a full house for the opening night, as religious zealots milled around outside with placards proclaiming us SINNERS who would BURN IN HELL. I guess it made a change from people saying 'Break a leg'.

When it comes to epiphanies and life-changing moments, the opening night of *Godspell* is one I will never forget. Despite the ongoing media outrage, the ten cast members had been in a hermetically sealed little bubble for months as we self-directed and diligently tweaked our audacious, taboo-busting production. It felt good to us, but we were too close to know. Would anyone else agree?

It soon became clear that the audience who had run the gauntlet of our fundamentalist detractors outside didn't just like the show – they adored it. Schwartz's great score went down a storm and the crowd seemed to respond to the moving narrative and our every idea. At one point they were laughing so much that I glanced behind me, convinced something must be going wrong, but no: it was sheer, spontaneous appreciation.

For the show's dramatic crucifixion climax, Jeremy Irons as Judas marched through the auditorium to me and I told him: 'Do what you must.' On his return, the cast placed me on a beer crate, fastened bracelets with trailing red ribbons to my wrists and spreadeagled me against the fence as I sang, '*Oh God, I'm bleeding*,' before carrying me through the crowd.

On paper it probably sounds ridiculous, especially as Christ was being sacrificed on the cross in a Superman T-shirt and stripy deckchair trousers, but the effect on the audience was hugely powerful. As I was held aloft and carried from the stage I heard both men and women crying, some of them uncontrollably.

Sometimes shows can be loved by the paying punters but slated by the critics, but when the reviews appeared, it was clear that *Godspell* had wooed the intelligentsia as well. To my delight, my own performance was praised beyond my wildest dreams, with the venerable critic Harold Hobson penning the following rhapsody in the *Sunday Times*:

> This inward happiness, this fragility, a joyous wine in a frail vessel is the mark of David Essex's Jesus in *Godspell*. This Jesus is a man who has found a splendid treasure and is eager to share it with everyone he meets. He is an agile but cheerful debater, with a ready answer to all objections, and a touching confidence.
>
> There have been many Christs in the world of art; the tormented Christ of El Greco, the benign shepherd of Murillo, the bland Christ of Rubens, the soaring Christ in majesty of Epstein; and Mr Essex's gentle and innocent figure, as capable of infinite and simple affection as it is incapable of seeing evil anywhere, is worthy to rank with them.

It is my opinion that Mr Essex's is the best performance in London, the least histrionic, the happiest, and the most moving. That it should be so at a time when we all marvel at Olivier's prodigious James Tyrone, one of our greatest actor's finest creations, is a measure of Mr Essex's achievement.

I may not have grasped all the reference points of this erudite write-up, but I knew perfectly well that being compared favourably with Sir Laurence Olivier was the kind of review that money couldn't buy. My own in-house theatre critic, Derek, was in raptures: he had never seen such first-night notices.

As they do, the media had totally changed their tune. *Godspell* was suddenly the hippest show in town. When I arrived for the next day's performance, the queues of people eager to buy tickets stretched away from the Roundhouse and right down the street. From being pariahs, we were offered three West End theatres within a week. Even the BURN IN HELL placards began to dwindle.

Having been on the verge of throwing my whole entertainment career in, I was now hot property, but the notable thing was that I felt vindicated not for me but for Derek. He had been the chivvying, constantly supportive figure who had pointed me towards theatre and sent me off into repertory when all I wanted to do was bang my drums. I had not always been kind to him but now I could not have been more grateful that he had persevered and had loosened my blinkers.

Life now rearranged itself into a high-adrenaline, exciting routine of eight sold-out performances of *Godspell* per week plus loads of media interviews and promotion. Journalists invariably asked me if I believed in Jesus and I told them the truth: that I thought he was a great teacher and he made a lot of sense to me, whether he was the son of God or not. I would circumnavigate the whole divinity aspect by saying that his teachings were more important than the folk tales and fairy stories about walking on water and the resurrection.

After years of being a nobody, it was certainly interesting to be having my opinions canvassed on such weighty matters, but there was no danger of my newfound fame going to my head. I had other things on my mind.

It was mid-December 1971 and Maureen was now eight months pregnant. Our energies were all focused on the birth. It's a sign of how ridiculous my overnight celebrity was becoming that the Archbishop of Canterbury, Michael Ramsey, got wind of my imminent parenthood and offered to baptise our firstborn personally. I was tempted but Maureen said no. I guess I can't blame her.

Her waters broke on the morning of 18 December and I drove her to Ilford Maternity Hospital in Newbury Park in my beaten-up £150 Mercedes. The nurses took charge and after an hour or so Maureen told me that I should head for the Roundhouse, as there was no way of knowing what time the baby would come.

We had two shows that day and the matinee passed in a dream-like haze as I waited for our company manager, Tony Howell, to relay any news from the hospital. *Godspell* had an interesting interval in that audience members were invited on to the stage to drink some frankly disgusting rosé wine and chat with the cast. Normally, overly earnest Americans would corner me and inquire: 'Do you believe in Jesus? Do you think he was the son of God?' This particular day, I was far too distracted to give any sentient or coherent replies.

The hospital had no news by the early evening and so it was in to the second show of the day. It was impossible to define what I was feeling: I was nervous, excited, distant and running on adrenaline, all at the same time. Midway through the first act, my antennae sensed a change of mood on stage and the cast's eyes all seemed to be on me.

Julie Covington passed me a note under the wire fence. It read:

> You can be a father to a son, but you have to be a father
> to a daughter.

A daughter! I had a daughter! My next line went clean out of my head as the actors all crowded around me, crying, kissing me and slapping me on the back, the script momentarily forgotten. What a moment! I would have loved to be there for the birth, but as I couldn't, there was no better way to celebrate becoming a dad than with these friends to whom I had grown so close.

The show over, I leapt back into the Mercedes and raced to the hospital, jumping a red light en route in my haste. A police car pulled me over and I admitted to the officer that I had not seen the light. I was about to explain why I was in such a hurry when he cut me short. 'Well, Jesus wouldn't lie, would he?' he reasoned. 'Off you go.'

Maureen was waiting for me on the ward, our baby in her arms. Everything people say about becoming a parent is true. I had never seen anybody or anything so fragile and beautiful, never felt an emotion so profound. As I held our daughter for the first time, I realised exactly what life is about.

Her name came to us fairly easily. We wanted to call her Verity, for Truth, because truth is so important in life. For her middle name, we went back to my mum's maiden name, Lee, for all of its gypsy connotations, but we decided to spell it Leigh. Verity Leigh Cook.

Having had a hard labour, Maureen stayed on the ward to recuperate for a few days as I saw off the last few pre-Christmas *Godspell* shows and readied the house for my family's return. The three of us had a wonderful, special Christmas together in Seven Kings, punctuated by daily visits from Verity's doting, delighted grandparents.

The New Year brought the news that *Godspell* was to transfer from the Roundhouse to Wyndham's Theatre on 25 January. I would, after all, become the first actor to play Jesus on the West End stage, but I also felt a small sadness at leaving Chalk Farm, where it had all happened for us.

Every night I would take the fervent applause of the audience, transported by my crucifixion, then bid the crowds of well-wishers good night and head home at midnight to my new family. After a few words with Maureen I'd pause at Verity's room to watch her breathe for a minute before going to bed.

Exhausted, like any new mum, by a hard day's childcare, Maureen would find it hard to get up for the 4 a.m. feed and nappy change so this became my task. It was always hard to drag myself out of bed, but being with Verity in the twilight hours was a joy. It felt as if we were the only two people in the world.

It was probably good that Verity had come along to help keep me grounded because I could easily have been getting very bigheaded. *Godspell*'s switch to Wyndham's went seamlessly and triggered another batch of reviews of the show by critics who would never have deigned to go to Chalk Farm.

The fourth estate wasn't the only institution to do a U-turn when *Godspell* got successful. The Church had initially viewed us with suspicion, wary of our motives, but when they realised our simplistic, childlike interpretations of the teachings of Christ were attracting 2,000 people a night, compared to the twenty or so scattered round the pews of their empty churches every Sunday morning, they also wanted a piece of the action.

We were invited to perform a section of the show in the crypt at St Paul's Cathedral. We did so, and the BBC came along and filmed it (rather badly, as it happened). It was a big deal to some of the cast members but, if I am honest, I viewed it as a bit of a nuisance.

The *Godspell* phenomenon had been, if you'll pardon the pun, a godsend to me, and with an eighteen-month contract I no longer had to worry about providing for Maureen and Verity, but there was still something itching at me: I was missing making music. A random encounter was to put that right.

Liz Whiting, a *Godspell* understudy, had an American boyfriend named Jeff Wayne who had visited London with his dad to work on a musical, *A Tale of Two Cities*, fallen in love with the country and stayed. Jeff, who was a big fan of *Godspell*, now worked writing and producing music for TV adverts, and asked if I would like to sing on an ad.

Even though it was only a TV jingle, I jumped at the chance, which I suppose showed how much I was missing making music. Jeff set to work to hymn the merits of Pledge furniture polish and I joined him in the studio to record the following immortal words for posterity: '*Let the sun come into your life / Bring in the sun / Pledge.*' Another advert had me adopting an American accent to plug Chrysler cars: '*Chrysler has the answer / Boo-boo-boom.*' For these half-day jobs, I was paid more than I would get for playing Jesus for two years. No wonder Jeff lived in a mews house off Baker Street.

Jeff and I also formed a hobby band for a bit of fun: I sang, Jeff played keyboards, we recruited a couple of session musicians, and Marti Webb and Julie Covington sang backing vocals. We only played a couple of gigs, so it was sod's law that when we did a half-empty show at the Revolution Club, Paul McCartney should be there, scrutinising us closely as we sang the Beatles' 'Long and Winding Road'. No pressure, then. Luckily, he clapped.

Godspell also enjoyed a degree of musical success, with the cast album and a single from the show, 'Day by Day', both going Top Ten, but these were slim pickings. Increasingly, I knew that my aim was to release records under my own name – and to write my own songs.

Yet this was for the future. For now, *Godspell* continued to dominate my career and my life. In fact our media profile went up a notch, if that was possible, when Tim Rice and Andrew

Lloyd Webber's musical *Jesus Christ Superstar* opened down the road from us at the Palace Theatre, with Paul Nicholas as Jesus.

There was very little similarity between the shows – *Godspell* was a sparse, simple affair while *Jesus Christ Superstar* was a huge, epic production – but this didn't stop the media trying to fabricate rivalry between us. The BBC even staged a TV debate, *Box Office Christ*, but their hopes for friction between Tim Rice and I were dashed when we agreed on everything and got on like a house on fire, as we still do forty years later.

As *Godspell* continued to sell out every night, there were more and more fans gathering at the stage door wanting photos and autographs, a new experience for me. I found it awkward to deal with, preferring the piss-taking banter of the porters in Covent Garden fruit and veg market, which would be springing into life as Jeremy Irons and I walked to an Italian restaurant, Luigi's, for an after-show meal.

Because we were dealing with sacred subject matter that was so important to many people, the cast tended to play *Godspell* very straight with no high jinks such as Cinderella's Wellington boot in Manchester. There was one exception. One night, Jeremy materialised to baptise me at the start of the show, as usual. He had his back to the audience, his eyes were closed, and on his eyelids he had written a distinctly un-Christian message: 'F*** Off'.

I would love to report that I kept a straight face. But I didn't.

8

THAT WAS THE
DAY THAT WAS

With *Godspell* my career had crossed the Rubicon. The entire dynamic of my working life shifted. After years of poor Derek slogging away and hitting brick walls as he tried to interest people in his young actor and singer, his previously silent phone was suddenly ringing off the hook with offers of work and media interviews.

Nevertheless, we tried to be selective. After all, I wasn't just a hot new star with a big hit behind him: I was also a newlywed and a doting dad with a wife and baby to care for, and I wasn't about to neglect them. Plus, of course, I was still doing eight shows a week of *Godspell*.

It needed to be a pretty special offer for me to take on another major, non-musical project at that juncture – and it was. David Puttnam, who was then no more than a little-known, upcoming film producer, phoned Derek to invite me for a screen test for a film he planned to make, called *That'll Be the Day*.

The film was to be about a working-class London lad, growing up in the fifties, who became obsessed with music and wanted to be a rock star. It resonated with me for obvious reasons. After a screen test on Hampstead Heath one afternoon with Puttnam, director Claude Whatham and an actress, David sent me the full script. I read it and was hooked straight away.

It wasn't just the story that excited me. The proposed cast was exceptional: former Beatle Ringo Starr, the Who drummer Keith Moon and rock 'n' roll singer Billy Fury (this time without his unwanted sidekick, Freddie Starr) had all signed up already. When Puttnam offered me the lead role, I had no hesitation. I was in.

Unfortunately, things were not that simple. Filming for *That'll Be the Day* was to take place on the Isle of Wight that autumn, and I was less than six months into an eighteen-month contract on *Godspell*. If I were to make the movie, I would need a leave of absence from the hit show – and why would they give me that?

Derek and I visited the office of Hugh 'Binky' Beaumont, the plummy and patriarchal impresario behind HM Tennant, the UK producers of *Godspell*. Binky (I wonder if he knew Bunny?) heard us out then hatched a possible plan. He would give me three months' leave from the musical if I would agree to add six months to my contract on my return, which basically meant I would spend two years playing Jesus.

Binky stressed that the scheme would need the agreement of *Godspell*'s American co-producers and promised to put it to them. Derek and I were in two minds, with Derek in particular feeling the deal had an element of blackmail to it, but when the US bosses agreed, we felt we had no choice but to go along with it.

Ultimately I felt the sacrifice – if that was what it was – was worth it because *That'll Be the Day* appealed to me on so many levels. The script was by a former *Liverpool Daily Post* and

Evening Standard rock journalist named Ray Connolly, and was about teenagers growing up in the late fifties to a background of the first flush of youth culture and of rock 'n' roll.

The genius of Connolly's script lay in locating the edgy glamour of *Rebel Without a Cause*-era James Dean and relocating it to a Britain where kids were growing up intuitively wanting more from life than the straitlaced, conventional existence that their parents' generation had been forced to lead. It was a rock 'n' roll movie that belonged in the John Osborne lineage of post-war working-class kids trying to escape a dreary destiny.

Maureen, Verity and I bought a ticket to Ryde on 23 October 1972 and decamped to a little house in Shanklin for the seven-week shoot. It was the best of both worlds: we got a precious family holiday, plus I had a fantastic time working on a project that felt personally meaningful and very significant.

The parallels between my life and that of my character, Jim MacLaine, were notable. Jim was a working-class suburban lad, restless and possessed of a visceral urge to find excitement in his life. A scene where he hurled his schoolbooks into a river and boycotted his exams vividly reminded me of scrawling Popeye all over my Eleven Plus paper.

It was equally hard not to identify with the scenes where Jim eschewed a conventional career, working as a casual labourer on a travelling fair, then married and became a young father. It was probably my affection for him that made me able to portray him as a lovable rogue, even when he became a cheating sex maniac. The movie ended with Jim abandoning everything to pursue his rock 'n' roll dream.

Despite my *Carry On* cameo of a few years earlier, taking the lead role in a movie was a new experience for me and there was a lot to learn. The early starts were a shock to the system, after being used to evening *Godspell* performances, and not even my weeks of early-hours nappy sessions with Verity could prepare me for the jolt of 5 a.m. alarm calls.

I learned to scale down my acting from the declamatory style of theatre – after all, if you raise an eyebrow on a cinema screen, it jumps twenty feet in the air – and I enjoyed the opportunity to give subtler, more nuanced performances. I also honed the crucial movie actor's skill of being able to sit around in a caravan for hours on end waiting to be called without going mad with boredom.

That'll Be the Day was a joy to make both because of the high quality of the script and the camaraderie of the cast. Claude Whatham was a skilled and helpful director, and any advance nerves I may have had about working with one of the Beatles vanished when Ringo proved easy-going, funny and warm.

Keith Moon's hell-raising reputation preceded him and he did his best to live up to it. He made a textbook rock star entrance to the proceedings, arriving via a helicopter that alighted on the hotel roof, scattering the tablecloths that had been laid out to mark the landing area on to the beach below. Keith emerged from the chopper to announce: 'The only way to travel, dear boy! I was in my front room in Chertsey twenty minutes ago and now I'm here. Where's the bar?'

Moon was aware that people expected him to be the life and soul of every party, swinging from chandeliers, so that was what he did. In private, though, I found him to be a decent, steady and very intelligent guy.

An upcoming young actor, Robert Lindsay, played Terry, Jim MacLaine's best friend at school who studied hard, took his exams and went off to university while Jim was frittering his life away. Robert was a nice guy, but we didn't get too close, largely I think because there was a tension between our screen characters that being too buddy-buddy could have removed.

Ringo, Keith and I enjoyed some very lively evenings after filming but I tried to keep a lid on my own behaviour. The film was a big deal for me – I knew its success or failure largely rested on my character – and it wouldn't help if I was turning up with a raging hangover every day, so most nights I retreated back to Maureen, Verity and our cottage.

Not every night, though. American singer Harry Nilsson was staying in the main cast hotel, partly because Ray Connolly had taken some inspiration for the script from one of his songs, '1941', but mostly because he was friends with Ringo. A few evenings degenerated into early-hours all-star jamming sessions: with Ringo, Keith and me, we had no shortage of drummers. The hotel just gave up and left us to it. Once or twice, I found myself creeping on to the set at 5 a.m. after a riotous all-nighter.

The Isle of Wight was a blast from start to finish and it remains a special place for me. Verity even took her first steps on the island. After seven weeks there, filming on *That'll Be the Day* continued at Pinewood Studios, north of London. It was while I was kicking my heels, as usual, in the dressing room there one day that I took the quantum leap that was to empower me as a songwriter and define my career from that moment.

In *That'll Be the Day*, Ringo's character, Mike, had the line: 'Only Americans can write rock songs.' I didn't believe that but it made me reflect on the extraordinary, pervasive influence that America and its iconography exerted over Britain's infant, impressionable youth culture. I sat down to write 'Rock On'. The first words came easy:

> *Hey, did you rock and roll?*
> *Rock on, ooh, my soul*
> *Hey did ya boogie too, did ya?*

Then images of Americana and its 1950s totems of hip poured out of me and into the song: '*Summertime blues … blue suede shoes … blue jeans … Jimmy Dean.*' Even as I scribbled the words down, the melody began to form in my head. 'Rock On' was one of the quickest songs that I ever wrote and it was to change my life.

Incidentally, it's long been one of the minor banes of my life that people have always got the 'Rock On' lyrics wrong. The sheet music for the song mistakenly had them as being '*Hey, kid, rock and roll*' and that version understandably stuck. But '*Hey, did you rock and roll?*' was what I wrote.

With *That'll Be the Day* in the can, it was time for me to return to Wyndham's and *Godspell*. While I had already spent a long time playing Jesus, I felt fresh after the break and it was good to see my fellow cast members again. Crucially, it was also my chance to reunite with Jeff Wayne and get serious about music.

After one of our Sunday-band get-togethers, I mentioned to Jeff that I had started writing my own songs and wanted to make an album. When he asked to hear one, I sang a number I had just finished called 'On and On', which he liked. A light bulb came on over my head and I made Jeff an offer: 'You work in the studio. Why don't you produce the album and I'll write it?'

Jeff seemed keen on the idea, and carried away with enthusiasm, I improved my offer: 'You can publish the songs, as well.' I didn't really understand what publishing rights were, and if I am honest I still don't, but Jeff was a far cannier music business operative than me and accepted eagerly. Derek was horrified when he heard what I had done, but a deal is a deal and I never attempted to back out of it, even if it would turn out to mean forfeiting countless thousands of pounds in earnings.

Jeff and I initially went into Advision Studios in Soho to record two songs: 'Rock On' and 'On and On'. Jeff had an extensive contacts book and with a few phone calls was able to gather an extraordinary collection of musicians. As a first-session band, guitarist Chris Spedding, bassist Herbie Flowers, drummer Barry DeSouza and percussionist Ray Cooper were peerless, and they were to contribute to my sound for years.

As the session unfolded, I felt grateful that my tender, fledgling songs were in Jeff's skilled hands. I sang 'On and On' with the rhythm section, leaving it to Jeff to organise the orchestra that would flesh out the song so fulsomely a few days later. Then we turned our attention to 'Rock On'.

We had arrived in Advision with little more than a lyric and a spindly melody but in these talented musicians' hands, my baby began to come to life. Herbie got the ball rolling, pulling out of the air the malevolent pulse of a bassline that began to define the song.

Something was happening here. I suggested that we add a 1950s Buddy Holly-style tape echo on my voice to the deliberately spartan, eerie-sounding track. Then when we reconvened in the studio the following week to finish the number, we piled on the weirdness.

Jeff had recruited a string section for this session, and we asked them to detune their instruments to give the track an even more skewed, foreboding air. They demurred, so we hit on Plan B: we would detune the classical players themselves by getting a few glasses of wine down them. In no time, they were sounding like an Indian mantra.

We were keen to make 'Rock On' sound more portentous yet so Jeff called up a multi-instrumentalist called Derek Wadsworth who played the didgeridoo. Derek arrived with it tied to the top of his station wagon and set up as Jeff and I eagerly awaited the alien noise that would add layers of mystery and mystique to the song. He blew into it. It sounded like a bull-elephant farting.

Once Jeff and I had picked ourselves off the ground and wiped the tears from our eyes, we explained to Derek that we didn't need his flatulent didgeridoo, but he supplanted it with an electric trombone that had a rather more sombre timbre. The studio engineer, Gary Martin, added layers of echoes and special effects. By now, 'Rock On' sounded alien, mesmerising and out of this world.

It was too far out for David Puttnam. When I offered him 'Rock On' to use in *That'll Be the Day*, he turned it down, explaining that he felt it was 'too weird' for the film. He did, however, include it on the soundtrack album that accompanied the movie.

Not that the movie needed any help from my song. When *That'll Be the Day* opened on 12 April 1973, its reception and reviews rivalled those that had been afforded to *Godspell*. The critics admired its edginess, teenagers loved its brooding angst and authenticity, and suddenly it was topping box-office charts as the hottest British film around.

When you have both the lead in a smash-hit musical and the star part in a number-one film, you are not going to remain anonymous. The first half of 1973 was when my previously low-key life was turned upside-down and I went from being a struggling bit-part performer to becoming some kind of phenomenon: what would today be known as a celebrity. It was quite a shock to the system.

The trend had been building slowly during my first stint in *Godspell*. There were increasing numbers of people, normally girls, waiting at the Wyndham's stage door after performances: there were more and more autographs to sign. It was tolerable, even nice, but after *That'll Be the Day* it went into overdrive.

For the first time, it became news if I walked down the street. People would do a double take; girls would stop me, wanting a chat or a photograph; drivers would beep their horns and wave furiously, or even screech to a halt. Despite being naturally shy, I had to get used to being public property.

This was a life-changing and curious side effect to my success and, without wanting to sound churlish, not something that I had ever remotely craved. I had never wanted to be famous. Even when I first set eyes on Georgie Fame in the Flamingo, I longed to be not the spotlit singer but the drummer, anonymous at the back of the stage. My ideal would have been a career hidden behind the cymbals, smoking a cheroot in a black polo-necked sweater.

This was something else entirely. The reception for *That'll Be the Day* also propelled the soundtrack album, including 'Rock On', to number one in the albums chart, where it lodged for weeks. I am not sure that even Derek, with his seemingly bottomless reservoir of faith in me, had ever envisaged success on quite this scale.

My newfound fame also had a knock-on effect on *Godspell*, and not only at the stage door. Where the audiences had previously been the sort of refined theatre-goers that I first saw at shows with Derek, now there was an influx of younger, excitable fans who wanted to see *That'll Be the Day*'s David Essex and probably couldn't have cared less about the teachings of Christ.

One casualty was the *Godspell* interval in which we invited the audience to come on stage for a glass of rosé and a chat with the cast. Whereas I used to be asked my views on theology and divinity, suddenly I was deluged with scores of fans asking me to sign photos as the rest of the actors milled around, ignored. Jesus spent the interval signing autographs, which seemed rather contrary to the message of the play.

It's a tremendous testament to the *Godspell* cast that they never seemed jealous of this imbalance of attention but remained fiercely loyal and protective of me. One night, Jeremy Irons and I had an after-show plate of pasta at Luigi's and he lugubriously reflected on his own obscurity next to my burgeoning fame. Yet I knew it would also happen for him: he was too good an actor to stay unknown.

Maureen was naturally delighted that I had become an overnight success after a mere ten years of slogging away, and thankfully it put an end to any financial worries. We were able to move from Seven Kings to a town house in Chigwell Row, Essex. I could even buy myself a £1,750 second-hand convertible Mercedes, as well as a Renault for Maureen to chauffeur Verity around in.

The upside of fame was that suddenly record companies were falling over themselves to release my music. Now I had some sort of name, labels that had never even returned Derek's calls before were locked in a bidding war for me. Eventually, after many transatlantic phone calls, Derek, Jeff and I signed a five-album deal with CBS Records.

CBS soon learned that they had signed a very stubborn artist. The label's executives felt that 'Rock On' was too avant-garde and, as David Puttnam had said, 'weird' to be my debut single for them. They preferred the more conventional 'On and On' to be the A-side, but I saw 'Rock On' as a statement of intent and was determined to get my own way.

However, once they had agreed to release it, the company pushed the boat out with 'Rock On'. Fashion and celebrity photographer David Bailey did the cover photo shoot, but I found the experience all a bit overblown and have never liked the photo on the sleeve of 'Rock On'.

CBS also hired the ballroom of Quaglino's restaurant in Soho to celebrate their signing of me and to launch the single. The room was packed with the great and the good of the music biz and the event could have got a little overwhelming, but luckily I had a good excuse to slip away – I had a *Godspell* show to do.

The reviews for 'Rock On' were mostly favourable. One critic waxed fairly lyrical: 'More than just a pretty face, more than a slender waist, this man has the guts to put out a positively thirst-quenching hit 45 – a rumble of bass, a voice laced in reverb and glance back to blue jeans, baby queens and James Dean. A feat of subtleties – it will mess with your head.' However, it was the promotional appearances that showed me how big 'Rock On' was about to be – and how my life was set to change for ever.

CBS had arranged signing sessions at a handful of London record shops. I anticipated fairly low-key events but could not have been more wrong, as became clear when Derek and I turned up at the first store in Streatham, which resembled a war zone – if wars were fought solely by screaming teenage girls.

It was absolute mayhem. The record store had also clearly under-estimated how many people would show up and their low-key security staff were hopelessly overwhelmed. I spent an hour trapped behind a desk signing singles and photos as girls sobbed and told me they loved me, then a lot longer waiting for the crowd outside to disperse so I could get out in one piece.

There were similarly chaotic scenes in Bond Street, where a thousand-plus crowd actually stopped the traffic in Oxford Street, and at a signing in Lewisham in south London, another occasion when the store's security consisted of a little old man who was no match for hundreds of shrieking, oestrogen-driven girls.

With his premises besieged by more than 2,000 delirious fans, the Lewisham record shop owner had no choice but to lock me in the storeroom for my safety and call the police. Even the boys in blue were unable to clear a way through the sea of teenagers. I was due in the West End for *Godspell*, and the situation looked desperate until my CBS plugger, Steve Colyer, had a brainwave.

Steve toured a few local premises' back yards and returned with a pile of dustbin lids. Wielding them as shields against the hordes like King Arthur's knights, we fought our way through the squealing mob to the car. Everybody was trying to grab at me and the dents in the battered dustbin lids told of the strength of their desire but somehow we made it, arriving at Wyndham's with ten minutes to spare.

How did it feel suddenly to be at the centre of this madness? It was exciting, of course, and an exhilarating adrenaline rush, but my main emotions were bemusement and embarrassment. Two years earlier, I had been signing on the dole and applying for van-driving jobs. Where had this come from? What did it mean?

I guess the years of failure that had preceded these days of success helped me to cope with it. I had spent enough time broke, unemployed, understudying and playing gigs to two men and not even a dog that I was grounded enough not to let this adulation go to my head. Or, at least, that was what I hoped. The truth was, it was hard to make any sense of such hysteria.

Godspell had made me but as my time on the show neared its end a few of the performances began to drag. A lot of Jesus's perorations began with 'I tell you this...' and once or twice I proclaimed those words then gaped at Julie Covington open-mouthed, my mind full of tumbleweed, until the helpful whisper of the prompter got my thought process back on track.

As my last night in the show – 15 September 1973 – neared, my life was pandemonium. Tickets for my final performance were changing hands for absurdly inflated sums. *That'll Be the Day* had taken up residency in cinemas up and down the land. And to top it all, 'Rock On' had reached number three in the BBC's Top Forty – and number one in the *NME* singles chart.

At the heart of the mayhem, I was concentrating on keeping my head together and getting through each day, but looking back, it is extraordinary to remember how my theatre, cinema and music careers had all come together at exactly the same time. I'm not sure that any artist has repeated that achievement, even to this day. So maybe Derek was right – I was an all-rounder, after all.

The *Godspell* producers had hired my *That'll Be the Day* co-star Robert Lindsay to replace me as Jesus, after I recommended him to them. It was clearly time to move on, but even so my departure from *Godspell* was hugely affecting.

In my two years on the show, the cast had grown spectacularly close. My last night as Jesus was charged with emotion, and as the clown disciples said their goodbyes to me in their individual ways during the Last Supper, I thought I would break down in tears. From such unpromising beginnings, directing ourselves when no theatre would touch us, we had been through so much. I even tried to capture the exhilaration and sadness of that last night in a song on my first album, *Rock On*, called 'September 15th'.

Normally when productions end, actors lavishly swap promises to keep in touch like people who have met on holiday and then go off on their merry way, never to meet again. It is testament to the extraordinary closeness of the *Godspell* cast that we still hold regular get-togethers more than thirty years on. It was a unique experience in all our lives.

They say Jesus saves: he had certainly saved me. *Godspell* had transported me from anonymity to fame and fortune and given my career the kick-start I had feared it wouldn't get. One thing was patently obvious: my life would never be the same again.

9

THE ONLY WAY IS ESSEX

With *Godspell* finally over, I was desperate to focus on my musical career. Theatre and cinema were great but, as ever, a big part of me still longed to sing the blues. I knew that I only had a short window to get things moving: before *That'll Be the Day*, I had signed a two-film deal with David Puttnam and shooting on the sequel, *Stardust*, was to begin early in 1974.

Firstly, though, it was time to re-jig Team Essex. Ever since he became my manager, Derek had been tremendous, but now the rules of engagement had changed. Almost overnight his charge had gone from being a hapless wannabe to a bona fide star, and every day he was swamped with requests for TV appearances, newspaper interviews and photo sessions. He needed help.

Derek had until then been a one-man band running my career from his spare room in Harlow in Essex, but now we set up an office in a mews building in St John's Wood, near the famous Abbey Road Studios. We also recruited a lovely and gracious lady named Madge Godwin, who had been working for *Godspell* producer Binky Beaumont, to be my PA. (Had somebody told me two years earlier that I would need a PA, I would have given a bitter laugh and gone back to signing on.)

For some reason, magazines seemed to have an insatiable desire for fresh photographs of me. Photo shoots were one of my least favourite activities, especially after the awkward David Bailey experience, but I got around that by doing a few sessions with an old mate, Colin Davey.

Colin had been at Plessey's with me, and unlike me had actually finished his apprenticeship to be an electrical engineer before leaving to become a photographer. These sessions, which thanks to magazines like *Jackie* finished up on bedroom walls all over the country, were basically two old mates having a laugh and trying to keep a straight face. We shot a lot of them in a studio in Leytonstone down the road from my old manor, until the local kids got wind that I was there and besieged the building.

Jeff and I were using every spare second we could find to record my debut album, which was also to be called *Rock On*. After the success of 'Rock On' and 'On and On' we kept the same team of musicians, and slowly but surely a record was unfolding that I would be very proud of.

That'll Be the Day was meanwhile being released around the world, and I became no stranger to the inside of aeroplanes as I was bounced off to various European cities to promote it. It was exciting to visit new countries and often pleasantly bizarre. On French TV shows, for some inexplicable reason, I always seemed to be preceded by a puppeteer or a juggler.

I was also called upon to attend a few continental premieres, but the possible boredom factor of seeing *That'll Be the Day* again and again was alleviated at the screenings where the local film distributors had over-dubbed the film in their own language, meaning that this Shipman County graduate could enjoy watching himself discoursing in fluent German or Spanish.

Nearer to home, the steady progression of 'Rock On' up the singles chart led to an invite to go on *Top of the Pops*. This was obviously a huge deal. Like every music fan I watched the show virtually every week and its guaranteed massive viewing figures and subsequent record sales meant it was hugely powerful.

Despite this, *Top of the Pops* was not to prove an easy experience. Archaic Musicians' Union rules intended to protect the rights of session musicians meant that artists who went on the show had to either re-record the track in a BBC studio the day before, or else play it live on the show with the *Top of the Pops* orchestra.

This second option didn't really work for Jeff and me because we used such unusual instrumentation. It was unlikely the BBC orchestra would possess an electric trombone like Derek Wadsworth's. So we re-recorded 'Rock On' the day before, trying to persuade the BBC's bored, jobsworth studio producer in his shaggy beard and brown coat to add the layers of dub and echo that made the track so unique.

We had further problems on the day. I turned up at Television Centre in my normal gear of black jeans and a black sleeveless T-shirt, and was halfway through my rehearsal of 'Rock On', singing live to the re-recorded backing track, when the show's moustachioed, autocratic producer, Robin Nash, came wafting down from the gallery.

'What are you wearing, David?' he asked, a distinct note of reprimand in his voice. 'I'm afraid you will disappear into the background, dear!' (This being the mighty *Top of the Pops*, there was obviously no question of altering the background to suit the artist's requirements.) 'Have you nothing white?'

I didn't have many white clothes, as it happened, but into my mind came a rarely worn cream suit hanging in the back of my wardrobe. I phoned Maureen, and a BBC car was dispatched to Essex to pick it up. I accessorised it with a carnation in the lapel, it looked OK on the screen, and I went on to wear that outfit so many times that it became part of my image.

With my career progressing so well on all fronts, I was finally making some decent money, and Maureen, Verity and I moved again. We bought a lovely house deep in the Essex countryside in a rather grand-sounding place named Havering-Atte-Bower, near to the less grand-sounding Romford. The estate agent told us it contained elements of Henry VIII's hunting lodge. More pertinent to us was that it would give us more privacy than the gaff in Chigwell Row.

Maureen, Verity and I had happy times in that house, although for now we weren't having enough of them. Now that everyone suddenly wanted a piece of me, my relentless schedule meant I was away a lot more than was ideal. I missed them, and looking back now, it can't have been easy for them either.

My next trip was to be even further afield: America. *That'll Be the Day* and 'Rock On' had come out there simultaneously and while the lack of a general release had hampered the movie, the single was taking off. Derek and I embarked on a whistle-stop promotional tour of eleven US cities in fourteen days.

For me, this was the big one. America had always loomed large in my life and imagination, from the blues music I devoured to the films, fashions and iconography I loved. The United States always seemed like the centre of the world to me, so distant and so glamorous, and here was my chance to see it at first hand.

Sadly, the trip was a little bit of a disappointment. I had such an inhumanly crammed promotional schedule that Derek and I saw little in two weeks apart from hotel rooms, TV studios and radio stations. I spent a fortnight having the same conversation every day with different journalists in different cities.

Nevertheless, one memory burns bright even today. I will never forget the moment that our yellow cab from JFK swung on to Brooklyn Bridge and I saw the skyscrapers of Manhattan for the first time. Like so many people, I fell in love with New York the second I set eyes on it, and it still feels to me like the ultimate city.

I realised on that trip that the American media had a different perception of me from their British counterparts. At home, the teenage fans and what were perceived as my heartthrob pop-idol looks were already leading some critics to perceive me as just a piece of fluff. It didn't matter that I wrote all of my own songs: for some people, I would always be a lightweight.

The best example of this, incidentally, came in the attitude of the most determinedly cutting-edge UK paper, the *New Musical Express*. When I first broke through, the *NME* plastered me on its cover and raved about me. As soon as the screaming girls appeared, they didn't want to know. One of their most august critics, Charles Shaar Murray, even dismissed me as singing like 'a constipated stoat' (which, frankly, I'd love to hear).

The US journalists took a less snobby and dismissive approach to me and I was granted an interview with the printed talisman of their counter-culture, *Rolling Stone*. Their extremely earnest, John Lennon-lookalike interviewer was particularly taken with the lyric that straddled the bridge section of 'Rock On':

> *And where do we go from here?*
> *Which is the way that's clear?*

He clearly felt this was a particularly profound encapsulation of the existential dilemmas facing modern Western society. Was it a depiction of the post-Vietnam generation, craving direction and moral purpose, he asked me? He may have been somewhat disappointed by my candid reply: 'No, it just rhymed.'

There again, he was even more aghast when our two-hour interview drew to a close and he discovered his tape machine had failed to record it. 'Could we do it again?' he pleaded. With my schedule, there could only be one answer: 'No.'

I also took a trip to Japan to meet the bigwigs at CBS there. It was a distinctly surreal visit. Their HQ was over sixteen floors of a skyscraper and the executives took me into a lift with them. On every single floor they stopped the lift and the workers on that floor, waiting eagerly outside the lift, applauded me frantically for three or four minutes as soon as the doors opened. This bizarre meet-and-greet exercise probably lasted nearly an hour.

Back in Britain, my relentless work schedule continued apace in November as CBS released *Rock On* and a second single off the album, 'Lamplight'. For whatever reason, Jeff and I were still looking to push back the sonic boundaries, and on 'Lamplight' we booked a blacksmith from Leyton to come in and play his anvil. Like the farting didgeridoo, it didn't work out, and I ended up bashing out the part on a fire extinguisher.

My newfound fame led to me picking up a couple of awards, and it really was a case of from the sublime to the ridiculous. The Royal Variety Club named me Most Promising Newcomer, which I gratefully accepted with a speech at their ceremony. I was less bothered about being named Rear of the Year a few days later. I didn't even turn up to collect that one. Maybe I was being arsey.

It was flattering to be asked to play Pete Townshend's part in a live concert version of *Tommy*, Pete's new rock opera for the Who. It was also a good chance to catch up with my old mucker Keith Moon. My main memory of our sole performance, at the Rainbow Theatre in Finsbury Park, north London, was that the theatre was so cold that the string section were wearing gloves.

That year, 1973, had been a whirlwind for me. As the year ended, the *Rock On* album was in the Top Ten, as was the 'Lamplight' single; *That'll Be the Day* was still hanging around the album chart; and across the Atlantic, 'Rock On' was climbing the Billboard 100. Maureen, Verity and I bunkered down for a desperately needed quiet family Christmas in Essex. It was just as well we did – because the next year was going to be even more mental.

10

A SPRINKLING OF STARDUST

The success of *That'll Be the Day* meant that David Puttnam had inevitably exercised the option in my contract obliging me also to appear in its sequel. *Stardust* – which originally had the working title of *Sooner or Later* – continued the story of Jim MacLaine but for me it was a far more emotionally punishing experience than its predecessor.

That'll Be the Day had ended with Jim walking out on his wife and child, buying a guitar and setting off on a mission to find musical fame and fortune. *Stardust* bore the tagline 'Show Me a Boy Who Never Wanted to Be a Rock Star and I'll Show You a Liar', but this could just as easily have read 'Be Careful What You Wish For – It Might Come True'.

Ray Connolly had once again written the script, and as soon as I read it, I had serious misgivings. They were concerned not with the quality of the writing, which was again very strong, but with the narrative of the story. To be honest, my reservations were so troubling that I'm not sure I would have made the film had I not been contractually obliged to.

In *Stardust*, Ray depicted Jim MacLaine becoming an overnight sensation rock star and teen idol, and reacting by turning into a bloated egomaniac, drug addict and recluse, completely out of touch with reality. It portrayed the damaging and deleterious effects of fame very starkly, and given that I was currently at the heart of a storm that the media had recently dubbed ESSEX MANIA, it was a little too close to home.

I wasn't the only one to feel that way. Ringo Starr, who had of course enjoyed and endured levels of celebrity way beyond my comprehension as part of the biggest band in history, didn't feel able to make *Stardust*, believing it would be too painful to be part of a fictionalised re-enactment of what his life had turned into in the Beatles. Adam Faith replaced him as Mike.

Before filming began in February '74 I made a quick trip to Los Angeles for a premiere of *That'll Be the Day*. California is very beautiful in parts but I found LA true to its stereotype of La-La Land, where everybody is trying to live the dream and it is hard to believe a word anyone says. Give me New York and the East Coast any time.

Maureen, Verity and I also snatched a short holiday in Mexico, where I doubtless impressed my family by going paragliding behind a speedboat, crash-landing into a tree and dangling from its branches like a doughnut. Otherwise, it was a relaxing break and, given the gruelling few months I had coming up, very necessary.

My LA trip had given me the idea for a song, 'America', and back in Britain, I went into the studio with Jeff and recorded the bare bones of the tune, the follow-up to 'Lamplight'. I had to leave Jeff to finish it as I headed off to begin filming *Stardust*.

Michael Apted had taken over as director from *That'll Be the Day*'s Claude Whatham and we began shooting in Manchester. I mostly enjoyed making the early part of the film, which showed Jim MacLaine enjoying life in his group the Stray Cats with band mates Paul Nicholas (another ex-Jesus, of course), Keith Moon, Dave Edmunds, Karl Howman and Peter Duncan.

The fact that Adam, Keith, Dave and myself were all musicians, and Ray had chronicled the rise of the Beatles as a Liverpool music journalist, meant that we were able to bring realism to our subject matter. Yet even such experienced, hard-bitten rock stars as Keith and Dave were gobsmacked by the scenes we encountered when the Stray Cats played Belle Vue.

The producers had booked this massive Manchester gig venue to film the band playing a show on their ascent to fame. They had invited David Essex fans to make up the audience, and as I had not yet toured since Essex Mania had broken, it was the first chance any of them had had to see me play live.

The first inkling of the levels of hysteria inside Belle Vue came before the Stray Cats came on. Cocooned in the dressing room waiting for the cameras to roll, we could hear thousands of girls chanting: 'We want David! We want David!' *Stardust* first assistant Garth Thomas begged them to yell 'We want Jim!' instead, but he didn't get very far with that one.

When we took the stage, pandemonium broke out. Everywhere I looked, girls were screaming, fainting, sobbing. In waves, they tried to rush the stage as the venue security men were hopelessly overrun. The noise was shrill and deafening. I couldn't hear a word I was singing, or the band was playing. All I could think was: is it supposed to be like this?

My main reaction, as ever, was shock and embarrassment. I had no idea how to process what was going on mentally, but the unadulterated frenzy provided some of the most powerful footage in the whole of *Stardust* and captured vividly what it was like to be the focus of such delirium. It was also something I was going to have to get used to.

It helped to relieve the pressure on me that Keith Moon was on his traditional hell-raising form as we filmed *Stardust*. Alcohol was invariably involved. One all-night shoot at Belle Vue degenerated into a fistfight between Keith and Ray Connolly. It was hardly Ali v Frazier, and the comedy value was enhanced by the camp, overwrought make-up man next to them jumping up and down and pleading with Ray: 'Not his face: please don't hit his face!'

We adjourned to the complex's ten-pin bowling alley, where Keith lost his footing as he attempted to deliver his first ball at 4 a.m. and slid all the way down the lane with his fingers still trapped in the ball, cartoon-style, demolishing the skittles and disappearing into the ten-pin mechanism. When we rescued Keith, his sole priority was claiming a strike.

Keith was also extremely fond of terrorising the Mancunian populace by means of a hidden speaker and microphone that his roadie had rigged up inside his car. He would pull up at a zebra crossing, wait politely for pedestrians, then scare them out of their wits with a booming roar of 'Get out of the road!'

Yet the increasing parallels between my life and that of Jim MacLaine were inescapable. For months 'Rock On' had been inexorably climbing up the US Cashbox singles chart, and one morning at four Keith and I returned to the Midland Hotel from yet another late-night shoot to find that Derek had phoned and left a message for me at the reception desk: 'Congratulations: you're number one in America.'

Many people would have been punching the air at this news but I've always been phlegmatic by nature, knowing from my years of rejection that fame and success are transient phenomena and not to be trusted, so my reaction was kind of understated. This was not the case with Keith Moon. 'Champagne!' he yelled as I showed him the note. 'You lucky sod! The Who have never had a number one.' The rest of the night became a bit of a blur.

Even Keith was a model of restraint, though, next to the US record label promotional guys who called up the next day and screamed down the phone as if my topping the Cashbox chart was the most significant historical event since the moon landing. Luckily, I always had problems taking that kind of call too seriously.

Jim MacLaine was growing ever more wayward, degenerate and sex-crazed in *Stardust*. Shooting a three-in-a-bed orgy with two girls was mortifying. I was terrified, made sure that I kept my pants on, and felt even more embarrassed when I looked up at the end of the scene to see an electrician looming over the bed, flexing his bicep and miming 'Phwoargh!' at me.

From Manchester, the filming moved on to Granada in southern Spain. Maureen and Verity travelled out with me, although their stay was to prove fraught and very unlike our idyllic time in Shanklin filming *That'll Be the Day*. Our accommodation in a tiny village near Guadix was little more than a hovel, and a livid Maureen confronted Michael Apted after a rat ran across Verity as she lay asleep in bed. Michael was apologetic but made a fair point: the location was so remote that there were no alternatives.

The remoteness was largely the point. At the end of *Stardust* Jim MacLaine, destroyed and driven mad by fame, buys a castle in Andalucia and holes up with his loyal sidekick and road manager Mike, becoming a recluse. The location for this was a remote Moorish castle, or *alcazaba*, in Guadix.

I found the film's closing scenes, where an embittered Jim feeds LSD to Mike's dog, suffers a nervous breakdown, goes insane and finally ODs, extremely harrowing to shoot. My upbringing and the fact I had a young family meant that I hadn't reacted to fame as Jim did by spiralling off into casual sex and drug abuse, but it wasn't hard to see how it could happen. Suddenly, I could see why Ringo couldn't face making this movie.

Maybe Adam Faith and I were getting too Stanislavski and method-acting about our roles, because Adam started making enquiries about actually buying the *alcazaba*. He was serious about it, and was only put off by the revelation that in buying the castle, you also became responsible for some troglodyte-like local people living in the caves beneath it.

There again, Adam, or Terry as his real name was, was always keen on buying property. When *Stardust*'s filming reverted to England, he took me to see another place he was contemplating purchasing. It was like something from a film set. As we pulled into a long driveway leading to a Hammer Horror-style Gothic mansion, a sudden thunderclap and flash of lightning rent the skies above it, adding to the melodrama.

Adam was considering buying a psychiatric hospital not unlike the one I had taken Michael to in my mini-cab days. After the sale, the inmates would be moved, but they were currently still in situ. As we walked in, a patient welcomed us by smearing baked beans all over his face, but driven by sheer enthusiasm, Adam was oblivious to the confused souls surrounding us as he strode around the building, pointing out where the snooker room and the master bedroom would be.

We finished off the *Stardust* filming in Los Angeles, where the Jim MacLaine/David Essex parallels became even more direct. In the film, US entertainment mogul Porter Lee Austin, played by Larry Hagman (who went on to enjoy huge success as J R Ewing in *Dallas*), brashly muscles in on Jim's rocketing career, persuading him to dump his British managers.

As we arrived in California, 'Rock On' was still number one in the US, which meant that a stream of similarly Machiavellian and opportunist operators came out of the woodwork trying to sign me up. Thankfully, I wasn't even remotely tempted. Derek had done far too much for me to deserve such treachery.

This trip to Los Angeles was memorable for yielding an encounter with the LAPD. One evening Ray Connolly, French *Stardust* actress Ines Des Longchamps and I were speeding down Sunset Boulevard, living out some daft American fantasy. The police pulled us over, and the shades-sporting officer's first enquiry to us was: 'Do you have any guns on you tonight?'

This struck me as a particularly preposterous question and I burst out laughing. The LAPD are not renowned for their sense of humour and in an instant the officer had me banged up against a nearby wall, my arms behind my back. Sadly, this reaction had the opposite effect to what he intended, and I quickly became near hysterical with mirth.

The situation wasn't helped when Ines, taking exception to this assault and with the French's traditional lack of respect for both authority and America, waded in and began belting the LAPD man with her handbag. He retaliated by making us walk in a straight line to ascertain that we weren't drunk, then finally gave up, deciding we were just goddamn eccentric Europeans and letting us go.

Away from the *Stardust* set, Larry Hagman was a larger-than-life Texan and a pretty mean Keith Moon-style party animal. At a riotous party at his beach house in Malibu, he proudly showed me his powerful telescope for stargazing and a bed whose party pieces included vibrating at speed. Keith decided to test the latter out and came near to breaking the thing, earning Larry's wrath, before we all disappeared into the ocean skinny-dipping.

It was moments like this that made me realise I had come a long way from Canning Town, very quickly, and I was in uncharted territory. If ever there was a time in my life when I could have done a Jim MacLaine and succumbed to sex, drugs and rock 'n' roll, this was it, and I guess *Stardust* was a salutary tale of how things could easily have played out if I had let them.

Having said that, I don't think *Stardust* was as truthful a film as *That'll Be the Day*. The latter had been a very British film, whereas I think with *Stardust* the producers had an eye on doing well in America, which may have been partly why we went to film there. It was a good movie, but it ended up being a little bit mid-Atlantic.

Nevertheless, for a few surreal weeks, shooting this troubling film, it was difficult for me to know where Jim MacLaine ended and David Essex began. That tension, plus the work-hard, play-hard attitude that suffused the set, meant that I ended the filming of *Stardust* exhausted.

Nobody knows you like your mum. Back in Essex, I drove over to visit my parents and my mum was horrified at my exhausted demeanour, gaunt face and dead eyes. *Stardust* had taken it out of me, in every way.

Hungry for more success, CBS were now on at me for a new album and single but I knew I needed a break or, at the very least, a working holiday. I booked a villa in the south of France and jetted out with Maureen and Verity for a few weeks' escape from the goldfish bowl of fame while I wrote my second album.

My record label plugger, Steve Colyer, joined us for part of the trip and inadvertently helped give birth to one of my biggest songs. As we sat around the pool on a sunny lunchtime, Steve strummed a sequence of chords. From nowhere, a tune popped into my head, followed by an opening lyric:

Oh, is he more, too much more
Than a pretty face?

'Gonna Make You a Star' was born that easily and simply, and that has always been my experience of songwriting. The best tunes tend to fall out of the ether, naturally and organically.

When you have to struggle and sweat over tracks, they tend not to be so special or successful.

While I was in France, 'America' was out as a single, and while it hadn't done much in Britain, the French couldn't get enough of it and it spent weeks at number one. I was flattered and puzzled by this until a French record executive explained it. It seemed the song's chorus '*America, America, ca, ca*' translated into French as '*America, America, poo, poo*'. This appealed to the people of France who, as I had seen from Ines, have never been big fans of the US. Maybe they thought the song was a work of biting satire.

The nation's police force were also big fans of the tune. While in the south of France, I went for a drink with a friend, Kenney Jones, the former drummer of the Small Faces. Somehow we got roped into judging a beauty contest in a nightclub in St Tropez, although we were quickly kicked off the panel after I insisted on marking the girls in fractions such as 39¼.

Kenney and I headed back to the villa but made the error of stopping on the way to pee against a handy wall. Big mistake. It transpired we had chosen to relieve ourselves against the wall of the local police station, and a burly *gendarme*'s arm suddenly materialised around my neck and dragged me away before I had even finished.

Inside the police station there was very little *entente cordiale* and Kenney and I were getting a severe ticking-off until one policeman suddenly recognised me: '*Ah, Davide Essex – America, ca, ca!*' The mood suddenly changed and I was offered a plea bargain – they would spare me a night in the cells if I gave them an intimate, impromptu concert.

This was the best offer I was likely to get so I got on a table and gave them a lively rendition of 'America', with *les gendarmes* enthusiastically joining in on the '*ca ca*' chorus as Kenney tried and failed to keep a straight face behind them. Thank *Dieu* it happened in the days before mobile phones and YouTube.

Writing 'Gonna Make You a Star' had got my second album, which with devastating imagination I had decided to call *David Essex*, off to a flying start. More songs followed, and back in London, Jeff and I went into the studio and set about committing them to vinyl.

Stardust was out that autumn and I decided to write a song with the same name for the film soundtrack. The words told the tale of the sorry decline of deluded rock star Jim MacLaine:

Ah look what they've done to the rock 'n' roll clown
Ah rock 'n' roll clown, look he's down on the ground
Well he used to fly high, but he crashed out the sky...

In my head was an eerie, resonant sound that I wanted to echo behind the crucial line: '*In a stardust ring see the rock 'n' roll king is down*'. Jeff and I experimented with weird synthesiser effects then a detuned bass, but it was percussionist Ray Cooper who hit on the idea of striking a gong and dropping it into a bath of water. Weird? Maybe, but this time David Puttnam was more than happy to put it on the soundtrack, and it played as the final credits rolled after doomed Jim MacLaine had shuffled off this mortal coil.

While Jeff and I were pushing back the sonic frontiers of music once more, Derek was busy trying to arrange my debut tour for that autumn. There were plenty of interested promoters but we settled on a keen, honest-sounding West Country boy named Mel Bush. There was no way of knowing then that Mel would go on to work with me for nearly forty years.

So autumn '74 would see the release of the *Stardust* film, its soundtrack album, the *David Essex* album and a major fifteen-date UK tour. That would surely be more than enough to satisfy any poor, unfortunate soul who was suffering from Essex Mania. Or would it?

11

'IT'S BECAUSE WE
F****** LOVE YOU'

After the prodigious success of 'Rock On' in America, Derek had received some approaches from various Porter Lee Austin/Larry Hagman-type figures for me to stage my first live tour in the US, but I wasn't really tempted. Bob Dylan once talked about Bringing It All Back Home, and I was determined that my first tour should be in my homeland, where it had all happened for me: Britain.

In actual fact, my first live date was to prove more significant still. When Mel Bush delivered the itinerary for my autumn '74 tour, the opening date jumped off the page at me: East Ham Odeon, not three miles from where I had been born and enjoyed such a wonderful childhood.

I knew the prognoses for the tour were good. *Stardust* had been released to a similar fanfare to that which had greeted *That'll Be the Day*. The *David Essex* album was to reach number two in the chart, while 'Gonna Make You a Star', that simple song dreamed up next to a French swimming pool, became my first number-one single. Yet movies and albums I was well versed in. Playing live was a new experience.

We weren't intending to stint on the production. Jeff Wayne had recruited a nine-piece band, plus backing singers, and we spent two weeks selecting a set list, running through the material and rehearsing the band until they were ultra-tight. Tickets went on sale and the entire fifteen-date tour sold out in two days. We felt prepared, and ready to go.

That didn't mean I wasn't nervous. As I sat backstage at East Ham Odeon before the first show, a million twitchy thoughts and memories ran through my head. As I heard the excited crowd streaming into the venue, I tried to focus on the slick, professional show we intended to give them.

There is a bizarre paradox with live performance of any kind: for two hours you are the centre of everybody's attention, a magnet for their adulation and love, yet the time immediately before and after you take the stage is an intense and lonely one. I'm not sure I've ever felt more nervy and psyched-up than that night in that East End dressing room.

Derek and I had hired Mel Bush's brother, Bev, to be my road manager for the duration of the tour, and eventually he tapped our secret coded knock on the door and told me, 'They're ready when you are.' So this was it. Showtime. I donned my jacket and made my way to the side of the stage.

Hidden in the wings, I could hardly believe the volume of the noise as the lights went up and Jeff and the band kicked into the first number of the night. However, even this cacophony seemed like nothing compared to the frenzy that erupted when I joined them on stage. It sounded as if twenty Concordes were lifting off all around us. Was this what it had felt like for the Beatles at the Shea Stadium? How could anything be this loud?

I felt stunned. The noise onslaught was so relentless that my mind seemed to be shutting down. Everything felt like it was in slow motion as, working from memory and instinct, I walked as if through quicksand towards the mike, certain that nobody would be able to hear a word I sang.

Somehow, I became aware of a shadow looming over me. As I twitched in shock, a girl who had jumped from one of the side boxes ten feet or so above the stage landed at my feet in a crumpled heap, yelling as she bounced on the boards. What should I do? Retreat? Pick her up? On autopilot, I moved to the other side of the stage, hoping security would sort it out.

I had fondly imagined that filming the fictional Stray Cats gig at Belle Vue in Manchester for *Stardust* had prepared me for being the object of mass worship and adoration. I could not have been more wrong. This was a hundred times more berserk than that ordeal, and this time there was no filter, no scripted Jim MacLaine, between me and the audience: they were screaming just for, and at, me.

How did it feel to be the cause of that baying mayhem, the sole reason for such an extraordinary mass explosion of passion? I simply didn't know. I had no idea how I was supposed to feel. I was grateful for the love being shown to me, of course, but also I felt grotesquely uncomfortable. What was so special about me? How could I ever be deserving of this?

In truth, I also felt a slight, strange resentment. Jeff and I had assembled this killer live band, worked for weeks on songs and arrangements, rehearsed and honed them until they were perfect, and now nobody could hear a thing through the shrill, piercing wall of screams. We might as well have been playing anvils and farting didgeridoos.

Nevertheless, you get used to anything, eventually, and as my tender ears gradually became accustomed to the cacophony, the show went well. The bouncers in front of the stage needed the sharp reflexes of West Ham goalie Phil Parkes to intercept the countless girls launching themselves towards me. I even saw the girl that had crashed from the box, still in one piece, come back for another go.

The noise levels hardly dipped all night, although they went up another notch for hits and crowd-pleasers such as 'Rock On', 'Gonna Make You a Star' and 'Stardust'. I staggered back to the dressing room at the end of the night as my incipient tinnitus kicked in only to realise that the greatest challenge still awaited us.

Put simply: we had to get out of the building. The thousands of fans might have streamed out of the theatre but none of them seemed to have actually gone home. Every exit of the Odeon was blocked solid as girls milled around, chanting my name and longing for a close encounter.

This was when Bev Bush came into his own. Together with the venue's security men, he devised an innovative escape strategy that involved creeping across the Odeon's roof to an adjacent building and exiting via their service entrance into a waiting car. Even then, a few intrepid fans intercepted us, and were rewarded for their anticipation with autographs.

I had never even remotely anticipated a reaction such as that, in my wildest dreams (or nightmares). The next day, my ears still ringing, I surmised that maybe the reaction was partly due to my first night being in East Ham and me being a local boy made good. Nope. The thrilling, sometimes terrifying scenes of lunacy followed me through the entire tour.

Even the scenes after the opening gig paled next to the mayhem in Liverpool. I was playing two sold-out, back-to-back shows at the Empire. The crowd for the first show decided to stick around outside the venue to hear the second set, which meant that when that performance finished, there were not one but two audiences blockading the venue: 6,000 people.

This was too much for even Bev Bush to overcome with one of his amazing exit strategies. The police were called, and roamed the area outside the Empire with dogs as the superintendent in charge hatched a cunning plan. Disguised in a police uniform, I would burst out of the venue with nine or ten 'fellow officers', jump into a police car and be rushed back to the Adelphi Hotel.

This might have worked were it not for the fact that the Scouse plods had no shoes for me to change into, which meant that I dashed into the throng in a too-big uniform and the same bright red, instantly recognisable boots I had been wearing on stage. I was twigged immediately, my outnumbered police escort was sent flying, and I would have been torn to pieces had a burly sergeant not put me over his shoulder, used me as a battering ram, and dumped me in the back of a police Land Rover. The Adelphi was clearly out of the question: for my own safety, I spent the night at the police station.

So Essex Mania *wasn't* just a glib phrase that the newspapers had invented. It really existed. As the tour hit south Wales, the band and I checked into our hotel and I was shown to my room. As I opened my suitcase on the bed and began to unpack it before heading off to the soundcheck, a girl emerged from my wardrobe. I gazed at her in shock.

She didn't bother to say hello: she cut straight to the chase. 'I love you,' she told me. I asked her what she was doing there, and she fell silent. This was a phenomenon I was to become very accustomed to in years to come: girls who, for whatever reason, were utterly obsessed with me would meet me and fall completely mute. Faced with the object of their desire, they simply wouldn't know what to do.

'You shouldn't be here,' I told her.

'I know,' my intruder agreed.

'How did you get in?' She gave no answer, so I opened the bedroom door and politely gave her a red card: 'I think you'd better leave.' She meekly filed through the door and trudged off down the corridor.

Of course, many rock stars, and men in general, would have behaved very differently when confronted with a nubile young lady leaping out of a wardrobe at them. My standard reaction was a million miles from that of a predatory Jim MacLaine, but that was just the way I was, and still am.

So why didn't I take advantage of the hundreds – thousands – of girls who would have liked nothing more than a night of passion with David Essex, the adored pop star? The main reason was very simple. I had a wife, and a young child. Maureen and I had our ups and downs, but I hated the thought of cheating on her or, particularly, doing anything that would diminish me in Verity's eyes. I loved them and I wanted them to respect me.

On a deeper level, I also had a very strong moral code that I guess must have been instilled by my parents. I knew that these girls who 'loved David Essex' didn't even know me, with all of my foibles and idiosyncrasies: they loved an impossible, glossy, unrealistic *ideal* of me, assembled from the music, the cinema screen and the pages of *Jackie* magazine.

I might have had my occasional romantic encounters on tour with Mood Indigo, all those years ago, but that was different. These girls were young and vulnerable and I knew at heart it would be wrong to abuse them and their 'love' for me.

In any case, it wasn't always girls who stalked me. Before my first-tour gig in Lewisham in south London, I was changing in my third-floor dressing room when a teenage boy appeared at the window, having shinned up a drainpipe. ''Allo, mate, I think you're great, you're my 'ero!' he informed me, before vanishing from view as abruptly as he had appeared. I was quite worried about him, but hearing no ambulances, could only assume he was OK.

I was also keen not to exploit fans with dodgy souvenirs and tacky merchandise. I never liked the idea of a fan club, and although I occasionally wrote a letter for it to send out to the members, I generally kept such activities at arm's length. I also cringed whenever I saw a David Essex tea towel, or opened a copy of *Jackie* or *Look-in* to find a pull-out poster of me. For one thing, fame had not destroyed my basic shyness.

The tour had been madness from start to finish, but even when the dates were over, with me thankfully still in one piece, the insanity did not end. Promotional appearances were equally high-risk, and possibly more so, as I didn't have a gang of security guards watching my back as I usually did at gigs.

Possibly my most perilous encounter with out-of-control fans came when I was due to go into Radio One for an interview with breakfast show DJ Tony Blackburn. Blackburn had talked this up on his show, and as we were about to leave, my promotions man, Colin, received a call warning that an enormous crowd had gathered outside Broadcasting House.

The most sensible reaction would have been to postpone the appearance, but desperate not to lose this high-profile publicity opportunity, Colin had a bright idea. I had a blacked-out Mini, and Colin suggested that I went with Bev in that while Colin travelled in the limo with one of CBS's promotional cardboard cut-outs of me. The theory was that the fans would mob the limo, leaving Bev and I to scuttle into Radio One unmolested.

It's hard to believe now that we agreed to this ridiculous plan, but we did. Arriving in convoy at Portland Place, we found thousands of girls waiting. Fans may be many things but they are not stupid and they paid little attention to the limo, instead converging on my poor little Mini as soon as they saw it appear.

In no time there were so many girls on top of the car that we thought the roof would give way. The weight broke the back springs. It was scary, and possibly the only time that I ever saw Bev panic. 'Stay here, I'll go for help!' he said and forced his way out of the Mini as I locked the door behind him.

I was now on my own, trapped in my poor battered Mini and engulfed in a sea of shrieking girls. Twenty or so faces pressed against the car's windscreen and windows, and fans fought behind them to get to the front. I was terrified, and at the same time – ridiculous as it sounds – I had no idea how to react.

What was the protocol? Should I smile at the girls? Frown at them? Ask them to get off my car? I settled for staring vaguely into the middle distance as if I were somehow oblivious to the carnage around me. But I couldn't help catching the eye of a black girl with her face squashed against the windscreen, who helpfully explained their motivation in this scene: 'You know why, don't you? It's because we f****** love you!'

Tony Blackburn was not to get his scoop interview. Bev fought his way back through the crowd, scrambled into the Mini and explained that the BBC commissionaires' response to his plea for help had been to tell him: 'Don't you bring him in here!' The good news was that the police were on their way. By the time they arrived, half of the West End seemed locked down.

It was yet more evidence that as 1974 ended and the dust settled on my chaotic first tour, I was arguably the most successful pop star and performing artist in Britain. For the first time, I became grateful for the years of failure and obscurity that I had endured when only Derek had any faith in me, because those hard-knock days of rejections were helping me to stay grounded.

I might have been enjoying number-one records, selling out venues and entertaining thousands of besotted fans, but I knew I was still the same East End boy who had driven mini cabs, trod the boards in rep and made up the numbers in pantomimes. No matter what *Jackie* magazine might think, I hadn't turned into a god.

It was ironic that America, the country that I had idolised as a teenager and whose music had first inspired me, had a far more measured and level-headed reaction to me. That was just what I felt I needed then, so when CBS returned to us still wanting US dates, I was ready.

There was only one place to kick off: New York. Our show at the legendary Bottom Line venue was packed, with people such as Rod Stewart in the audience, and I loved the fact that we could hear ourselves think during the show and the audience actually listened to the music.

Around the same time in New York City I attended the Grammy Awards at the Uris Theatre on Broadway. I was nominated for a Grammy for best new artist and also presented an award and sang a duet to a TV audience of millions with jazz legend Sarah Vaughan, which put Derek into seventh heaven.

The Grammies is a very stiff and formal ceremony that seems to last for days and after a couple of hours I was pretty bored of hanging around the venue booted and suited. I had lost Derek and had no security with me but decided to stretch my legs and have a fag, so I wandered out through the theatre's front door – and was immediately besieged by 500 autograph hunters.

I was trying to sign something for everyone but it was all getting a bit overwhelming when a black limousine suddenly pulled up alongside me, a window lowered and a voice emerged: 'David, get in here!' I had no idea who it was, but opened the door and hopped in, to find myself sitting next to John Lennon and Yoko Ono.

We had a short chat as we cruised the New York streets. John asked me, 'Are you going to the after-show party?' I don't think so, I told him. It's not really my thing. 'No, me neither,' he concurred, and after some more amiable chitchat they dropped me back at my hotel and headed off to the Dakota Building.

Back on the road, my States tour was short but memorable. In St Louis we played to 28,000 people in a vast stadium, supported by US soft rockers Journey. They had overrun their slot by twenty minutes and showed no signs of stopping when Derek, losing his rag, pulled out the main plug and plunged the stage into darkness.

Georgia yielded rock 'n' roll antics when a band member – no name, no pack drill – decided to pee into the hotel's ice-making machine. The management didn't take kindly to this, and we had to make a run for it into the woods around the hotel as the local sheriffs fired their guns over our heads.

In Los Angeles we played the Roxy on Sunset Strip. Led Zeppelin came down to see us, and when we hung out with them after the show, Zep told us that FBI agents were guarding their apartments and remained very diligent about protecting famous people after the Manson Family murders.

Well, that had been five years ago and nothing untoward was about to happen to us now, right? Wrong. Taking my leave of Zep, I returned to the Beverly Wilshire Hotel, where Maureen and Verity had already gone to bed. Slipping between the sheets next to Maureen, I was drifting off when I saw a figure by the bed.

'Verity?' I asked, sitting up. No: we had a burglar. Maureen also woke up and took a swing at the intruder with her handbag as he bolted from the end of the bed. She succeeded only in smashing me full in the face as he ran from the room.

We then went into slapstick mode. I jumped out of bed to give chase, but was naked, and so grabbed what I thought were my jeans. Wrong again. They were Maureen's, and as I hopped around trying to get them on and then off, I crashed my toe against the leg of the bed. Eventually I stumbled to Verity's room, where she and her nanny, Shirley, were safe and sound.

Zeppelin's talk of the Manson murders was still echoing in my head as I nervously opened the door to the suite's lounge, half-expecting to see naked hippies waving knives. It was empty, but immediately the phone rang. It was the LAPD, telling me they had apprehended two men running down the fire escape from our suite.

I met the police officer in the lobby and he quickly proved that the LAPD hadn't made any gains in the humour or people-skills departments since I had met them on Sunset Strip a few months earlier. First, he insisted I had to identify the two intruders. I explained that this would be hard as I had only seen one of them, in silhouette in the dark, but I would have a go.

The cop led me to his patrol car where two men were sitting in cuffs in the back. I peered in the window, which one of them promptly spat on. The officer then produced a small packet of brown powder. The thieves had dropped it as they ran away, he told me. It was heroin: as I was a rock star, he assumed it was mine?

I hastily assured the cop that I had never seen heroin before and had no idea what it even looked like, adding that Maureen and I would like to locate our missing cash and credit cards, if possible. I wished I'd never spoken, as the officer then insisted on me accompanying him on a painstaking search of the entire hotel.

We took the lift to every single floor. The officer would spring out, his gun levelled in classic LAPD style, survey the scene then nod to me that the coast was clear, at which point we rooted around each corridor, including emptying the sand buckets. We never found a thing – but there again, we never searched the cop.

Outside of this unwanted encounter with the LA criminal underworld and a bone-headed cop, the US tour had been an unqualified success. Yet I never repeated it: it was to be my sole tour of America.

It's hard to say why, exactly. I had always loved the idea and the ideal of the country, and I'm aware that most artists regard breaking America, with the global fame that ensues, as the entertainment industry's Holy Grail. I guess with my three-headed music, film and theatre career I always seemed to be busy with projects in Britain, and after hassling Derek and me for a while for a return visit, the record label just got bored and stopped asking.

So why didn't I try harder to conquer the States? I suspect the answer is extremely prosaic: at heart, I am very, very English.

12

FAIRGROUND ATTRACTIONS

At least one good thing came out of my Los Angeles trip. While in the City of Angels, another song had come to me from nowhere, almost fully formed: a simple, upbeat little number called 'Hold Me Close', further proof of my theory that the catchiest, most successful tunes arrive via inspiration, not perspiration.

It got me off to another good start with the writing of my third album. The 1970s were the days when record companies expected their main artists to produce an album every year, not one every two or three years as is the case nowadays, and CBS were keen to move quickly to capitalise on the success of *David Essex* and its three hit singles.

For the concept behind the album, I went back to the future – to the lure of the fairground, and my gypsy roots. Travelling fairs have always excited me, ever since I worked on the funfair in Canning Town in my early teens, and I guess *That'll Be the Day* had brought that lifestyle to the front of my mind again.

Even as a kid, I was aware that fairs had a unique glamour and sense of danger. I loved the way that the fun and frivolity of the rides and candyfloss were delivered with an edginess that hinted at an undercurrent of violence in the rough-and-ready workers and the loud rock 'n' roll music. Even the smell of fairs had a unique, heady allure.

The album was to be called *All the Fun of the Fair*, and the opening track, of the same name, set the scene:

> *Roll on up, see the main attraction,*
> *Get your money ready to step inside...*

Unusually, I was able fully to concentrate on *All the Fun of the Fair* without having to juggle the commitments of a film or a theatre production at the same time, and the album was a joy to record. Jeff and I were on the same wavelength, the band were tight from spending months playing together, and we brought in Liverpool soul band the Real Thing to add some rich, honeyed backing vocals.

Jeff and I might have loved making the album but we were not working as quickly as CBS wanted and their delivery deadline passed. Eventually the record company lost patience and fixed a date for the playback for executives who were flown in from all corners of the globe.

It's a sign of how tardy we were that we had to keep the CBS big cheeses waiting in the studio reception for an hour and a half as we finished off the last track, 'Hold Me Close'. I only had time for two vocal takes and Jeff had to speed-mix it in thirty minutes, so it was kind of ironic that it went on to be such a big hit for me.

Record-label album playbacks are always fraught affairs, with all the yes-men and lesser executives trying to gauge the mood of the big boss man before deciding how to react themselves. The CBS head honcho enjoyed hearing *All the Fun of the Fair* so we were good to go. Against their better instincts, they even let us persuade them to release 'Rolling Stone' as the lead single.

I was keen to push the fairground theme further when we took the album on tour that autumn and suggested to Derek and Mel Bush that we used a funfair for the stage set, with a Big Wheel as the centrepiece. *All the Fun of the Fair* was the first tour that ventured outside Britain and America and it was a lot of fun.

We played some great European dates, with the French reliably enthusiastic and not just for '*America, ca, ca*', and Holland and Scandinavia really welcoming us. As we rocked Stockholm, I vaguely wondered how my old flame Beth was, and if she even knew what had happened to me in recent years.

I've never gone down great in Germany, and I didn't make the situation any better on our first night, in Frankfurt, when I muttered a dumb aside to the band about 'Don't mention the war'. The crowd picked up on it, and booed. It wasn't my finest moment.

The levels of hysteria at the UK dates had not diminished, though, and Bev Bush became a master at spiriting me out of the venues after shows via increasingly torturous routes to avoid me being lovingly torn to pieces. For my part, I remained both flattered and, mostly, flummoxed by this bizarre adulation. Creeping through back exits and down corridors, I felt more like a member of the SAS than a pop singer.

Driving to a gig one Tuesday lunchtime, with Johnnie Walker unveiling the new singles chart on Radio One, we learned that 'Hold Me Close' had gone to number one. If you had a single out, Tuesday was always the day you learned about its performance. If a song had leapt from number fifteen to number three, say, I could expect congratulatory Tuesday morning phone calls from Derek, Steve Colyer and a host of other people. If I had to call them for news, I could safely assume things had gone less well.

The highlight of the British autumn '75 dates was a week at Hammersmith Odeon in London. To mark the occasion, Mel commissioned an enormous billboard painting of me to cover the entire front of the theatre. He needn't have bothered: Hammersmith council ordered us to take it down after one day in case the drivers on the adjacent flyover were distracted by a fifty-foot man looming over them.

My first trip to Australia was a great way to round off the tour, and I'll never forget until the day I die a wonderful Melbourne night when we played a vast tennis stadium. The crowd seemed to stretch to the horizon and my bass player, Mike Thorn, leaned over and whispered in my ear: 'Is this a dream or is this real?' I think, to be honest, I was asking myself that question every day.

Maureen and Verity were not accompanying me to nearly so many dates now, partly because Verity had started nursery and was nearing school age but also because I preferred it if they didn't.

I had very good reasons for this. In Britain, some of my nuttier fans were jealous of Maureen, and I had enough to worry about at my shows without wondering if someone would take a swing at her. As a protective father, I also hated the thought of Verity being frightened by the madness of Essex Mania, or hurt in one of the baying crowds trying to get near to me.

I also had a deeper, more selfish reason. Given the lunacy of my day-to-day existence, I valued the privacy of family life with Maureen and Verity more than ever. They were my refuge and I was desperate to keep the two worlds separate. Yet Maureen was keen to be involved, and while she understood the pressure I was under, there were times that she felt excluded.

In three years, Maureen had seen her husband go from signing on and doing cash-in-hand odd jobs to being a pop star and a sex symbol. She trusted me and she could hardly have been more supportive, but human nature being what it is, she must have felt insecure on occasion. Tensions had crept in to our marriage.

Fame also exerted some pretty insane pressures on us. We had decided to move from Havering-Atte-Bower back into London and so bought a place in Primrose Hill. Somehow this became public knowledge, and when we turned up to move in, we found the whole street packed with teenage girls playing my hits on cassette players. We had to sell it without even living there.

Instead we bought a house near Abbey Road and built a big wall around it to stop people seeing in, but even so it was clear we would also need a place far from the madding crowds. In 1976 we purchased a farm down in Kent, and while Maureen, Verity and I didn't do any hop picking, we had some idyllic times there.

By now, we had acquired two dogs: a mongrel named Scruff and also Rover, the LSD-scoffing hound from Jim MacLaine's *alcazaba* in *Stardust*, whom I had adopted and brought home to be a family pet. For her part, Verity's favourite down-on-the-farm pastime was dressing up to sing Top Forty hits to the cows.

I needed the respite that the farm gave me. After so long in the spotlight, I think that I was subconsciously craving anonymity, and I relished retiring to the backroom to produce albums by the Real Thing and my friend Steve Colyer. Possibly nostalgic for the camaraderie of the Everons and Mood Indigo, I was also keen to merge into the band a little more rather than always being David Essex, Solo Star.

Unfortunately this put me at odds with Jeff when we came to record the next album, *Out on the Street*. I was keen to use the same band I toured with and make a far harder-edged, rockier album. Jeff didn't agree at all and we suffered our first fallout over artistic differences.

Selfishly and stubbornly, I stuck to my guns and Jeff went along with my vision, despite the new friction between us. It made the recording sessions somewhat fraught at times. Jeff may have felt he was vindicated when *Out on the Street* sold less than my first three albums and stalled outside the Top Thirty, but I think it still stands up musically.

The first single from the album, 'City Lights', was more than five minutes long so didn't get much radio play and only got to number twenty-four in the chart. This didn't stop Paul McCartney hearing it. One evening in an Italian restaurant, I heard somebody crooning it and looked around to see Paul, at a nearby table with Linda, singing and beaming at me. Maybe he was stalking me.

The music world was changing in 1976 and 1977, with punk rock exploding on the scene with its scorched-earth policy of disdain towards everything that had gone before it. Punk was a bit of a cartoon but I had no problem with it, especially as Chris Spedding, the guitarist who had worked with me for years, was to become a pivotal part of the scene, producing the Sex Pistols' first demos.

Punk struck me as a bit of a media hype but it was all about knocking the Establishment and I guess that was what I seemed like to them. The Clash gave an interview to *Melody Maker* in which they sneered that they were keeping it real and 'not driving around in a white Rolls-Royce like David Essex'. This struck me as ironic, as I hadn't been in one of those since Alfie sorted it out for us the day I married Maureen.

Mostly, though, the punks were nice enough to me if I bumped into them at a TV show or radio station. They might try hard to be aloof and angry when we met, but they generally sought me out in a quiet moment later to politely ask for an autograph.

There was very little that was punk rock about the extravaganza that I mounted at the London Palladium late in '76. I had been very impressed by a club that I stumbled across in Paris called *L'Ange Bleu*, which obviously took its cue from the Marlene Dietrich film of the same name.

I loved the dark humour and theatricality of the 1920s Berlin cabaret that Dietrich had come to embody and decided to import a little of this decadent glamour to the West End. Its appeal to me was not a million miles from the allure of the fairground that I had celebrated in *All the Fun of the Fair*.

The Palladium show was magnificently over the top, with baby tigers, llamas, clowns, and a risqué dance troupe named Hot Gossip who were dressed as Tiller Girls. I had seen them in a club and booked them via their choreographer, a rising star named Arlene Phillips.

I had met Arlene before. A few years previously, Ken Russell had told me I was to play opposite Twiggy in a film called *The Boyfriend* and dispatched me for refresher tap-dancing lessons with Arlene. Ken then binned me in favour of a ballet dancer. When I saw his finished film, I could not have been more relieved at my lucky escape. Ken clearly didn't rate me: he also asked me to sing 'Pinball Wizard' in his movie of the Who's *Tommy*, then dropped me for Elton John.

The Palladium spectacular was magnificently bonkers, although the aura of twisted mystique was arguably sullied slightly by the llamas depositing great steaming piles of crap on the stage every night as I sang 'If I Could'. There again, it was the same stage where I was French-kissed by a brown bear in *Dick Whittington*. Maybe I should have expected it.

Derek and I had made a conscious choice at this stage to step back a little from the promotional treadmill. I definitely felt in need of a little more downtime, and after the non-stop musicals, movies, albums and tours of the last few years, we also figured the public might need a break from wall-to-wall David Essex.

Although we were still resisting their entreaties to tour there, Derek and I headed back to the States for some high-profile TV shows. We did *The Johnny Carson Show*, although I never got to meet Heeeere's Johnny! I did, however, get to sing a duet with

Cher on *The Cher Show*, although the 'comedy' sketch I had to perform with Jerry Lewis was an absolute stinker. Ticking off the American icons, I also did *The Merv Griffin Show* a few times. It didn't mean that much to me, but with his encyclopaedic knowledge of showbiz, Derek was in raptures that we were rubbing shoulders with these light-entertainment legends.

There was talk of me taking the lead role in a new musical film being shot in America called *Grease*. Producer Robert Stigwood met me to sound me out and shortly afterwards I bumped into the movie's female lead, Olivia Newton-John, in London. She enthusiastically told me, 'I really hope you do it – it would be great!' but I never heard any more, and when the film finally appeared, John Travolta was clearly perfect for Danny.

My fifth studio album was to be the last of my contract with both CBS and Jeff Wayne Music. After the minor fallings-out and frosty relationship that had developed between Jeff and me on *Out on the Street*, I decided that I would produce the record myself. This was the direction I wanted to go, and also our friendship was too valuable to risk damaging it with work disagreements.

This also suited Jeff, who had his own epic project to occupy him. He asked me what I thought of him writing and recording a musical version of H G Wells' classic sci-fi book, *The War of the Worlds*. I told him it was a fantastic idea, and he went off to begin work as I set about recording *Gold and Ivory*.

It was the first record I made outside of Jeff's Advision base, and the band and I decamped to Richard Branson's Manor Studios near Oxford. Working without Jeff felt a little like taking the stabilisers off a bike, but I had an experienced band and penned a couple of songs with Steve Colyer.

Producing my own record was a challenge as it is impossible to be objective about your own voice, and initially I found myself reverting to type and spending hours getting the drum sound exactly right. Nevertheless, making the album was a liberating and enjoyable experience.

The Manor complex housed some hidden secrets. Keyboardist Ronnie Leahy was convinced it was haunted, and I pooh-poohed him until the early hours of one morning, when I had just retired to my bedroom after a late-night recording session.

I had just fallen asleep about 2.30 a.m. when for some reason I woke up again and became instantly aware of the grey figure of a man in seventeenth-century clothing warming himself by an imaginary fire. Oddly enough I wasn't scared at all as I lay and watched him rub his translucent hands together with his back to me. He did this for two or three minutes before dissolving into thin air.

Had this really happened? Was it a dream? I wasn't sure until the next morning, when I related what I had seen to the band and the girls serving breakfast. As they dished up the bacon and eggs, the staff confirmed that, yep, guests saw this guy all the time. Ronnie looked vindicated.

I loved making *Gold and Ivory* and it sold respectably, making the album chart Top Thirty and going down well with my hardcore fans. At this point my records were not shifting the phenomenal amounts that they did during the height of Essex Mania, but I was happy with the music, and the upside was that I was able to live something that resembled a more normal life.

In any case, the lower sales were no deterrent to CBS, who were desperate to re-sign me to a new contract now that our five-album deal had expired. I had earned them unthinkable sums of money over the last few years and they pulled out all the stops, even getting world champion motorcycle rider Barry Sheene to present me with a Yamaha 250cc off-road bike as a sweetener.

Mel Bush was by now my co-manager, alongside Derek, and the two of them entered into intensive negotiations with CBS. They clearly did a good job, because they reported back to me that the company were offering a $1m advance for a new five-album agreement, and wanted to fly their top executives and lawyers in from the US for a face-to-face meeting to clinch the deal.

One million dollars! It sounded an absurd amount of money, and of course it was, but this headline figure was misleading. I was not living on caviar and bathing in asses' milk at the end of the seventies. Government policies meant I was paying 98 per cent tax as, unlike most of my rock-star contemporaries, I had never spent months abroad each year to escape it. An accountant suggested a tax-avoiding bank account in Lichtenstein and for a while I toyed with the idea, but it felt wrong and in the end I bit the bullet and paid up.

Nevertheless, the CBS offer was obviously enticing, and Derek, Mel and I converged with their top men at their swanky new HQ in Soho Square, London. The meeting lasted hours. Eventually a deal seemed to be in place and the lawyers began to read aloud the contract that had been prepared for my signature.

It all sounded like legalese to my bored ears until one clause leapt out at me: that CBS would have 'creative control'. What?!

I queried this, and the American executives had a spectacular answer: they meant to make me bigger than Elvis in the States, but to do so they would need to exert creative control.

This reply set every alarm bell ringing in my head. Having just survived the ravages of Essex Mania in Britain, I was by no means certain that I wanted to be 'bigger than Elvis' and go through the whole thing to the power of a hundred in the US. And to hand over creative control of my career to faceless executives: surely this was a deal-breaker?

I retired with Derek, Mel and our lawyers to a side-room. The lawyers held the view that the sums on offer were so huge that we should sign the contract and fight the creative-control issue on a case-by-case basis. Derek, as ever, was more sensitive to my needs and understood the depth of my objection.

When we reconvened in the boardroom the Americans handed me the contract. I read the offending clause one last time then quietly gave my verdict: 'I can't sign this.' Their looks of blank incomprehension seemed to require a further explanation, so I continued: 'I can't sell my soul. Now if you will excuse me, I have to go. I have a plane to catch.'

Three hours later, Maureen, Verity and I were high in the sky en route to another South of France getaway. As I gazed down at the Channel from 35,000 feet, I figured the best way to view the $1m I had just tossed away was to say that you can't miss what you've never had.

Maureen and I always had a great time in France but this didn't mean the underlying tensions between us had dissipated. Our occasional tiffs were becoming more frequent and more intense and like many couples before us, we eventually found ourselves pondering a trial separation. I loathed the nights that I bedded down alone in the Paddington mews house that held Derek and Mel's office.

Nevertheless, through all of this I always assumed that Maureen and I were simply going through a bad patch and would survive it, and this idea was strengthened when she told me that she was pregnant. We were both delighted: surely another child could only bring us closer together again?

Jeff had meanwhile been beavering away on *War of the Worlds* and called to ask if I wanted to be involved. It was an extremely tempting offer. Jeff had persuaded the Welsh Hollywood legend Richard Burton to narrate his concept album, and my old friend and *Godspell* colleague Julie Covington to sing on it.

I flew back to London and went back into Advision, where I was incredibly impressed with *War of the Worlds*. Jeff had done a typically amazing job on the music and arrangements and his father Jerry and stepmother Doreen's dialogue brought H G Wells' narrative to life. It was an honour to sing the part of the Artillery Man on the record.

Richard Burton was filming in Los Angeles so Jeff and I flew out to record his contribution. We were both fairly nervous about working with such a Hollywood god and had prepared for our meeting meticulously. Before we left London, I read out Richard's lines so that Jeff could time and record the music to play beneath his dialogue.

Out in LA, filming commitments meant that Richard blew out our first two recording-studio appointments. When he finally arrived, Jeff eagerly explained that he had prepared the music for him to read over, both for the atmosphere and to let him gauge the time of each speech. In his glorious, rich baritone, Richard declined: 'No music, thank you. I'll just read it.'

We were in the presence of a master. Richard was a genius, a consummate professional, a walking party and great company, and I'm proud to report that we became friends. His fondness for a drink would invariably trigger a torrent of brilliant theatrical anecdotes.

He had me in tears of laughter when he told me about playing a Shakespeare season in Stratford-on-Avon with his fellow Welsh actor Hugh Griffiths and spending a long liquid afternoon toasting Hugh's birthday. That evening, his role in one of the Bard's dramas required him to wear chainmail.

Caught short on stage after his long pub session, Richard had no choice but to pee quietly down his leg and on to the boards. The audience never noticed, but the same couldn't be said for Sir Michael Redgrave, who strode on stage to deliver a bare-footed soliloquy and found himself paddling in Burton's hidden golden shower. Richard said Sir Michael had never forgiven him.

The War of the Worlds enjoyed phenomenal success when it was released in 1978, topping charts around the world and going on to spend more than four years in the British album chart. It was quite a compliment when Richard Burton claimed he was as proud of his platinum disc as he would have been of an Oscar.

For my part, I had rather more pressing matters on my mind, and was soon even prouder than Burton. On 20 April 1978, Maureen gave birth to our son, Dan, at the Queen Charlotte

Hospital in Hammersmith. It was the first and only time I was present for the birth of one of my children, and that may be a good thing, because I hardly covered myself in glory.

I was there encouraging Maureen all the way through, but just as the baby emerged, there was a split-second when neither of us knew what sex it was and we just stared at the midwife. As she beamed and told us, 'Congratulations – you have a little boy!' my knees inexplicably buckled beneath me and I crashed to the floor like Peter Sellers at his zaniest.

Bouncing back to my feet, I told the bemused occupants of the delivery suite, 'Sorry – I'll be back in a minute!' and bolted to the next room, where I decided to call family and friends to tell them the good news. You had to dial nine to get an outside line from the hospital phone, but nobody had told me and I was obviously in no state to work it out.

I thus diligently spent the following twenty minutes attempting to dial my parents' and Derek's numbers, only to be interrupted by the hospital receptionist on the line asking if she could help me. 'No thank you, I'm trying to make a phone call,' I would reply politely, before repeating the entire process. Clearly fatherhood does strange things to the brain.

We chose the name Daniel partly because Maureen has Irish antecedents, including an Uncle Danny, but mostly just because we liked it and I thought Dan Cook sounded like a good, strong, manly name. Certainly more manly than his dad, who the next evening cemented his reputation as the Frank Spencer of the delivery ward.

I have never been a big drinker, and after a lively evening with Steve Colyer and a couple of other music-biz friends wetting the baby's head, I returned to the Queen Charlotte. Overcome by happiness and, more to the point, lager, I snuck up to Maureen's ward, climbed in bed with her fully clothed, and passed out.

Understandably, the ward sister found it hard to keep a straight face as she admonished me the next morning. I guess that I should think myself lucky she never phoned the *Sun* to tell them all about it, as would probably happen today.

13

THE CHE MUST GO ON

Nobody has ever looked as cool as Che Guevara. As a teenager, it was his moody visage that hung off my bedroom wall, not that of Bobby Moore or Martin Peters. I can't claim that I was ever steeped in the intricacies of Latin American revolutionary politics but somehow the image of Che, like that of Jimi Hendrix, seemed to epitomise the radicalism of the sixties, the era of change.

After years of solo music work, guesting on the lavishly theatrical *War of the Worlds* album and meeting Richard Burton had rekindled my interest in the theatre. So when Derek and Mel got a call asking if I might be interested in appearing in a new Tim Rice and Andrew Lloyd Webber musical called *Evita*, it was a bit of a no-brainer.

There was already a buzz about the show, with its rock opera concept album in the charts and my good friend Julie Covington enjoying a hit with one of the lead songs from the production, 'Don't Cry For Me Argentina' (although she turned down the chance to play Eva Perón, which went to Elaine Paige). I went to meet the director, big-name Broadway producer Hal Prince, who had produced or directed *West Side Story, Fiddler on the*

Roof and *Cabaret*. He told me his vision for the show, I sang him 'I Think I'm Going Out of My Head' and he asked me to play the part I coveted: Che.

I accepted eagerly, but then had to fight for my vision of the role when rehearsals began in May 1978. Hal, Tim Rice and Andrew Lloyd Webber all felt that I should play Che as a young student to reflect the reality of him being a lot younger than the Peróns, whereas I wanted to capture the Che that everyone instinctively imagines: the iconic, romantic, bearded revolutionary in battle fatigues. Thankfully, I won the day.

Where *Godspell* had been an intimate ensemble piece, stitched together by a cast who felt like a family, *Evita* was a far more lavish and starry production. One similarity, though, was that John-Michael Tebelak had been laissez-faire to the point of being comatose directing *Godspell*, and now Hal Prince showed an equal lack of interest in directing me.

Hal channelled his energies into working with Joss Ackland and Elaine as the Peróns and gave me enormous freedom to interpret the role of Che as I saw fit. I would wander on stage, deliver my lines and wander off. The only feedback I remember Hal giving me during the entire rehearsals came when he told me, 'You are marvellous when you're angry.'

This suited me as I researched and read more and more about Guevara. It was impossible not to be drawn to this fascinating icon, a poet and asthmatic whose ideals led him to abandon his medical studies and take up arms as a guerrilla opposed both to the tyrants in his native land and in Cuba, where he famously instigated the revolution alongside Fidel Castro.

Che seemed a role that I had been born to play and I like to think that I brought quite a presence to it. It helped that my Romany ancestry had given me the same kind of blue-eyed, dark-haired looks captured in his classic portrait, and my naturally laconic nature lent an edge to his idealistic intensity. There was no need for histrionics: if anything, I under-acted, to draw people in.

I steeped myself in Che to the degree that I consciously didn't socialise with Joss and Elaine, fine actors and good people both, in case it diluted the onstage antipathy between us. As the first night neared, the rehearsals became overwrought and there were quite a few tantrums: thankfully, none of them involved me.

The first previews of *Evita* at the Prince Edward Theatre piqued already strong media interest near to fever pitch and the opening night on 21 June was a success beyond our wildest dreams. The audience loved this huge, passionate, melodramatic production and it felt as if the standing ovation at the curtain call would never end. Hal Prince might have left me to my own devices but his vision for the overall production had been immaculate.

The critics largely mirrored the audiences' approbation, with Derek Jewell of the *Sunday Times* declaring *Evita* to be 'quite marvellous' and praising Andrew Lloyd Webber's score as 'an unparalleled fusion of twentieth-century musical experience'. They were also highly complimentary about my interpretation of the brooding, enigmatic Che. We were off to a flyer.

Meanwhile, now I was free of CBS and their sinister creative control, Derek and Mel had been shopping around for a new record deal for me. They negotiated an agreement with Phonogram Records, who suggested that my first single for them should be a song from *Evita*.

This seemed an eminently sensible idea, and the very talented Mike Batt came in to produce 'Oh What a Circus', backed with another of Che's tunes in 'High Flying, Adored'. The single was both high flying and adored, and went to number three in the chart: my first Top Ten hit in three years.

As Tim Rice and Andrew Lloyd Webber productions tend to be, *Evita* was a society event as well as a glittering spectacle, and the beautiful people of show business, music and even royalty all beat a path to its door. During my six months in the show, my cramped post-show dressing room attracted some venerable names keen to offer their congratulations.

Princess Margaret came back to tell me, 'What's good about your part is you're not on all the time.' This comment could be taken in two ways, and I very much hope that she meant it as a compliment. Her remark to Elaine Paige was even more gnomic: 'It must be awful, dying every night.'

I would never have imagined Bob Dylan to be a fan of opulent West End musicals but he materialised in my dressing room to announce that he'd enjoyed the evening a lot. It probably meant a bit more to me, though, when he added '...and "Rock On" is really good, man.'

Yet in truth I often found something inescapably awkward about these brief backstage audiences with the glitterati. Maybe it was partly because I had only just come off stage and was still in my revolutionary, anti-Establishment Che mindset, and my shyness obviously played a part as well.

Fundamentally to blame, though, is an inverted snobbery bound up in my East End roots. It is hard to explain away except to say that faced with a legendary figure whose presence is expected to inspire awe, my reaction can be a strange, nebulous resentment. So Steven Spielberg is in the audience – so f****** what? It's the same rebellious urge that still, even today, makes me feel itchy in posh restaurants.

So while it was nice of charming Hollywood royalty Cary Grant to tell me I had incredible charisma, his words kind of went in one ear and out the other. Katharine Hepburn came and went in a flurry of whispered 'Wonderful, darlings!' and although I know I met Ingrid Bergman at *Evita*, I don't really remember a thing about it.

American cinema legend and *My Fair Lady* director George Cukor was a lovely guy, your perfect granddad, and we met up again later once or twice. I have also stayed in touch with John Travolta, who had just had a huge hit in *Grease*. It was funny to remember that, at the height of Essex Mania, I had briefly been touted for that role.

There was talk of me having further involvement in *Evita* but it came to nothing. Tim Rice and Andrew Lloyd Webber thought of using Elaine Paige and I to open the show in New York, but eventually it was decided to cast American actors.

A few years later, Oliver Stone was scheduled to direct the film of *Evita* and he and I met up to discuss his hard-hitting vision of the movie and how I might play Che. I was very impressed with Stone's no-nonsense demeanour and his work-hard, play-hard attitude led to a couple of lively nights out.

Unfortunately, Oliver got bumped from the project in favour of Alan Parker, who made a weak film that I thought totally lacked the revolutionary fervour that the story demanded. To be frank, I thought it was pretty crap, although Madonna was a good Eva Perón and didn't deserve the snippy reviews she inevitably got.

Still, I picked up a flurry of British theatre awards for *Evita* and thoroughly enjoyed my time on the show. A proper old-school trouper, I even laboured through a week's performances with German measles. Typically prurient, the *Daily Mail* warned any pregnant theatregoers to sit at the back of the circle.

Evita was still a hot ticket when I bowed out from the show on 4 November 1978, to the extent that tickets for that night were changing hands for £500 on the black market. It had been a thrill and re-established me in the theatre world. So, with typical contrariness, I set about returning to music and cinema.

14

BACK ON THE BIKE

After the success of *That'll Be the Day* and *Stardust*, Derek and
Mel had been offered quite a few film roles for me to consider.
They were a decidedly mixed bag. The chance to star opposite
Joan Collins in *The Stud* held little appeal. There is a distinctly
Victorian aspect to my nature, and I had no wish to do soft porn:
after all, when I had filmed sex scenes in my previous films, I
had always kept my underpants on.

I was far more taken with a project called *Silver Dream
Racer*. Ever since I had hammered Dad's James Captain down
the A13 at the age of fourteen, I had been obsessed with motorbikes. When I was offered a film that would give me the chance
to cane 750cc monsters around the famous racetrack at Silverstone, it was too tempting to resist. I signed up to begin filming
in summer 1979.

In the meantime, I was spending as much time as possible on
the farm in Kent with Maureen, Verity, Dan and the nanny,
Shirley. Dan's arrival hadn't miraculously resolved all of the
niggling problems between Maureen and I, and our arguments
dragged on, but Verity was delighted with her new little brother
and we seemed to be holding things together.

There again, I was away quite a lot because I had a new record label, Phonogram, and an album to make for them. I managed to assemble a great band including Phil Palmer, Chris Spedding and my old mate Kenney Jones, not to mention key contributions from the London Philharmonic Orchestra.

Despite this, *Imperial Wizard* proved to be a very stop-start album to record. I produced half of the record, with Mike Batt and Chris Neil also weighing in, and we had some bad luck when a snowstorm sabotaged deliveries of the lead-off single, also called 'Imperial Wizard', which lost momentum and stalled at number thirty-two in the chart.

Yet I had a lot of fun making the record, with one real highlight coming when I wrote a folk-type song, 'Are You Still My True Love?' and recorded it with a Chieftains-like Scottish reels-and-fiddles group called the Whistlebinkies. I remain very proud of *Imperial Wizard*, and regarded it as a good sign when it charted far higher than had either of my last two albums for CBS.

Around this time I also made an appearance with Cat Stevens, who had just converted to Islam and adopted the name Yusuf Islam, and his brother David Gordon on a concept album called *Alpha Omega*. I worked on a song named 'World' with Yusuf and David and even sang on stage with Yusuf at Wembley. He is a special, charismatic man, and our friendship has endured.

After that, the *Silver Dream Racer* movie was a blast from start to finish. It was to represent quite a commitment, as I had signed up to write the film score as well as play the lead role, but if I am honest, the appeal to me was all about the motorbikes.

I was to play Nick Freeman, a fixated and idealistic young rider who inherits a prototype superbike when his brother is tragically killed in an accident, and sets about riding it to the world title against all the odds. I realised from the outset that the script was hardly Shakespeare, but then Shakespeare would not have given me the chance to power around Brands Hatch.

My co-stars in the movie were Beau Bridges, who was a nice guy despite having no interest in bikes, and Cristina Raines, who was a tad highly strung but turned in a great performance. Clarke Peters played my wisecracking sidekick, Cider: Clarke is a tremendous actor who recently went on to have huge success as Lester Freamon in cult US TV show *The Wire*. Motorbike champion Barry Sheene also visited our set a lot and became a friend.

Yet the real stars of *Silver Dream Racer* were the bikes. We used a lot of privateer bikers in the film – independent riders with no financial backing from top manufacturers like Yamaha or Suzuki – and I was amazed by their love for their machines. These were men who kept their bikes in their front rooms and seemed to adore them more than they did their wives and kids.

Despite the producers' extreme misgivings, I was determined to do as much riding as possible and I largely succeeded. I will never forget the day when the amazing Silver Dream Machine itself turned up on the set in Brands Hatch. A firm in Wales called Bartons had custom-made two bespoke bikes for the film: a 750cc version and a smaller 500cc one.

The 750cc monster turned up in bits as filming was going on at the other side of the racetrack and our mechanics assembled it. Seizing my chance, I leapt on and accelerated around the track in a flurry of testosterone and blue smoke. The distraught producer was hyperventilating as his male lead and the movie's irreplaceable main prop both unexpectedly roared past him doing more than 100 m.p.h.

Silver Dream Racer's main plot tension, such as it was, was that Nick's American girlfriend, Julie Prince, played by Cristina, loyally supported her man in his motorbike dreams even though she knew they could kill him. So it was to prove: the film's lurid climax saw Nick triumph in the world championship final only to lose control of the bike, crash into a wall and die.

I was thus horrified to learn recently that a new DVD edit of the movie ends when Nick crosses the line and punches the air in delight, cutting out the tragic denouement because such a dark ending is seen as too bleak for American audiences. To say the least, this banal edit seems to miss the whole point of the story.

While I was making the film, Triumph had recently closed their motorbike factory at Meriden, near Coventry, and a work-ers' co-operative had emerged in its wake. I supported them and tried to publicise their endeavours in my interviews around the film, and the workers showed their gratitude by giving me my much-loved Triumph Bonneville, one of the last ever built at the plant. It's a great British bike that I still ride to this day.

Director David Wickes hooked me up with film composer John Cameron to write the *Silver Dream Racer* score and John was invaluable in teaching me the nuts and bolts of writing inci-dental music. As well as a tutor, John became a great friend and a frequent future collaborator.

Sadly, away from the film set, my greatest friend of all and I were about to go our separate ways. Maureen and I had battled as hard as we could to save our relationship, and for a while Dan had seemed like the cure that could heal us, but in the end the fault lines just ran too deep and we decided we had to split up.

It's difficult, and very painful, to analyse in the cold light of day exactly why a marriage comes to an end. Maybe we had met and married too young. Maybe the extraordinary pressures of Essex Mania had taken their toll: certainly, Maureen had never cared for my efforts to keep my public and private lives separate. Or maybe, like so many couples, we just gradually drifted apart.

Whatever the root cause of our break-up, it speaks volumes for the love and respect that I feel for Maureen that my admiration for her grew even as we were going separate ways. At all points of the horribly painful process, she put the children first, as did I: she behaved with immaculate honour and dignity throughout.

Obviously, Dan was too young to understand what was going on, but Verity was eight, a vulnerable age. It probably helped that she was used to me being away for long periods on film shoots and tours, but Maureen and I made it our sole priority to present a loving and united front to her, and that is what we did. We still took family holidays together and I am incredibly proud that Maureen and I remain friends even to this day. It probably says a lot about the love we feel for each other that it took us seventeen years to get around to getting divorced.

In the immediate aftermath of the separation, though, Maureen and the kids holed up on the farm down in Kent while I moved into a flat at the office in Paddington and worked on the *Silver Dream Racer* score. Sadly, bad news will always out, and when the tabloids got wind of our split, their vulture-like reporters and paparazzi besieged my office for days.

I said nothing because there was nothing to say, but that didn't prevent the redtops from speculating feverishly. One day Derek answered one of the many knocks on our door from journalists demanding exclusive interviews and offering me the chance to 'set the record straight', and came back upstairs roaring with laughter.

It seemed the man from the now-defunct, dear old *News of the World* had solved the thorny question of exactly why Maureen and I had ended: it was because I was having a homosexual relationship. Sadly, the *Screws* were unable to identify the other party in this sordid gay affair. This was a pity because, as I told Derek in between our gales of hysterical laughter, I would really like to know.

In the wake of the break-up, it was good that I had some work to focus on. In addition to the incidental music, I had penned a few motorbike-themed anthems for the soundtrack of *Silver Dream Racer*, and I was delighted when 'Silver Dream Machine' hit number four around the movie's April 1980 release.

Silver Dream Racer also gave rise to one of my more bizarre foreign promotional trips. The movie was chosen to represent Britain in a film festival in Poland, so director David Wickes, Derek and I flew out to Warsaw to support it.

Derek and I found we had been billeted in a squat, ugly Soviet-architecture hotel in the city centre. Having checked in, I was shown to a room the approximate size of a postage stamp, and as I have always suffered from mild claustrophobia, I asked for something bigger. This did not go down well.

'In Communist Poland,' the hotel manager loftily informed me, 'everybody has the same.' I replied that this was fine but I was not able to stay there and would check out straight away, at which point he performed a spectacular volte-face.

'One moment, Mr Essex,' he requested, before producing a key and showing me to a massive, oak-panelled suite that was usually exclusively reserved for visiting senior politicians and party apparatchiks. Clearly, it was true that on *Animal Farm*, some animals were more equal than others.

Outside the hotel, Warsaw appeared so grey and depressing that it could have been a 1950s US Cold War propaganda film about the evils of Communism. It rained non-stop, and the streets were full of dowdily dressed, defeated-looking people queuing to buy bread. Furthermore, it was Chopin's birthday, and the state radio appeared to be broadcasting his most famous tune, the funeral march, 24/7.

Thankfully, things picked up at the film festival. David, Derek and I attended a screening of *Silver Dream Racer*, but arrived to discover that it had not been dubbed into Polish. Instead, a male interpreter stood behind the screen, microphone in hand, translating the dialogue as it was spoken.

This deep-voiced intermediary voiced every character, male and female, with no change in his intonation, which meant that when the love scenes between Cristina Raines and I came on, we were seducing each other in two throaty baritones. It was impossible not to weep with laughter, so David Wickes and I did. Our hosts were not terribly impressed.

For some reason, *Silver Dream Racer* did spectacularly well in South Africa, where it seemed to run for years. However, a trip I made to this country around the same time to play a few gigs was to prove somewhat controversial.

South Africa's hateful apartheid system was still in place and the United Nations had imposed economic sanctions against its regime, as well as discouraging sports teams and entertainers from visiting the country. Yet Britain and America had a policy of 'constructive engagement' with South Africa, and I decided to accept an invitation to tour there.

This in no way meant that I condoned apartheid: after all, I was a man who owed his whole career in music to his love of black American blues musicians. Instead of boycotting the country, I felt I could make a more effective point by taking with me the Real Thing, the all-black soul band and good friends of mine.

We played quite a few dates in South Africa, including Cape Town and the huge Las Vegas-style entertainment complex at Sun City. Travelling between shows, we simply ignored the train companies' ridiculous segregation policies: if the Real Thing were not allowed to travel with me in a whites-only carriage, I went to join them in the blacks-only section.

Apartheid was clearly abhorrent and we played to both white and black audiences as we traversed the country. Yet inevitably these subtleties were lost on some of the more knee-jerk critics, and on my return to England, Sheffield council banned me from playing anywhere in the city, while Harry Belafonte placed me on a UN blacklist.

This was hugely ironic to me. I loathed racism and felt as if I had just challenged it, not collaborated with it. Also, the scenes in South Africa had been no worse than those I had encountered on my first trip to America's deep south, when a gloves-wearing waiter in Nashville had served me coffee with cling-film over the cup. 'Why is this here?' I had asked him. 'Because I am black, sir,' he had replied. So where were the sanctions there?

The South African furore blew over fairly quickly and I have many great memories of the trip. Cape Town is magical, and one day Bev Bush and I hired motorbikes and drove to the point where the Indian and Atlantic oceans meet. As we rode along the edge of a cliff, five or six monkeys suddenly rushed our bikes. I had one on my handlebars, Bev had one on his head, and we were lucky not to get bitten or go crashing to a watery grave.

Bev was also my accomplice shortly afterwards when I gave my definitive – but secret – statement on the evils of apartheid and racism. For some reason, east London used to boast a statue of a former Boer commander, and after a few drinks one night, Bev and I located some black paint and painted his face black. It was probably the most perplexing unsolved local mystery since the days of the Canning Town Arsonist.

15

MY LIFE AS AN INTERNATIONAL DRUG SMUGGLER

When the most central strand of your life is gone, it takes quite some getting used to. Maureen and I had been together for what felt like a wonderful lifetime and Verity and Dan had been our very heartbeat, our *raison d'être*. Our separation had been totally civilised and amicable but it still hurt, and becoming a single man at thirty-three was quite a lifestyle change.

In the short term, I needed somewhere to live. I had had quite enough of kipping at the office. I was looking for somewhere in central London that felt like home and that the kids would like when they came to stay with me, and when I found a fairly big flat near to Hyde Park, I bought it and moved in.

At the time Phonogram wanted another album from me and I teamed up again with John Cameron, with whom I had written the *Silver Dream Racer* score, to work on *Hot Love*. We kept the motorbike theme going, to a degree. For one self-written track, called 'On My Bike', I lugged my Triumph Bonneville into a vocal booth in the studio and nearly asphyxiated myself revving it up to provide a sound effect. I got so carried away that only a quick-thinking engineer kicking open the door of the booth averted an incipient case of carbon monoxide poisoning.

Hot Love was to prove one of my least successful albums but for a while, things also got a little steamy in my private life. A lot of people had probably assumed that I was sexually promiscuous all through the crazy years of Essex Mania. A decent-looking pop star, with screaming girls throwing themselves at him every day: what man *wouldn't* take advantage?

I *hadn't* been living that life, in fact, due to being married, my personal sense of morality and, overwhelmingly, wanting Verity to love and respect me, but now I was single and had no reason not to indulge in a few flings. With the Hyde Park flat as my base, I set about belatedly playing the field.

Thirty-three is admittedly quite old to begin sowing wild oats but I saw a lot of girls and formed a lot of liaisons during that period. It was very lucky that my Hyde Park flat happened to have two entrances the badly planned evening that I showed one young lady out of one door as another woman arrived at the other.

I suppose they were quite wild times, looking back, but I guess I was just doing what most men would have done in my situation and, if you will pardon the phrase, making up for lost time. Even then I think I behaved with respect towards the women. We all knew what was going on and I never led any of the ladies on, made promises I couldn't keep, or said that they were 'The One'.

Because of this, I was surprised and a little disappointed when one or two of the girls then sold kiss-and-tell stories to the newspapers. Their accounts of what had transpired between us never remotely matched the truth, and on a couple of occasions I had never even met the women. Plus, on a basic level, I just think kiss-and-tells lack respect and dignity.

It was fun, sort of, but also there was an inescapable ache and hollowness at the heart of my promiscuous period. I had just come out of a loving marriage with a soul mate with whom I had made two children that were the light of my life. How could casual relationships not seem essentially empty after that?

After the split, I bought Maureen and the kids a house by the Thames in Chiswick and a routine developed whereby I would pick up Verity and Dan on Friday evenings and return them on Sunday nights. We would head down to the farm in Kent or stay in London, where I was meticulous in ensuring that they never encountered any of my new female friends.

So now I was that dreaded thing: a Weekend Dad. We always had a great time, even when they were pretending to like my fry-ups and sausage and mash, and it was noticeable how much Verity had become like a little second mother to Dan. Yet, for me, there was always an ineffable sadness hanging over the weekends, because they were so short and the time with the two of them was so precious.

The low point always came on the quiet Sunday evenings when I drove them back to Chiswick and they reunited with Maureen. Driving away, I would inevitably feel hugely alone and outside of the family unit that I belonged in. Frequently, I pulled away from their house, stopped the car at the end of the street and wondered: how did it come to this? What went wrong?

I wanted to spend more time with them, and Maureen and I agreed it would be healthy to all still hang out together, and so I bought a family holiday home. We had always previously headed off to the South of France but we fancied a change of scenery, so I bought a farmhouse, or *finca*, in a tiny cactus-filled village called Mijas in the mountains above Marbella in Spain.

It was a beautiful old building complete with its own olive trees and I hired a local builder to add a top floor and a swimming pool. The view from the house was magnificent, taking in both Gibraltar and the North African coast, and we had some blissful family holidays there during the years after our marital split.

The location was so remote that I could walk unrecognised and unmolested, unlike in England or France, and I wasn't the only person heading out there for some seclusion. There were English, Dutch, German and Italian people living on our side of the hill, and most of them had a story to tell.

My nearest neighbour was a charming and charismatic Italian named Giovanni, or Gio, who said he had flown fighter planes for the Israelis in the Six-Day War, been an intelligence officer unearthing Nazi war criminals, and spent time raising hell in Paris with Jacques Brel. He had also flown a plane under a bridge in Malaga, to the huge annoyance of the local authorities, but now spent his time drinking and feeding the vicious guard dogs that patrolled his high-walled property.

Gio and I occasionally spent days with the nomadic goat herders who roamed the hills above Marbella. Gio, a brilliant cook, would rustle up breakfast over an open fire and then act as an interpreter as the shepherds told me how they would wander an area a hundred miles wide to graze their herds, spending the night in any semi-derelict buildings they might stumble across. Hearing their rustic stories under the blazing Spanish sun was a fantastic experience, and I loved it.

Giovanni, sadly, was to meet a sticky end. After one drinking session with the herders, he fell and broke his leg badly. After the local hospital inserted metal pins to hold it together, he never bothered to return and have them removed, and they rusted and fatally infected his bloodstream. It was a fittingly cavalier way for him to go.

Mostly, though, time at the *finca* was all about Verity and Dan. They loved the swimming pool, although its existence was a matter of some controversy for the Spanish locals on the other side of the hill, who complained that it was an extravagance in an area of little rainfall where water was precious.

Conceding their point, I got water for the pool delivered in a tanker from town rather than draining the local well, but the locals repaid this considerateness by stealing my water under cover of darkness. They also controlled the electricity for our side of the hill, which meant that we were sometimes plunged unexpectedly into darkness.

Nevertheless, these holidays were wonderful and exactly what we needed to ensure that Verity, Dan and I remained interwoven into the fabric of each other's lives and didn't drift apart. Danny and I had some great boys' adventures there as he grew older, especially the hours that I bounced across the mountains on a Honda 250cc off-road motorbike, with Dan an excited passenger on the pillion in front of me.

One day I lost control of the bike on a mountain track and, about to plummet down the side of a hill, threw Danny off before the bike and I vanished over the edge. Recovering my wits as I lay prone beneath the bike and a pile of ash, I looked up to see Dan, twenty feet above me, indignantly shouting, 'What did you do that for?'

Back in Britain, *Hot Love* had been a bit of a flop, and while the national tour to promote it later in 1980 had been fun, it had also been fairly gruelling. At the end of it, I was invited to be the first commoner to turn on the Christmas lights in Regent Street, which was a surprise and an honour. I even designed them, in collaboration with jewellery company Butler & Wilson. The following year Regent Street reverted to type and Princess Diana did it.

After a tumultuous time in both my career and my private life, I felt as if I needed to get away. Yusuf Islam had offered me the opportunity to spend some time in his apartment in Rio and I decided to take him up on the offer and to extend it into a wider trip across South America. Packing a bag, I took off on a solo excursion across Argentina, Uruguay and Brazil like an aging gap-year student.

Travelling alone is not for everyone but I loved it. Maybe it goes back once again to being an only child. Freed from the tiresome obligation to make conversation with a companion, you can be like a spy in a movie, observe everything at close hand and soak up the exoticism and *foreignness* of your surroundings. Maybe it is selfish, to a degree, but it is hugely satisfying. Sometimes, I think it's the only way to travel.

I flew first to Argentina, where I had been advised to keep a low profile, as *Evita* had not exactly been a huge hit with the ruling Junta. There again, they had a lot to answer for. As a member of Amnesty International, I was aware that the Argentine military regime was suspected of eliminating thousands of its citizens: the so-called Disappeared Ones.

Nevertheless, when I landed in Buenos Aires the city seemed surprisingly European, even down to having a Harrods. As I settled in and began to meet the locals, I found them warm and welcoming. On the other hand, I suppose a couple of years later after the Falklands War it might have been a different story.

It wasn't hard to find confirmation of the kind of stories I had heard through Amnesty. In a bar I met a young man, who told me in whispers how his younger sister had been kidnapped and held to ransom. She was kept tied up and blindfolded in a cave for three weeks until her wealthy father paid the ransom: he knew that the military regime was to blame.

He later introduced me to his sister, who was clearly traumatised and had been mentally scarred by her horrendous experience. It was heartbreaking to see, and when I returned to Britain I made sure to recount her tale, and those of other people that I met, to Amnesty.

After the European feel of Buenos Aires, the Uruguayan capital of Montevideo was far more of an exciting culture shock and definitively Latin American. It was not unlike Cuba, particularly in the proliferation of pristine 1950s American gas-guzzler cars that are lovingly preserved by their owners and sail like galleons through the dusty streets of the city.

It was in Montevideo that an extraordinary adventure began which, had it turned out differently, could have defined my life, ended my career and led to me languishing in a second-world jail for more years than I would care to contemplate. It began early one morning as I strolled by the Atlantic, musing that it was time for me to up sticks and head down to Yusuf's place in time to catch the world-famous Rio Carnival.

I nodded hello to two men who were leaning on a rather beaten-up Ford Mustang and they returned my greeting and then spoke to me in Spanish. When I indicated that I didn't speak the language they asked me in broken English where I was from, and were delighted to hear England: 'Ah! Manchester United!' (What a shame they didn't say West Ham.) Continuing our pidgin-English conversation, they asked where I was heading and I told them I was bound for Rio. 'So are we!' they told me. 'Would you like a lift?'

You only live once and this was exactly the sort of spontaneous adventure I had headed off to South America on my Jack Jones to enjoy. Of course I would! I headed back to my guest-house to pick up my bags and reconvened with my newfound friends by the beach an hour later.

We pointed the Mustang towards Brazil and I got to know my companions better. Jesus was a handsome, long-haired man in his thirties with twinkling brown eyes, and proudly told me that he was from Chile. Mario was a slightly chubby Costa Rican in a worn blue suit whose English apparently extended no further than 'Bobby Charlton' and 'Let's boogie!'

Montevideo to Rio is a seriously long journey but it passed in a haze largely because Jesus and Mario seemed to have a limitless stash of industrial-strength marijuana. I have never been a big dope-head and never even smoked my first joint until I was thirty, but taking occasional puffs on the endless spliffs that Jesus and Mario passed between each other, I was soon happily out of my box.

The three of us shared petrol costs and the driving, and travelled long into the night. When we became exhausted, we would stop at some seriously basic roadside motels. This was a truly cheapskate trip: we all shared not just a room but a bed, which meant that I could lie awake all night listening to Mario talking in his sleep in Spanish.

One morning shortly after we hit Brazil, my need for speed got the better of me again and we were pulled over by a traffic cop. Jesus and Mario leapt from their cannabis-induced stupors and reached the policeman even before he had got off his bike. After their long, earnest conversation had ended in handshakes all round and the policeman riding off, they returned to the Mustang looking mightily relieved.

'I must drive,' reported Jesus. 'He has let us go, but you must never drive again in Brazil! I told him you are English and so you are used to driving on the wrong side of the road.'

I thanked them for their sterling efforts, but as they lit up yet another monster pure-marijuana spliff, I couldn't help feeling a tad surprised by the alacrity with which they had intercepted the traffic cop. 'Jesus,' I asked, 'where is Mario getting all of the grass from?'

With a conspiratorial grin, Jesus pulled away one of the panels of the car to reveal a hidden compartment groaning with weed. So I was in the middle of an international drug run with two men for whom the Rio Carnival was the biggest payday of the year. As Mario skinned up another joint and proclaimed 'Let's boogie!', I wondered just how *that* one would have played in the *Sun* or the *Daily Express*.

My bandit friends dropped me off on a street corner in Rio and vanished and I was immediately struck by the vibrancy of the city. Carnival was a week away and heady excitement was in the air. I hailed a taxi to Yusuf's apartment and enjoyed my first good night's sleep since I had left Uruguay.

The next morning I left Yusuf's hillside home, which was spartan but lovely with beautiful views from its balcony, and set out to explore this new, magical and enchanting metropolis. Rio was certainly a city of extremes. Multi-million-pound luxury flats and apartments nestled alongside the Copacabana beach; a few hundred yards away, families languished in tin shacks in filthy shanty towns.

The Brazilians, though, were friendly and passionate. Rio was a city that seemed to live for music, whether in the samba bands that occupied every street corner or the rhythmic ease that made even people walking look as if they were dancing. I fell in love with Rio, a city that confirmed my view that South America is a very special corner of the world.

It is, though, a small world, as I learned when I had a couple of coincidental encounters during my first week there. One day in the street I bumped into Jim Capaldi, the drummer of the band Traffic and singer of the chart hit 'Love Hurts'. Jim was living in Rio, where he had married a Brazilian girl. He had a daughter who spoke only Portuguese, and was learning the language so that he would be able to talk with her.

Jim and I arranged to go for a drink and the evening featured a very bizarre scene. We met in a hotel and took a lift that promptly broke down between the eleventh and twelfth floors. With some people in the crowded lift beginning to panic, two English rockers wrenched the doors open and pulled its grateful inhabitants to safety like action heroes.

I also visited the iconic statue of Christ that towers over Rio and bumped into Phil Lynott, the singer of Thin Lizzy whom I had met when he had also featured in Jeff Wayne's *War of the Worlds*. Phil was in Brazil on his honeymoon so I took care not to become a gooseberry, but we became firm friends until his sorry death a few years later.

While I was staying in Yusuf's flat, a few of his friends called on me and elaborated on the merits of Islam. I listened carefully as they gently attempted to convert me, and leafed through the copy of the Koran they gave me, but ultimately I figured I lack the fervour and belief to fully embrace any organised religion.

As I walked around Rio I had realised just how central Carnival was to the city. Even the poorest families prepared their costumes and sent their children to the samba schools all year round, and as the momentous event dawned the mood in the city hit fever pitch.

There was something diabolic about the fervid change in the atmosphere as Carnival devoured Rio. Thousands and thousands of garishly garbed men, women and children sambaed through the streets to inescapable, hypnotic rhythms in an explosion of life, power and passion. I had heard that every year people died at the height of Carnival frenzy, and now I could believe it.

As an outsider it seemed clear to me that Carnival, this uniquely cathartic and crazy celebration, served as a pressure valve and exorcised the feelings of societal exclusion and inequality that could otherwise cause the people to rise up against their leaders. Whether this was a good thing was a different question entirely, but it was certainly a brilliant, unforgettable experience. I felt as if I had landed in Hades.

Experiencing the riotous music of Brazil at Carnival had made me want to broaden my own musical palette and I returned to London eager for new ideas. My long-time bassist and friend Herbie Flowers introduced me to American producer Al Kooper and we began work on the record that was to become *Be-Bop the Future*.

Al and I began the album in London and finished it off in Los Angeles, working with ace US musicians such as the guitarists Steve Lukather and Jeff 'Skunk' Baxter. The critics were quite taken by this change in musical direction, but unfortunately the record-buying public appeared not to share their enthusiasm.

My trip to LA, however, was to indirectly yield the inspiration for my next theatrical project. Derek had flown out to join me for the end of the *Be-Bop the Future* recording sessions, and on our way back we stopped off in my all-time favourite city, New York.

Derek and I went to see an off-Broadway production of *Childe Byron* by an American writer named Romulus Linney. Both of us were hugely impressed by it: Derek with his voluminous and insatiable knowledge of drama, and me just because

I thought it was an incredibly powerful and visceral piece of theatre.

The play recounts the tale of the life and death of Lord Byron, England's famously licentious mad, bad and dangerous to know libertine poet. It opens with his daughter Ada, whom he had never known, at death's door. Sedated with laudanum, she hallucinates her father into being and demands that his ghostly presence confesses his errant ways.

Having begun as a two-hander between Byron and Ada, *Childe Byron* then allows a larger cast to act out the various excesses and indiscretions of Byron's scarcely believable life as the poet and his daughter watch and react. It seemed to me so special that I immediately knew I wanted to stage it in London.

The American producers were happy for me to do this, and the Young Vic theatre and director Frank Dunlop came on board very quickly. I had not initially resolved to play Byron myself but as I threw myself into researching the life of the wild George Gordon Byron, the drinking, drugging Romantic poet who exiled himself to Greece to fight the Ottoman Empire in the Greek War of Independence, the role simply became irresistible.

Frank Dunlop and I cast the talented actress Sarah Kestelman as Ada and before rehearsals began we decided to take a trip to the house where Byron had spent his formative years. Byron had had an equally debauched antecedent in his Uncle Jack, widely known as Mad Jack, who was the squire of an estate named Newstead Abbey near Nottingham.

Mad Jack had clearly fallen foul of the same strain of extraordinary psychosis that was later to possess Byron. His party pieces at Newstead Abbey had included ordering his servants to take to the lake in the grounds in rowing boats to re-enact historical battles, and then firing cannons at them. This was when he was not lying naked while locusts crawled all over his body.

Clearly a man of trenchant beliefs, Mad Jack had also shot dead his best friend in a duel after an argument about the optimum formula for making dog food. It is perhaps no surprise that accounts held little interest for him: he died a destitute recluse, leaving his equally erratic nephew to inherit the title Lord Byron and the bankrupt Newstead Abbey.

This fantastic back-story had Frank, Sarah and I champing at the bit to experience Newstead Abbey for ourselves, so after a three-hour drive from London we were hugely disappointed to arrive to find the impressive mansion closed. We were desperate to examine the house and hunt for its ghosts, the Headless Monk and the White Lady, and I was determined our trip should not be in vain.

Frank gave me a leg-up and I began to shin up a drainpipe (well, it is certainly what Byron would have done) when my progress was rudely interrupted. The abbey's caretaker, a gentleman named Sam Pierce, had materialised and was not impressed to find a random hooligan attempting to break into his property.

Frank, Sarah and I managed to placate Mr Pierce and once I had explained our mission, he kindly let us inside the house. We were enchanted by its stately, evocative interior, and I still am: even today, if I find myself in Nottingham, I will always pay it a visit. I tend not to go in via the drainpipe nowadays, mind.

Childe Byron ran at the Old Vic for a month from 15 July 1981 and was very well received by critics and public alike. There was talk of transferring to the West End, but I was in two minds about extending what was a very dialogue-heavy and demanding role, so in the end it never happened.

One night in particular will live in my memory for ever. After we had met in LA years earlier I had kept in occasional touch with Richard Burton, and we spoke on the phone a month before the play opened. 'What are you up to?' he asked me, and when I replied that I was set to play the poet Byron, he said, 'Get off! Where's that?' A short while later, he rang back and announced that he would like to come and see it.

The night that he attended I was very conscious that I was being watched by possibly the greatest actor Britain had ever produced and I could only hope it wasn't inhibiting my performance too badly. The curtain call seemed particularly enthusiastic, and I gazed out into the auditorium to see Richard Burton leading the standing ovation. I am surprised Derek didn't explode with joy.

Richard then came backstage to see me and lavished me with further compliments, even adopting a broad Cockney accent to tell me, 'I didn't know you could speak posh, you clever sod.' How do you react to something like that? In truth, it was quite a relief: a big part of me had expected him to pat me on the head consolingly and say, 'Never mind, son, better luck next time. I'm a *proper* actor. Just carry on with the singing, OK?'

16

THE WORLD IS MY LOBSTER

Finding myself a single man in the early eighties, it was more tempting than ever to gather up a band and hit the road. The work ethic nurtured by my East End roots and the experience of clocking on and off at Plessey's all those years ago mean that I have always played very long British tours – lining up fifty dates where most bands will do fifteen. Yet as the eighties dawned, I decided to take things a little more international.

My 1982 album *Stage-Struck* saw me return to chart action after the damp squib of *Hot Love* and spawned a Top Twenty single in 'Me and My Girl (Nightclubbing)'. Elton John's manager John Reid liked the album and, with Derek and Mel's blessing, took over my management temporarily to see if he could foster more interest in the country I had always neglected: America.

It was a short-lived liaison but John was a larger-than-life figure who left me with some very funny memories. One night I was over at his house when West Ham were playing Elton's football team, Watford. John grandly announced that he would bet his Bentley Mulsanne against my Range Rover that Watford would win. Gambling is not one of my vices, so I declined the bet. At which point – wouldn't you just know it? – West Ham won.

Derek and Mel were firmly back in the management saddle when Mel called to tell me he had booked me five nights in the Thai capital of Bangkok. Mel had been meeting in London with a decidedly shifty Asian tour promoter, who promised to pay half of our fee before we flew out and the other half after the last show.

This deal seemed reasonable, but appeared less so as our flights neared and we had still seen no money. Mel was perturbed but the band and I were keen to go, and phone reassurances from our Far Eastern friend were enough to persuade us to take a chance and head out to Bangkok.

Thailand was as much of a shock as South America had been, but in different ways. Bangkok was hot, bustling and engagingly exotic, and seemed to house the busiest and most preoccupied people in the world. There again, Jesus and Mario would have been impressed with the quality – and quantity – of their Thai sticks.

Herbie Flowers and I may possibly have indulged a little too enthusiastically in those lethal weapons the night that we spent what felt like hours whizzing up and down in a hotel lift, too stoned to get out and laughing uncontrollably at every puzzled fellow passenger who entered. The trip acquired an even more surreal edge when a box of dozens of pairs of awful synthetic underpants was delivered to my hotel door with no explanation. It later became clear from a TV advert that their manufacturers were my 'tour sponsor'.

Neither the pants barons nor the tour promoter had come up with any money by the day of the first show but I decided to play it anyway as it was sold out and I didn't want to let people down. The venue was a large cinema in the centre of Bangkok, the gig was a blast, and it moved me to see people who didn't speak English mouthing every word of my lyrics.

The second night also went well, but as the halfway point of our supposed five-night run came with no sign of payment, it looked to Mel and me as if we had been had. I had decided to honour all the shows and attempt to resolve the money problems later, but we arrived at the cinema to find hundreds of very disappointed-looking people milling around. Something was clearly amiss.

By the venue entrance, a cardboard sign in two languages stated:

DAVID ESSEX SHOW CANCELLED – ELECTRICAL PROBLEM

We went inside and discovered that this 'problem' didn't seem to have stopped the management showing a film, which was being avidly watched by two people. It transpired the Australian gig-sound company, who were less tolerant than us of not being paid, had removed all their gear. The band and I, guitars in hand, collapsed in fits of giggles.

Matters were rather more professional when we undertook a mini-tour of the United Arab Emirates. The facilities there were breathtaking and my main memory is of learning to ice-skate on a rink in the middle of the desert.

Australia has always been one of my favourite countries for live tours but I've had one or two run-ins with the local wildlife.

Playing golf in Perth one morning, I was poised to tee off when a stray emu emerged from a bunker and attacked me, leading me to fend it off with a five-iron. Another time, as we drove a hire car across the outback, a kangaroo launched itself at our vehicle. Skippy was fine; we spent the night in a very broken car.

I also enjoyed a few early eighties on-the-road misadventures rather nearer to home. One British tour kicked off in Ireland, so we decided to rent a house near Limerick for pre-tour rehearsals. The mansion that we chose was massive, remote and extremely eccentrically furnished.

One night off, our driver Michael procured us six bottles of the local firewater, poteen, a white spirit made from potatoes. It tasted like I imagine Domestos would but was clearly powerful stuff and we were swigging freely as we adjourned to the games room that featured a snooker table with a few balls missing, a dartboard with five plastic darts and a three-stringed harp.

As the poteen kicked in, the evening degenerated into one of those surrealistic image montages that Roald Dahl would reject as overly fanciful. I vividly recall two band members eschewing cues to play snooker with their willies; my sax player, Alan Wakeman, waltzing up and down a small set of stairs to Bing Crosby Christmas songs; and, in the corner, somebody with a lampshade on his head. No one took the slightest notice of anyone else. Everybody was off in his own warped little world.

For my part, I spent the evening making comically ineffectual attempts to hit the dartboard with the plastic darts and trying to apologise for our antics to the Irish housekeeper, Mary, who was stoicism personified: 'Ah, the boys have to relax!' When

Michael the driver appeared from the village with two local girls, they took one look at the Bacchanalian scenes unfolding around them and walked out. I can't say I blamed them.

Back in England, another interesting avenue opened up when the BBC asked me to host a talent show. I was initially reticent to take this on, but was persuaded that it would be a valuable outlet for struggling new performers: after all, if it had been around in my day, I might have been spared Prince Zelim in Guildford and Dandini in Manchester.

The David Essex Showcase was filmed in Harrogate and was a gentle, supportive affair a long way from the sneering tone often adopted by shows like *The X Factor* today. We weren't too bad as talent scouts, either: Richard Digance, Mari Wilson, Thomas Dolby, Talk Talk and the Belle Stars all scored a break with us.

My own music career was in decent shape and I enjoyed getting together with Mike Batt again for 1983's album *The Whisper*. The record didn't pull up any trees sales-wise but it did spawn one of my biggest hits. Mike and Tim Rice had written some lyrics for me for a song that used the metaphor of the seasons to examine a declining relationship.

Mike had just finished scoring the *Watership Down* movie and working with Art Garfunkel on 'Bright Eyes', so when we went into Air Studios to record 'A Winter's Tale' he initially asked me to sing it as Art might. I didn't fancy doing that and I didn't need to, as 'A Winter's Tale' just missed out on being a Christmas number one and even now, thirty years on, still seems to pop up on the radio every festive season. I guess I know how Noddy Holder feels.

My working life seemed to be ticking over nicely at this point but every man needs a hobby and in the early eighties I acquired a very exciting – and, in truth, rather expensive – one. Together with my old friend Kenney Jones, I learned to fly a helicopter: specifically, a Bell 47, the old-school chopper you used to see on the opening credits to Korean War-themed US TV comedy show *M*A*S*H*.

We became pilots under the tutelage of an ex-Army man named Captain Ken Stephens, who noted that we had both picked up the physical co-ordination aspect of flying quicker than most of his trainees, probably because we were both drummers. Even so, this didn't prevent me from hearing 'You bounced it!' – Ken's trademark description of a bumpy landing – rather more often than I would have liked.

My first solo flight was extremely harrowing, as was my first solo cross-country trip from Goodwood Airport when I almost had an airborne near-miss with three military jet fighters. After we qualified, Kenney and I bought an old ex-Army Bell 47 and shared its upkeep and flying hours between us.

This airborne crate was to give me untold happy hours. I took Dan up in it from a very early age and he adored it, as any boy would. In truth, I suspect his favourite trip was the one when a technical fault led to us making an emergency landing in a cornfield in Kent to the horror of the farmer, who thought the SAS were paying him a visit.

After I had moved back from Essex into London, I had given my mum and dad the house at Havering-Atte-Bower (it had seemed only fair, as they were having to endure occasional coach parties of my fans turning up to gawp at the outside of their Chadwell Heath gaff). I used to chopper down there to visit them and land in the back garden, until Mum banned me from doing it as the rotor blades were blowing the tops off her rhododendrons.

I will always cherish the day I persuaded my mum into the Bell 47 and took her on a sunset flight over the fields of Kent where we had picked hops all those centuries ago. She absolutely loved it, as did my dad when we took a low-level flight over his old stamping ground of the east London docks.

As I sat by my dear old dad, it was lovely to reflect that our father-son bond felt exactly the same as when we had bumped across the same streets on his pushbike together thirty years earlier. I guess we had just moved to a rather more rarefied altitude.

17

IT'S UP TO YOU, NEW YORK

My father was about to take an even more momentous trip with me than a nostalgic helicopter swoop over Canning Town. As the eighties hit their stride and we moved towards the middle of the decade, I became increasingly aware that I wanted to spend more time in New York.

Partly this was to give myself a bolthole. I had now been famous in one form or another for more than a decade, and while I had long become used to being public property and appreciated the love and affection that people in the street normally showed me, there were moments that I longed to be anonymous again. Also, the tabloids had been showing a rather tiresome interest in my private life since Maureen and I had split. But this was only half of the story.

New York had always drawn me like a magnet. Ever since I had first set eyes on the city, it had electrified me. Manhattan felt like the centre of the world, a teeming, multicultural, artistic and creative melting pot where anything and everything was possible. My infatuation had not dimmed with repeat visits and I decided it was time to buy a place there.

My dad had always longed to visit New York so I asked him to join me on my mission. My mum would probably have liked to come as well, but she was happy to see her two boys going off on an adventure together as we flew off to America.

Anybody's first visit to New York is amazing and so it was wonderful for me to see the city anew through my dad's eyes. He took to it like a duck to water. His TB-damaged lungs didn't stop us from sampling diner breakfasts on Broadway, wandering through Little Italy and Chinatown and heading up to the top of the Empire State Building.

Ever practical, my dad wasn't convinced that it made sense for me to buy a place there. I still had the *finca* in Spain, he pointed out – how often would I even get to NY, anyway? But I was determined, so we visited the neighbourhood estate agents, or realtors, as they prefer to call them.

We visited a loft apartment at 620 Broadway, near to Greenwich Village. It was in a rundown part of Manhattan where old textile warehouses were being converted into studio complexes: some of them could only be sold to artists. It was a scruffy area trying – with considerable success – to become fashionable.

Entering the sales office, we were greeted by a small, nervous Jewish guy who rammed a wig on top of his bald bonce as soon as he saw us, triggering memories of my old mini-cab boss from all those years ago. The archetypal neurotic salesman, Sidney had all the spiel and patter as he strove to convince us of the glories of the complex.

The Woody Allen-like Sid took us to a first-floor apartment that must have been 3,000 sq ft and had enormous windows that overlooked Broadway. He gabbled on about partition walls and adding balconies but all I could think as I surveyed the flat was, 'Wow! What a place!'

Sidney was hellbent on making his sale – 'If David Essex buys here, it will attract other buyers!' he claimed, unconvincingly – but he had no need to burst a blood vessel. I was in. We made a deal: Sid would organise a team of Mexican builders to split the space into two apartments, and I would use one half as my NY pad and rent the other half out to help cover expenses.

Now I was a proud Manhattan property-owner, I began spending two to three months per year in New York and had a fantastic time. I loved walking unrecognised through its insatiable streets and avenues; taking in the theatres, art galleries and gig venues. Like many people, I always feel most alive in New York.

I also had some interesting encounters there. Hearing I was in town, Andy Warhol invited me over to his house for lunch. Not being an acolyte of the Factory or the Velvet Underground, he didn't mean that much to me but I was interested to meet this iconic figure. I found an awkward, inscrutable man who hardly said a word. I'm not much of a talker either, so our lunch was a bit of a non-event.

It meant more to me to tick off one of my heroes when I went to see Little Richard play a Manhattan gig. I was so excited I even broke one of my cardinal rules and went backstage to meet him afterwards. Very gay and very camp, Richard was charmingly flamboyant and praised 'Rock On' to the skies. Another early idol of mine, Bo Diddley, was also there. Bo gravely informed me, 'I'll tell you one thing – you keep your money!' and walked off.

Yet my most significant New York encounter by far came early in 1984. At a loose end one evening, I glanced through the local *Village Voice* arts newspaper to see if there was anything going on. A gig caught my eye: a band with the lurid name of Rash of Stabbings were playing at CBGB's around the corner from me.

A rock 'n' roll fleapit on a squalid avenue called The Bowery, CBGB's had become internationally famous a few years earlier as the crucible of New York's punk scene, with Patti Smith, the Ramones, Blondie and Talking Heads all regularly playing gigs there. Rash of Stabbings sounded as if they would be just as punky as any of them, or more so. I decided to take a butcher's.

It might have surprised the Clash with their misplaced sneers about my white Rolls-Royce but I've always been into all sorts of music, punk included, and when I got down to the charmingly grotty CBGB's, it was hard not to be excited by Rash of Stabbings' primal, thrilling racket. One member of the group, though, stood out a mile.

Their diminutive, pretty lead singer, with one side of her hair shaved and the other side tumbling over her eyes, was attacking their material like a woman possessed. She had to strain to reach the microphone and her guitar looked a size too big for her, but her stage presence was so explosive that it was impossible to take your eyes off her.

I thought Rash of Stabbings had something special and was so taken with them that I went back to meet them after their set to see if I could maybe produce a record by them. It turned out they were from Providence, Rhode Island and their lead singer, Carlotta Christy, was the main writer and driving force of the band.

We swapped details and arranged to meet again and Carlotta and the band's manager came back up to New York a few days later to discuss the possibility of me adding them to my producing CV. That never materialised but I found Carlotta's energy and intensity as captivating in person as I had watching her on stage.

Carlotta was one of the most quirkily artistic and creative people I had ever met, whether in music, art, drawing or simply the way that she approached everyday life. She was from an Italian-American background but not at all loud or extrovert. There were hippy and wacky elements to her character, but most of all she was a strong, fascinating, unique individual.

She was still living in Rhode Island, where Rash of Stabbings had a cult following on the local post-punk hardcore scene, and over the next few weeks we got closer and closer. It began with meetings in New York and daily phone calls, and when I went back to the UK for a while, the phone conversations continued.

After three months or so we were an item and I went down to Rhode Island to meet her family. They were typical larger-than-life Italian-Americans, with everyone talking at once and the volume wrenched up to eleven, and my ears would be ringing after a visit. The loudest of all was her Uncle Frank, who would roll up in his classic 1958 Cadillac.

I seemed to be living at 35,000 feet, flying back and forth to the UK to see Verity and Dan and for various work projects, and I started to find I missed Carlotta more and more while we were apart. I was also having severe problems with my Manhattan apartment, as my plan to rent out half of the floor space had turned out to be a bit of a nightmare.

This was not actually Sidney's fault but rather a consequence of the colourful characters I had inadvertently chosen to rent it out to. My first tenant was an Italian dress designer who seemed perfectly pleasant when I vetted him and handed over the keys before heading back to England for a while.

I returned to a torrent of complaints from the building's Residents' Co-Operative. It transpired the designer had a rather fiery girlfriend who would show up and argue with him into the early hours; rows that frequently ended with the bruised, partly clothed girlfriend roaming the complex screaming insults into the night before sleeping in the lift. I had no choice but to give him his marching orders.

His replacement was a seemingly amiable young guy called Sol who claimed to have invented the electronic garment tags that stores use to prevent shoplifting. We got on well, although the alarm bells sounded one time that Sol invited me into his flat. While I was there, the entry phone went off and three massive dudes walked in with a football-sized rock of cocaine: one of them was in stockings and high heels. I could turn a blind eye to that, but when the neighbours complained that Sol had imported a pet wolf to the building, he had to go.

I was fast becoming the bane of the Residents' Co-Operatives' lives, and the nadir was reached when I attempted to do a good deed. The complex's janitor was a kindly, amiable black guy named James who lived with his wife in a minuscule space in the basement next to the heating system. Feeling sorry for them, and given that I was in London more than New York, I gave James the keys to my apartment and told him that they could stay there while I was not around.

My warm glow from this Good Samaritan act lasted until I got a call from the NYPD a few weeks later. The cops informed

As Jim MacLaine in *Stardust*.

Keith Moon and me
jamming while filming
Stardust.

Actually recording 'Rock On' with the wonderful Herbie Flowers on bass guitar in the background.

Arriving at the
premiere of
That'll Be the Day.

And with Maureen
later that evening.

Essex Mania in an Oxford Street record shop.

Another dressing room.

In concert at the Hammersmith Odeon, 1975.

The West Ham team – heroes all. I'm the one with the ball.

Billy Bonds, me and Frank Lampard.

Che Guevara in *Evita* at the Prince Edward Theatre in London's West End.

The evil Don Pedro in the film *Shogun Mayeda*.

At the launch of *Beauty and the Beast*, with two Russian Olympic skaters.

Mum, Dad, Billy and Kit.

Mum, Dad and
my son Danny.

Danny on his bike.

My wonderful children: Verity, Kit, Billy and Dan.

With Mum, filming *Heartbeat*.

Verity and me frigging about in the rigging on *Robinson Crusoe*.

Me, George the dog and the boys.

A day out at Buckingham Palace to see the Queen, and receive my OBE (Mum bought a new hat!).

Me and my two sons from *EastEnders*, Matt Lapinskas (Anthony) and Tony Discipline (Tyler).

Romance is in the air between Eddie and Carol (Lindsey Coulson).

All the Fun of the Fair at the Garrick Theatre in the West End.

The wonderful London cast in full flight.

Levi Lee in *All the Fun of the Fair*.

me that using my loft as a base, James had ransacked the unoccupied apartments in the building of all of their owners' possessions. His relatives had then driven up from Louisiana in a truck, loaded the goods on to it – including all of my stuff – and disappeared with him into the night.

As a parting gift, James and his cohorts had also left my flat littered with syringes from their drug use, with blood from injections spattered all over the walls. My neighbours were contemplating a lynching by this stage and I felt I had no choice but to sell up. At least I passed the loft on to a very conservative Chinese Wall Street financial adviser, and even managed to make a profit while doing so.

My New York property-owning adventure had come to an end but I was leaving the city with more ties than I had brought to it. Carlotta and I had already tentatively discussed living together in London and we decided to give it a go. When I flew out of JFK after selling the flat, she came with me.

18

WHAT SHALL WE DO WITH THE DRUNKEN SAILBOAT?

Throughout my life and career, people have always seen me as terminally laid-back. I remember once in the eighties turning on the TV and seeing an impressionist doing an impersonation of me. His routine consisted of saying 'I'm David Essex … zzzzz!' and slumping forward as if asleep or, more likely, comatose.

It made me laugh and I can understand this reading of my nature but I don't actually think it's accurate at all. My body language and laconic speech rhythms may appear pretty laid-back but in actuality I have always been intense and driven to find new challenges and take myself out of my comfort zone, in work and in life.

While I had been zooming back and forth between London and New York in 1983 and '84, I had been working on an ambitious and fairly audacious new project. Being a writer of songs, and having appeared in a number of other people's musicals, it seemed to me that the logical conclusion was to write a stage musical of my own.

I didn't have a subject matter in mind and vaguely wondered if I could translate some of the dark-hued, seductive *Grimm's*

Fairy Tales to this format. I was fairly unimpressed the day that Derek suggested that an alternative might be to write a musical around the famous mutiny on the *Bounty* of 28 April 1789.

As every schoolboy knows (except for any unlucky enough to attend Shipman County), the mutiny on the British Navy ship the *HMS Bounty* in the South Pacific was led by a seaman called Christian Fletcher against the domineering and inflexible Captain Bligh. The mutineers cast Bligh adrift on the high seas and settled on the paradise island of Tahiti.

I was initially sceptical about this suggestion, but Derek pointed out that as well as the central dramatic conflict between Fletcher and Bligh, the narrative presented opportunities to write violent, spectacular music to illustrate sea storms and the chance to use the exotic rhythms of the Polynesian music of Tahiti. The more I thought about it, the more this epic story felt appropriate to turn into a musical.

It has always been a personal bugbear of mine that the sections in musicals where characters segue from spoken dialogue into song can seem forced and contrived, so I was determined that every line in *Mutiny!* should be sung. We still needed to flesh out the story, and Derek suggested a meeting with a Brighton-based playwright named Richard Crane, who had already written a version of *Mutiny on the Bounty* for children.

Richard was around my age, mustard-keen and steeped in knowledge of the mutiny and we hit it off straight away. Over the following months, as I zigzagged from London to New York, he worked at the storyline while I began crafting the music and lyrics.

We soon picked up a couple of heavy-duty accomplices. The Royal Shakespeare Company's Terry Hands agreed to direct the show and recruited the Ballet Rambert's leading choreographer Christopher Bruce to plot the dance sequences. We were a long way from having a show, but it was reassuring to have two such big hitters on board so early.

I read up religiously on the story of the *Bounty* but I felt that to truly bring the tumultuous tale to life we needed more first-hand experience. The mutiny had come after the ship's crew had spent five months in Tahiti and been so enchanted by the island that they could not tear themselves away.

What was it about this magical, mysterious island that could drive men to such heinous acts of insurrection and rebellion? There was only one way to find out. We would have to go to Tahiti.

As soon as Terry, Christopher and I landed at Tahiti's sole airport at Faa'a, the spellbinding appeal of the island became clear. It was one in the morning, and a spectral moon glowed through a necklace of twinkling stars as nature's fragrant aromas suffused the warm night air. It was impossible to imagine how welcoming Tahiti must have appeared to Bligh's crewmen after the ordeal of their ten-month journey over harsh seas on the *Bounty*.

Our two weeks on this beauteous isle were hugely productive. Chris studied the local traditional dances, Terry tracked down and talked to actual descendants of the original mutineers and I listened to and started to write music. I composed the single 'Tahiti', which was to go Top Ten, on my hotel balcony with a rented keyboard as the island of Moorea glowed on the horizon in the sunset.

We leavened this hugely enjoyable work with a little pleasure, venturing into the capital of Papeete to experience its highly idiosyncratic nightlife. The city is also a major port and base for the French Navy, whose sailors had traditionally enjoyed the embraces of the accommodating South Seas women while on shore leave until the Catholic Church altered local attitudes towards casual sex.

The love-starved Gallic sailors now had to look elsewhere to sate their appetites, as became clear when we visited a place called the Piano Bar. Initially I thought its bar was lined with gorgeous women, but soon realised that they were lady-boys.

As Christopher, Terry and I sat at a corner table and drank in the scene, not to mention a few cocktails, the boy-girls could tell that we had a different agenda to the drunken sailors and four of them came to sit with us and keep us company. This aggrieved a French sailor who had evidently had his eye on one of them, and he charged at us with a bottle – at which point a lady-boy in a leopard-skin mini-skirt leapt to her feet and took him out with a right hook that Ali in his prime would have been proud of. As a gaggle of boys in dresses heaved the battered matelot head first into the street, we made our excuses and left.

Seeking to avoid the pursuing British Navy back in the nineteenth century, Fletcher Christian and his gang of mutineers had taken refuge on the spectacularly remote Pitcairn Island, and I was keen to continue my journey there to speak to Christian's descendants. I was told my only option was to wait for a passing boat that might call at Pitcairn to deliver post and supplies. How long would this wait for a ship be? I asked. 'About six months.'

Yet although Pitcairn proved beyond our reach, the expedition to Tahiti yielded countless ideas and inspirations for *Mutiny!* Back in London, I finished the score and John Cameron and I set about recording a soundtrack album to be released prior to the show's staging to try to drum up interest in the production.

Having decided to play Fletcher Christian myself, I needed a Captain Bligh. My first choice was Frank Finlay, the marvellous and authoritative actor who had been so kind to me when I was an extra in *Assault* all those years ago, and I was delighted when Frank agreed and showed enormous enthusiasm for the project.

I scored another coup when I showed my score to the leader of the Royal Philharmonic Orchestra and he congratulated me and agreed that the orchestra would record the soundtrack album with me. Buoyed by this vote of confidence, I decided that I would initially conduct the orchestra myself, to attempt to impart my vision for the music.

I am not sure I have ever felt so nervous as when I stepped on to the conductor's podium in front of sixty-five of the *crème de la crème* of the nation's classically trained musicians. It was such a big deal for me, and yet I gazed around and saw three-score bored-looking people who looked like they wanted to be anywhere but here as they mulled over phone calls they had to make and what to have for dinner that night.

The disconnect between their seeming indifference and the rich, exquisite waves of music that washed over me as the Royal Philharmonic struck up was staggering. How could these people tease such a magnificent noise from brass and strings yet look so unmoved by it? I found working with this brilliant orchestra so nerve-wracking that I started smoking again, fifteen years after I had stopped. Sadly, that filthy habit remains with me to this day.

Mutiny! was taking shape but there now began a hugely frustrating period in its genesis. It was hard to find a West End theatre to stage the show. After we missed out on the Theatre Royal Drury Lane to *42nd Street*, Terry Hands reluctantly had to drop out of the project to return to the Royal Shakespeare Company.

Losing a director is pretty disastrous but – as had happened so many times in my career – Derek came to the rescue. He suggested that we go to see a show at the National Theatre based on *The Rime of the Ancient Mariner* directed by the renowned Michael Bogdanov. It obviously had a nautical theme, which seemed relevant, and we were delighted when Michael agreed to replace Terry.

Michael brought enthusiasm and expertise to *Mutiny!* but he also wanted changes. He felt we should add spoken dialogue to the production, and although this went against my instincts, I agreed. Even more significant were his alterations to the staging. Under Terry Hands' instructions, set designer William Dudley had built an abstract set using billowing sails and evocative space. Michael wanted a boat: a Big Boat.

William fulfilled this brief, and then some. He somehow created an extraordinary replica of *HMS Bounty* that was not far off the original vessel's actual size. Pitched on a complicated hydraulic system deep beneath the stage, its rigging and sails flew in the flies above the stage as the cast literally built the boat in front of the audience. William's *Bounty* was an amazing achievement – yet the physical requirements it would make of whichever venue was to house the show made the search for a theatre even more difficult.

Eventually the show's producers announced they had secured use of the Piccadilly Theatre behind Piccadilly Circus. Despite its central-sounding name, I had strong reservations as the venue was a little hidden away in a side street and had a history of shows closing early because of poor attendances. But beggars can't be choosers. The Piccadilly Theatre it was.

As we waited for the theatre to become free, we tweaked and tinkered with the show for close on two years. I filled the time with a couple of albums and tours, flying to as many dates as possible in my new toy, the helicopter. It was often a challenge to find landing sites near to the provincial venues I was playing.

One hair-raising flight between gigs in Bournemouth and Northampton saw me hit an electrical storm around Bath. With nowhere to go, I had no choice but to descend to 500 feet and do a few airborne laps of Bath before the storm cleared enough for me to continue my journey.

Having given up my New York apartment, I was making fewer transatlantic flights, particularly after Carlotta moved over to live with me in Manchester Square, central London. She had understandably taken a while to decide to make the move, as Rash of Stabbings had been poised to sign a major record deal with A&M in America.

It was great to have her over with me, and any trepidation I had about her meeting the other all-important woman in my life, Verity, receded when thankfully the two of them got on great from the start. I also knew it was important that Carlotta had an outlet for her creativity, and encouraged her to carry on making music in my small home studio in Manchester Square: I was to record some of her songs on future albums.

Carlotta was a true bohemian and we gave each other a lot of space in our relationship. It was never constricting and that was how we both wanted it. If she became homesick, she would fly home to Rhode Island for weeks or even months at a time. I'd go to visit her, or she'd fly back, and we would pick up as if we had never left off.

She understandably absented herself quite a lot in early 1985, as *Mutiny!* finally began to come together and seemed to occupy my time 24/7. Christopher Bruce's Ballet Rambert connections ensured that we had terrific dancers and Michael Bogdanov and I also oversaw open casting auditions.

One day in particular resembled an early episode of *Britain's Got Talent*, with hundreds of hopeful amateurs and, without being too unkind, well-meaning incompetents tumbling on to the stage. I was fighting giggles long before one hapless individual arrived to yodel gratingly out-of-key versions of the songs from *Chitty Chitty Bang Bang* while busily fire-eating during their instrumental breaks. Sliding from my chair to the floor, I crawled to a cupboard at the back of the theatre to give vent to my hysterics, only to find one of the producers had beaten me to it to do exactly the same thing.

The rehearsals proper began in May '85 in a hall in Wandsworth in south London, and were a riot. *Mutiny!* was to be a very physical show, with sea storms, hornpipes and vigorous dance routines in the ship's rigging. Frank Finlay was an example to us all, hurling himself into the show with the brio of a wet-behind-the-ears teenager despite being close on sixty.

While the acting side of things was going well, the technical rehearsals were turning into a nightmare. Our *HMS Bounty*'s vast proportions meant that a team of construction workers had to dig deep beneath the Piccadilly Theatre to house the ship's complex hydraulic system. The workers dug so deep they had to be careful not to hit the tube's Piccadilly Line.

When our rehearsals shifted from Wandsworth into the theatre, it immediately became clear that the set was a Health and Safety minefield and potentially highly perilous. As the hydraulics pitched the *Bounty* from side to side as it rounded an imaginary Cape Horn, it was all the dancers could do to hang on to the rigging: if they fell, it was a serious drop to the boards below.

Michael turned to the Jameson's whiskey bottle as he attempted to direct our renegade ship, which sporadically crashed into the back wall of the theatre, shattering stage lights and sending the broken glass cascading onto the cast below. These technical difficulties meant our opening date had to be postponed twice.

The producers were becoming understandably impatient and even though we still didn't feel entirely ready, *Mutiny!* opened on 24 July 1985, the day after my (extremely apprehensive) thirty-eighth birthday. Thankfully the technical gremlins stayed away, *HMS Bounty* remained afloat, and after all the grief we had been through, the standing ovation at the curtain call sounded like the music of the spheres.

This approbation was reflected in the comments of the guests at the after-show party, with some people saying that it was the best musical they had ever seen, so the newspaper reviews the next morning were a punch in the stomach. They were terrible: the first time a project I had starred in had been utterly savaged.

The gist of the criticism seemed to be that as a mere pop star, I had ideas above my station in attempting both to write and star in a musical, a feat of creative multi-tasking that had previously only been achieved by such luminaries as Noël Coward and Anthony Newley. The slating seemed extreme, gratuitous and unfair, but luckily the public voted with their feet, the standing ovations kept coming and *Mutiny!* sailed on a successful eighteen-month run.

Carlotta was back in America for much of *Mutiny!*'s run and our unrestrictive, kind-of open relationship was on a bit of a break. I found myself growing very close to Sinitta, the young American singer who was the female lead in the production as Fletcher's girlfriend, Miamiti. She was a great girl, full of life and vitality, and eventually our onstage relationship grew into a real-life affair.

Sinitta and I had a lovely time together, and when we went our separate ways as Carlotta and I hooked up again, we did so with a lot of mutual affection and no bad feelings. It seems a shame to me that her music career has always been defined by her novelty eighties hit, 'So Macho'. It has been the same millstone around her neck as the Wombles have been for the ultra-talented Mike Batt, and '*Oh my, thigh high, dig dem dimples on dem knees*' could have been for me all those years ago, had I been unlucky enough for it to be a hit.

Mutiny! gave me a huge sense of achievement in having dreamt up, written and performed such a vast project in the West End. Nevertheless, it was a very demanding show to be at the heart of, especially as the looming *HMS Bounty* was such an erratic and unpredictable co-star.

In the end the troublesome vessel didn't give us too many problems apart from occasionally gently bumping the back wall of the theatre, although once it overshot its stage mark for a crucial scene. This meant that we found ourselves accidentally acting out a burial at sea with our backs to the puzzled audience.

As our ever-professional Captain Bligh, Frank Finlay delivered a magisterial address to the back wall of the theatre: as Frank is slightly short-sighted it is possible he had not even realised that anything was wrong. We might even have got away with it had not one cast member, Bill Snape, slipped on the misplaced set and farted loudly as he fell, triggering a giggling fit among the funeral party, including the Union Jack-covered corpse.

Eighteen months was the longest time I had been in any show since *Godspell* and I must admit that *Mutiny!* took its toll on me. Towards the end of the run, I was definitely beginning to flag: I seemed to have a permanent cold and was pretty run-down.

I remember that Cliff Richard was starring in a musical nearby called *Time*, and one matinee show he brought the whole cast down with him to check out the friendly competition. It was a pity that I was feeling so rough that particular day that I growled through my entire performance like Lee Marvin on downers.

I could easily have lapsed into seeing out the end of the run on autopilot were it not for a very necessary wake-up call. After one lacklustre matinee show, an American tourist left a letter on Savoy Hotel-headed notepaper for me at the stage door. It basically said, 'If you don't want to be in this very fine show, then why don't you leave?' He was completely right: he had detected that I was merely going through the motions, and his comment shocked me back to the top of my game.

Nevertheless, I must admit that I was relieved when the curtain came down on the last *Mutiny!* one Saturday in November 1986. By the following Monday, I was high in the sky and on my way to a distant and wonderfully distracting corner of the globe. It felt very much like time for another solo travelling adventure.

19

TWO HEADS ARE
BETTER THAN ONE

After the stresses and strains of eight *Mutiny!* shows a week, a trip to India seemed exactly what the doctor ordered. Intrigued by the much-vaunted spirituality of this mysterious, sprawling land, I resolved to see as much of it as possible and headed off with little except a few changes of clothes in my backpack.

I was also determined to stay in guesthouses and B&Bs owned by local people as much as possible. I have spent far too much of my life in anonymous chain hotels and did not want to ape Lou Reed, who once told me that he had decorated his New York apartment like a Holiday Inn so that he would feel at home when he was on tour. I trust he was joking.

When you first arrive in India, all the preconceived clichés seem to be true. The rutted roads are a kinetic chaos, with fume-belching trucks, tuk-tuk taxis, boneshaker bicycles and lowing cows all competing for space. Poverty is rampant, and in the big cities like Mumbai (or Bombay, as it was then) and Delhi, spices and sewage intermingle pungently in the humid air. Yet the country is addictive and fascinating.

Arriving in Delhi, I got my bearings and sampled a local curry or two – basically bones in spicy gravy – before heading over to Mumbai. I made friends with two Air India air hostesses and one of them invited me to stay with her and her boyfriend, who allowed me to take my life in my hands and take his motorbike into the city's traffic. There is no rush hour in Mumbai: *every* hour is rush hour.

There were intriguing sights everywhere I looked. In Mumbai I saw vultures circling over a building occupied by holy men with beards down to their waists and talon-like long fingernails. My hosts later explained that when these ultra-religious men died, their bodies were left in a place called the Towers of Silence for the vultures to devour. The birds were waiting for their supper.

Nobody visits India without seeing the Taj Mahal but the most memorable feature of my train journey to Agra was gazing out of the window of the packed carriage to see countless local men crouching and unloading some generous post-breakfast bowel movements by the side of the tracks. At least the dazzling white temple itself was just as breathtaking as its advance reputation suggests.

My next port of call was the famous 'pink city' of Jaipur where my wish for unusual places to stay was more than satisfied. A friendly tuk-tuk driver delivered me to a palace that was run by a maharajah who he said was a little down on his luck and would rent out occasional rooms to tourists he took a shine to.

The palace was like a museum to the long-lost days of the Raj, with elephants' tusks mounted in the hallway, gold paint flaking everywhere and flea-bitten peacocks roaming the grounds. My red-and-gold bedroom held a spectacularly hard four-poster bed and a zoo's-worth of stuffed hunting trophies, including a rather baleful-looking stuffed tiger's head.

I was told dinner would be served in one hour, and after a gong sounded I wandered down to the dining hall. As the only guest, I was the sole occupant of a twenty-person dining table, but that didn't stop the maharajah supplying ten staff to serve me. The food was good, but the fact that four or five over-servile waiters appeared at my elbow every time I so much as twitched made me feel ridiculously self-conscious.

The next day started well but then declined very, very badly. I trekked off to see some Hindu temples, even riding an elephant on the way, but made the mistake of buying an ice cream from a roadside vendor. Some grotesque projectile vomiting ensued, and by the time I made it back to the palace I had never felt so sick in my life.

For the next two or three days I hardly moved from the rock-hard bed. The maharajah brought a local doctor to see me and he gave me an injection from a giant needle and some brightly coloured pills that sent me off on a long, strange trip into the dark recesses of my mind. The tiger on the wall was by now looking particularly malevolent.

After a ropey few days I recovered enough to head off to Goa, a different experience entirely. This serene coastal area was full of hippies and Portuguese architecture, a souvenir from the former colonial power, and in the women's looks I saw reminders that Goa had spawned many gypsies and Romany people. I also just about survived a scare when a badly over-crowded ferry sank as we were crossing a river.

My Indian odyssey came to an end in Srinagar at the foot of the Himalayas, a beautiful spot where I rented a floating houseboat. Vendors would call in tiny boats, selling anything that you could require, including a tailor who measured me for a shirt and then delivered it later the same day. It was bizarre to sit in this tranquil paradise and hear gunshots from the disputed Kashmir border between India and Pakistan just a few miles away.

Halfway up a mountain in Kashmir I met a holy man dressed in sun-faded orange robes. We sat and talked for hours about life, death and his theories of reincarnation. He told me he felt I was a kindred and much-travelled spirit and asked if I was a holy man in my own land. Maybe I should have told him that I once played Jesus.

India reinvigorated me and I returned to England fully refreshed in time for Christmas with Verity and Dan. Carlotta flew back to London and I began 1987 by recording a musical version of a poem by former Poet Laureate Sir John Betjeman for an album that was compiled by Radio One DJ Mike Read. 'Myfanwy' was a minor hit.

I was keen to return to music and touring and began work on an album to be called *Touching the Ghost*. The title referred to the nebulous, almost mystical process of songwriting: I have always felt that trying to define where the initial spark of inspiration that builds into a song comes from is like trying to touch a ghost.

Feeling more inclined to work with a producer than produce the record myself, my mind drifted back to my old sparring partner Jeff Wayne and I realised how much I'd like to work with him again. I did not know how he would react, given the fractious experience of *Out on the Street*, but he was receptive when I phoned him, and when he jokingly greeted me at the door of his studio with a box of plasters and bandages, I knew we'd be OK.

We picked up exactly where we had left off a decade earlier, as the best friends always do, and making *Touching the Ghost* was a lively and creative process. I was also hankering for a return to the road so Mel Bush assembled one of his trademark fifty-date tours for the autumn.

The jaunt was about to begin when Carlotta dropped the bombshell that she was pregnant.

In all honesty, I was simultaneously thrilled and perturbed by this unexpected revelation. I was excited at the idea of becoming a dad again, and starting a family with Carlotta, but part of me worried how Verity and Dan would take the news. I knew that I couldn't bear either of them to feel that they were no longer quite as important in my life.

Carlotta shared my concerns: she had become close to both of my kids, particularly Danny, and didn't want to hurt them. With typical considerateness, she suggested that she return to Rhode Island for the pregnancy while I waited for a moment to break the news. I agreed and she flew back to America.

Carlotta, her pregnancy and my kids dominated my thoughts all through my autumn tour and she and I spoke on the phone every day. After the tour Christmas was upon us, and I decided to wait until the festive season had passed before trying to explain to Verity and Dan that they were not losing a dad but gaining a brother or sister.

It was a good thing that I did, because just after New Year 1988, Carlotta phoned with a scarcely believable, utterly unexpected news bulletin.

'Are you sitting down?' she asked me.

'Why?' I inquired.

'It's twins.'

'No!'

'Yes!'

'Right,' I said, lamely. 'Blimey.'

It was a lot to take in but the more I thought about it, the happier I was about it. Bizarrely, this extraordinary news made it a little easier to spill the beans to Verity and Dan. Happy-go-lucky as nine-year-old boys always are, Danny thought the news was cool, although Verity seemed surprised and a little guarded.

The first chance that I got, I jumped on a plane to see Carlotta and check everything was OK. She was fine, although nearly as wide as she was tall, and we headed down to her local hospital for a scan. They had more news for us: it was two boys. I loved the prospect of two more sons, and Verity was relieved to know she would still be her daddy's only girl.

Back in London, my stalwart PA Madge had a meeting request from a BBC drama producer named Susi Belbin. Mel and I headed down to Television Centre and the charming, husky-voiced Susi asked if I would consider taking the lead role in a sitcom called *The Lock-Keeper*.

Derek had always been understandably keen to keep me away from the cheesier, lowest-common-denominator elements of TV work and I'd always trusted his instincts but the meeting was a good one, and when Susi presented me with a handful of work-in-progress scripts, I promised to go away and read them.

When I did, I liked what I read. The comedy felt whimsical and gentle compared to the crass stereotypes and set-pieces of traditional sitcoms. I also thought the lock-keeping hero, Davey Jackson, an easy-going Cockney wide boy with a dodgy past and a gypsy soul, could almost have been written for me. Even Derek admitted the scripts were OK so I decided to give it a go.

Susi concurred with my suggestion to change the title from *The Lock-Keeper* to *The River* and we cast fresh-faced and talented Scottish actress Kate Murphy as the leading lady and Davey's love interest. I was also commissioned to write the theme tune to the series, and was sitting at my piano striving to do exactly that late at night on 19 May 1988 when the phone rang.

I never get late-night phone calls, so one thought flashed into my mind immediately: Carlotta! I was right. It was one of her Italian-American family – and I was in such a state of shock that I can't remember which one – telling me that Carlotta had gone into labour a month prematurely and been admitted to a Rhode Island maternity hospital.

'I'm on my way,' I said. A sleepless night of worrying followed until I headed towards Heathrow Airport before the sun was even up. The first flight I could commandeer got me to Boston by five in the afternoon East Coast time.

A family friend called Jim met me at the airport and broke the momentous news. Carlotta had given birth around two hours earlier, while I was probably somewhere over Greenland. I was sorry to have missed the births, but this feeling was quickly lost in the overwhelming relief that Carlotta and the twins were OK.

The two-hour drive to the hospital seemed to last weeks and as soon as we got there I ran through the labyrinth of corridors to find Carlotta. She was looking a little the worse for wear and decidedly battered by what she had been through but she only had thoughts for the boys, who had both been whisked into an Intensive Care Unit. The words struck dread into me.

'Can I see them?' I asked, and a sympathetic nurse walked me through to the ICU, where medics were attending to seven or eight babies in respirators. She took me to the far end of the room and there they were: my two new sons, the elder weighing just three pounds fifteen ounces, and his younger sibling (by fifteen minutes) one ounce less.

They had drips and seemingly dozens of other leads and tubes attached to their tiny hands, feet and noses. They looked weak and helpless and as if they must be in pain from all the gadgets attached to them, and as I looked at the sweet little woollen hats on their heads to keep them warm, I felt as if my heart was breaking.

My voice trembled as I addressed a doctor who was standing by another ventilator nearby. 'Will they be all right?' I asked him. 'It's a little early to tell,' he replied in a detached, professional manner: they were really not the words I needed to hear.

As I gazed at the twins, another nurse appeared and stuck yet another needle into one of my boys, who cried out in pain. I felt a huge instinctive rush of anger towards her but controlled my passions and repeated the question. She turned towards me and smiled.

'Of course they will,' she assured me. 'It's not unusual for twins to be premature and underweight. Now, don't you worry!' At which point, I felt the most extreme mood swing towards her imaginable, combined with a sense of intoxicating, exhilarating relief.

Carlotta and the twins were in hospital for two weeks as they recuperated and regained their strength and I visited every hour I was allowed. As I sat by her bedside we talked over names. Her family home in Rhode Island was on a former Native American reservation so we playfully worked our way through a few cowboy names and settled on Kit Carson and Billy the Kid. That was it, then: Kit and Bill it was to be.

The three of them were safely back in the arms of Carlotta's doting family a week or two later when I flew back to London to begin filming *The River*. It was a wrench to leave them behind so soon, but on another level, I was used to such partings: it was what I had been doing my entire life.

The series was filmed at a village called Wootton Rivers near Marlborough in Wiltshire, which doubled as its fictional setting on Chumley-on-the-Water. A genuine picturesque lock-keeper's cottage was the main location for shooting this sweet story of an unlikely romance flourishing in a village of British eccentrics.

The river looked gorgeous on the TV but was actually so rank and stagnant that Auntie Beeb issued the cast with a directive that if anybody were to jump in, they should ensure that every orifice was fully covered. The BBC didn't make it clear exactly how this challenging task was to be achieved.

The River was a hoot to film from start to finish, with a friendly cast and scenes that frequently broke down in gales of giggles. The scripts required Davey to own a cute little piglet, but as shooting progressed we had to recast this part three times as the piglets had an unfortunate habit of rapidly maturing into hulking great porkers.

The last episode of the six-part series ended with Katy and I sailing off into the sunset on the remains of an exploded narrow boat. Viewing figures had been healthy and there was talk of a second series but my heart was not in it – and my thoughts were elsewhere.

Flying back to America, I bought a house for Carlotta, Kit and Bill on the borders of Connecticut and Rhode Island, about an hour from her family and within striking distance of the sea. I spent months there with them in that beautifully rugged locale, only flying back to finish off the *Touching the Ghost* album. It was my first release on my own Lamplight Records label.

For the next year or two, I shuttled back and forth between Connecticut and London, juggling work and family. It seemed to work for all of us. During a visit to Los Angeles I met with some TV producers who offered me the lead role in an imminent science fiction series.

It was a tempting offer, and had it been for six months I would probably have done it, but the contract required me to relocate to LA *ad infinitum*, which simply didn't fit my plans. American TV producers are not renowned for taking no for an answer, and eventually camped outside my Connecticut home offering me the world to reconsider. I did – and the answer was still 'No'.

As the eighties wound to a close, I flew back to England to appear in the Royal Variety Performance. It was an honour, and I got to meet the Queen afterwards. She told me, 'Well done,' which I guess was an improvement on her sister's comments at

Evita. I was to meet the Queen again years later, in very special circumstances.

The Royal Variety Performance was slightly marred for me by the ego-driven backstage arguments about dressing rooms and running orders, and I have found similar problems when I have appeared on Children in Need. They are both excellent events to raise money for charity but too many artists seem only bothered about achieving maximum exposure and plugging their latest product.

I have always had mixed feelings about the celebrity-charity interface and generally prefer sending a private cheque to a good cause rather than taking part in mass organised profile-raising jamborees. There are exceptions to this rule, though, as I learned in 1990 when the Voluntary Services Overseas organisation asked me to be their Ambassador of the Year.

20

A LOT OF WORK
FOR CHARYDEE

The Voluntary Services Organisation, or VSO, sends people to the developing world to pass on their particular skills to local people to help them to help themselves. It is a remarkable and honourable organisation, but I had to think long and hard about whether to get involved with them.

Their initial approach was a letter from a VSO official called Dick Rowe, whom I liked as soon as I met him. Dick talked me through the organisation's laudable aims and *modus operandi* and I explained that while I felt honoured to be asked, I had severe misgivings about celebrities hijacking charitable causes just to enhance their own image.

Once Dick and the VSO chief, David Green, had made it clear to me that I could make a positive difference and not be merely a semi-famous name on their headed notepaper, I was in. I was to replace Lord Lichfield as the ambassador and the handover ceremony, held at his photographic studio in London, seemed to feature dignitaries from every developing country extant.

My first task was to meet some volunteers and observe their fieldwork at first hand and Dick decided that we should go to

Uganda. It was a country that I knew little about save for the atrocities wreaked there by Idi Amin two decades earlier, but on the flight over Dick told me of its years of tribal conflict and civil war and its crippling Aids epidemic.

We were met in Kampala by a tremendous VSO field officer named John who drove us in a jeep through the bustling early evening streets of the capital. Cars, scooters, bikes and absurdly overloaded buses vied for road space as in India, while in the crowded markets women balanced impossibly precipitous loads on their heads.

As we drove to the VSO compound in the Kampala suburbs, I realised what a green, lush and verdant country Uganda was. It was severely crime-ridden, though: John told me that the last VSO field officer in the capital had been murdered for petrol in the very compound that we were heading for.

Over the next two weeks, we travelled across the country and I admired the sterling and inspirational work done by the team of volunteers. We visited a teacher training college in Nkozi, a ninety-minute drive from Kampala. The students were on holiday, but the principal walked me around the campus.

He showed me to the campus theatre, which was used by the college's music and drama department. It was little more than a small tin-roofed building with a raised concrete stage. 'Maybe you can come and teach here?' he suggested. It seemed a great idea straight away.

There was a heart-rending trip to an orphanage for kids whose parents had been killed in civil strife or died from Aids. Some of them ran around the room seemingly happily while many others sat in corners, too traumatised to speak. A saintly volunteer named Mary and her two Ugandan helpers moved among these damaged children, teaching them how to play. One of the older boys took a shine to me as soon as I arrived and insisted that I gave him a piggyback for the duration of my visit.

In Kampala's hectic central market I met an American girl who had left a high-flying finance job in New York to organise a group of local lepers into a co-operative. This admirable woman had transformed them from street beggars into traders selling small items for a stall and making a modest profit. They even had an office made from cardboard boxes and it was humbling to be invited in, shake their hands and – a very African protocol – sign their visitors' book.

Equally impressive was the middle-aged ex-head teacher from Birmingham who tore around rural Uganda on a motor-bike working for women's rights and helping Aids victims. She was a formidable woman, and even her frequent bouts of malaria were unable to poleaxe her.

The mantra I heard from so many volunteers in Uganda was 'We came to teach but we learned so much' and as Dick Rowe and I boarded the flight home at Entebbe Airport he asked if I would like to return again one day. 'I'd love to. Maybe I'll take up that offer at Nkozi,' I told him. He laughed, but I think both of us knew I was not joking.

A few months later the fantasy became reality. Dick informed me that Nkozi College had made a formal request for me to do some teaching there and I turned my thoughts to what lessons this very un-trained teacher could impart. In the meantime, I launched another VSO-related project.

I approached the body with the idea of producing a fund-raising album featuring musicians from many of the forty-eight countries in which it operated. Peter Gabriel and his Womad record label and another fine label Ace were also willing to help, and with the VSO's enthusiastic support, I began to tackle the logistics of the idea.

We agreed that I would travel to Uganda, Belize and the Caribbean, visit volunteers and their projects and while there enquire about local musicians. If I liked what they were doing, I would try to find cheap local studios and record them out there.

It sounded an impossible project but came together remarkably adroitly. On the Caribbean island of St Lucia I found a man called Boo Hinkson singing calypso in a hotel and went to his home studio to record a track called 'Calypso Classic'. I learned where he got his nickname from the day that a cat crossed our path and poor scared Boo literally jumped into my arms.

Back in Uganda the country's biggest group, Afrigo Band, kindly came to record for me in a Kampala studio called Sunrise normally used for Christian programmes. Traditional musicians Dr Semke and Abolugana Kagalana were so keen to be involved that they turned up a day early and had to sleep in the studio overnight.

It is easy to become cynical in the music business but seeing the joy on these musicians' faces as they heard their songs recorded and played back to them for the first time was wonderful. It made me think, in a strange way, of the first time I had heard myself singing 'And the Tears Came Tumbling Down' on a seven-inch single on my parents' gramophone in Essex, almost thirty years earlier.

Although I was loath to intrude on the record myself, I figured it was worth it if it marginally increased its commercial appeal, so back in England I added a track called 'Africa – You Shine' with my keyboardist Ian Wherry, African guitarist Abdul Tee-Jay and some brilliant South African female singers, Shikisha. I called the finished album *Under Different Skies* and released it in 1991. Like all world music albums, it was hampered by the lack of radio and media outlets for such music in Britain, but it achieved its aim of raising some much-needed funds both for the impoverished musicians and for the VSO.

While I had been making the record the wheels had been set in motion for my return to Nkozi College and now I had decided what I would teach there. I resolved to direct the student teachers in a production of *Godspell*. I knew resources were tight, but even in my West End performances as Jesus the crucifixion props had been no more than a beer crate and two red ribbons.

Before flying out I got hold of a few little magic tricks for Jesus to perform and some T-shirts, and I also knew I would need a pianist. My keyboardist Ian Wherry couldn't make it but a very talented musician called Helen Ireland agreed to come and spend two months in rural Uganda.

I will never forget our arrival at the college, on a warm night with a huge moon and students sitting talking, laughing and playing drums outside. Helen and I were given a tin shack to share and a Ugandan teacher named Celestine was to be our assistant.

Celestine showed Helen and I to our new two-bedroom home and lit a candle: as usual, the electricity was not working. I was just drifting off to sleep when I heard a scream from

Helen's room. Freeing myself from my mosquito net, I jumped from my bed only to feel the floor moving beneath my feet.

Scrabbling to light a candle, I discovered that the entire floor of my room was a shifting carpet of cockroaches. Tiptoeing to Helen's room, I found she had the same unwanted guests. She was not keen, but it is surprising what you can get used to, and over the coming weeks we managed to co-exist warily with our intrusive insects.

The next morning we awoke to a definitively African scene. The families in the mud huts dotted around us were stirring and making breakfast over open fires. There was the crisp smell of burning logs and the sounds of monkeys, goats and exotic birds. Celestine had kindly brought us a can of water from the well so we washed and prepared to meet our new students.

In the makeshift theatre that I had seen on my first Nkozi trip, thirty-six trainee teachers greeted us by singing an uplifting, sonorous welcome song. They were fifty-fifty male and female, with an average age of about twenty-three. I explained that we were to rehearse and perform a musical and they appeared delighted, even though I am not entirely sure they had even heard of the genre before.

Celestine had managed to borrow a piano from a local church so with Helen at the keys we set about the casting process. I had decided to choose ten clowns, including Jesus, and use the other twenty-six cast members as a powerful singing Greek chorus.

Everybody wanted to play Jesus, girls included, but I settled on a boy called David. Both he and Judas seemed to have a lot of potential, and after a long day Helen and I returned to our grub-laden hut far more confident and less apprehensive about the task ahead.

Our domestic life soon settled down into a routine of me doing the cooking, Helen washing the dishes and my tinny transistor radio crackling out the BBC World Service. On one of the few nights that the electricity worked, I left our outside light on for the convenience of the family in the nearest hut. Woken by laughter at three in the morning, I looked through the window to see our neighbours gathered around this outside light, feasting on the flying ants that had been attracted to it. Apparently they were a good source of protein and quite the local delicacy.

During the days, Helen worked tirelessly to teach our willing cast the songs from *Godspell* as I tutored the principal cast members. It was a very emotional process for me, both for the flood of memories of my days in Chalk Farm that it brought back and because the African actors were growing in confidence and into their roles. I certainly tried to be a more proactive director than John-Michael Tebelak.

It soon became clear to me that these Ugandans were natural storytellers and performers. If anything, my role was to try to prevent them from over-acting wildly and turning every scene into an over-the-top melodrama.

Some ladies from the village helped with the costumes and a local carpenter constructed the rudimentary set of planks and sawhorses. The nearby shop gave us a plastic bottle crate for the crucifixion. Occasionally I would take a break to organise other workshops or coach football sessions with some footballs I had persuaded West Ham kindly to donate to the trip.

The cast's sense of camaraderie reminded me of the us-against-the-world attitude we had nurtured in the Roundhouse all those years ago, and by the time of the first show we were ready. The audience was made up of other students, locals, doctors and nuns from the local hospital, and VSO volunteers from other Kampala projects.

We were to play three nights at the college theatre and they were a triumph. I was so proud of my cast on the opening night and the audience were moved to tears by the crucifixion scene just as they had been in London. Absolute troupers, the actors even survived the sticky moment when a goat decided to join them on stage and butted and baa-ed its way through the Greek chorus.

We had got a touring itinerary, of sorts, with a date lined up at another local college and then the big time: the National Theatre in Kampala. I had booked a truck to transport the cast and set to the next venue, but when it had not arrived two hours after it was due, I stopped putting it down to usual lackadaisical African time-keeping and started getting worried.

Celestine vanished to the local hospital to make a phone call and returned to confirm that the truck had broken down and would not be making an appearance today. 'Does anybody else have a truck?' I asked him. 'Not that I know,' he replied. I left the cast happily playing football and headed into Kampala to try to find a solution.

Passing a construction site, I spotted some builders emptying sand from an extremely beaten-up truck. 'I want to borrow your truck,' I told them, and while their initial reaction appeared to be that I must be mental, some cold hard cash helped to change their minds and I headed back to Nkozi with my prize.

The *Godspell* cast cheered as I chugged on to campus in a cloud of black smoke and we loaded up the piano, set and actors and set off for the outskirts of Kampala. The journey was quite something. With somebody else taking over driving duties, I transferred to the piano stool on the back of the open truck and resolved to teach the students Ben E King's 'Stand By Me' en route. With the rich voices of thirty-six Africans intoning a tribal-sounding version of this Tamla Motown classic as a long-haired white guy bashed at the keys, we were certainly a sight to stop the traffic.

The show was at a rival college to Nkozi, which meant that the cast were both nervous and determined to put on a great performance. This was easier said than done as two or three of them had got malaria, and one female clown was too ill to perform and was replaced by her understudy.

Adversity can be a great motivating force and to my delight the cast ratcheted their performance up another notch with both Jesus and Judas on spellbinding form. The audience transformed from too-cool-for-school to transfixed and then tearful, and as the company bedded down in a borrowed dormitory that night, there was much excited talk about hitting the big time with the National Theatre show the following night.

Yet this show looked to be ill-starred when we arrived at the theatre to be told that the stage manager was away for the day at a funeral. This being Africa, he had no assistant and the theatre managers had not thought to provide anybody else to help us. We would have to work the lights, the sound system and just about everything else ourselves.

The technical rehearsal was understandably slow-going as Helen, Celestine and I pushed buttons and twiddled knobs on the National Theatre's fairly rudimentary production console. I found a big ladder and vanished up to the ceiling to set the lights. The students were restless but patiently did what had to be done before show time.

In the dressing room, I gave them a football-manager-style pep talk, pointing out that it was by far the biggest show to date and they had to rise to the occasion. However, I was only too aware that this also applied to me as I tried to keep the technical aspects of the performance afloat.

I even had to ring the bar bell to summon the audience into the auditorium, at which point it became clear they were of a very different calibre to the previous shows. Here were Kampala's glitterati, together with senior representatives of VSO, consulates and various other aid organisations.

I had kept the lighting low as John the Baptist opened the show by entering through the auditorium to baptise Jesus so that when the clowns burst into 'Prepare Ye the Way of the Lord' there would be an explosion of light and colour. It worked, and from there the audience were with us all the way.

It was hard for me to evaluate individual performances as I hunched over the unfamiliar lights and sound switches but the cacophony of clapping at the curtain call told its own story. The British Consulate invited us to a post-show reception in their honour and as my jubilant cast nibbled canapés in the palatial grounds, I knew it was an experience they would never forget. That went for me as well.

The National Theatre were so taken with our *Godspell* that they asked us to play for a week and after the stage manager returned I was able to sit back and enjoy the subsequent performances. It was also nice for Helen and I to get out of Cockroach City and have a week in the VSO compound in Kampala that boasted twentieth-century luxuries such as electricity and running water.

This last week was great fun but contained yet another lesson that I need to do something about my pesky need for speed. Driving a jeep with a VSO volunteer in the passenger seat, my accelerator foot grew itchy as we crawled along behind a very slow-moving Ugandan Army jeep full of soldiers. I pulled out to overtake them, at which point the soldiers all levelled their guns at me and the volunteer quickly grabbed the steering wheel and diverted us down a dirt road. He then patiently explained the Ugandan Highway Code: if you overtake a military vehicle, they will shoot you.

Helen and I had the most emotional departure imaginable from Uganda. We travelled back to Nkozi to say goodbye to all of our friends, and to the cockroaches, then were driven to the airport. As we waited to board the plane at Entebbe, Helen pointed out of the window and simply said, 'Look!'

Our students were ranging the airport's perimeter fence, holding signs declaring 'COME BACK SOON' and 'WE LOVE YOU' and waving furiously. They had walked more than twenty miles to do this and it made me feel both awed and humbled.

Twenty years on, I still receive occasional letters from the Nkozi class of '92. Most of them have now become teachers, although a couple of the girls became nuns. I will also never forget the biggest compliment of all, paid to me by the boy who played Judas: 'You are a white man with an African soul.'

I made numerous other trips with the VSO including a jaunt to Grenada in the Caribbean, which has a high incidence of mental illness, and also to Malawi, where I managed to contract Tick Typhus fever and on my return spent a few days in a state of mild delirium in the Hospital for Tropical Diseases in King's Cross. I also played a fund-raising concert at the Barbican that was attended by the Duke of Edinburgh, who took a definite shine to Verity backstage and had a long chat with her.

Despite my initial reservations, I found my work with the VSO so fulfilling that I even extended my tenure as ambassador to three years, only reluctantly handing over the baton in 1993 to Olympic gold medal javelin-thrower Fatima Whitbread. It had been absolutely one of the most rewarding adventures of my entire life.

21

IT'S ALWAYS
ABOUT THE FAMILY

Outside of the VSO, as the nineties dawned I chose my work projects carefully and selectively. With Verity, in particular, and Danny having been born at the height of the hysteria of Essex Mania, there had inevitably been times when I had to be away from home for longer than I wanted as they were growing up. I had missed a handful of crucial formative moments in their childhood developments and I was not going to make the same mistake again.

So outside of my trips to Africa, I made sure that my work schedule always left me plenty of time to zoom back across the Atlantic and hang out with Carlotta, Kit and Bill in Connecticut, as well as spend quality time with Verity and Dan in London. It was a busy period but a happy one.

One film offer appealed immediately to my subversive, slightly twisted sense of humour. A Japanese film company contacted us asking me to play an evil duke, Don Pedro, in a ninja movie called *Shogun Mayeda*. By now a teenage martial arts fan, Dan was hugely impressed as its star, Sho Kosugi, was a legend in that field.

Sho apparently wanted me because he had enjoyed my Che in *Evita* so I flew to Hollywood to meet him. The script seemed lively, my scenes would be shot in Yugoslavia and I fancied being a bad guy for a change, so I agreed to do it.

Yugoslavia was about to be no more, of course, and when I flew out to Belgrade in 1992 you could sense the ethnic tensions and general unrest that were soon to lead to civil war. Even within the film unit there was a degree of suspicion and contempt between workers from different areas of the Balkans.

We filmed in Dubrovnik, Belgrade and Montenegro, which were all beautiful, although some of the local customs were not to my liking. In Montenegro, near to the border with Albania, I saw a gypsy with a dancing bear, although the bear's gyrations were clearly mainly to try to alleviate the pain of being led around via a hook that its handler had viciously twisted into its lip.

As well as being its star ninja, Sho was also one of the film's producers, and *Shogun Mayeda* was a proper martial-arts action movie and very physical to shoot. Its team of Japanese fight co-ordinators spoke absolutely no English and so as they taught me the fight sequences, we had no choice but to develop a whole new language to describe the moves.

This bizarre argot sounded as if it belonged between the pages of a comic book as it mostly consisted of childish phrases such as 'Ka-Boom!' or 'Whoosh!' Sometimes during filming, I had to stop a scene to politely enquire of my tutors whether they required a 'Ka-Boom!' or a 'Whoosh!'

The movie's director was very old and inanimate and in truth didn't entirely seem to know what he was doing, and the whole project's surreal air was heightened by the fact that the cast also included Christopher Lee, the venerable and veteran actor best known for playing Dracula in a stream of old black-and-white Hammer Horror films.

Christopher Lee was charm personified and quite possibly saved my sight after a fairly dreadful mishap on the set. The scene we were shooting required Don Pedro and his gang of evil Spanish cohorts to fire muskets at our Japanese foes, and I guess I should have taken heed when the towering Serbian special effects guy materialised on set covered in numerous burns and bandages.

We shot our guns at the enemy and the director raised himself from his torpor to request another take. The battered-looking FX man refilled my musket but was clearly a little generous with the proportions because when the order to fire came, my gun went off like a cannon, blowing back and shooting gunpowder and flint into my eye.

The pain was excruciating but being both a trouper and a bloke, I declared that I was OK and indicated I would carry on filming. The film crew seemed perfectly satisfied with this, but Christopher Lee stepped in and insisted that I should go to hospital. With a look of inconvenience, the director reluctantly agreed and packed me off with an interpreter.

The first hospital we visited was closed for a holiday, which seemed unorthodox, but at the second one a white-coated doctor examined me pretty quickly. He clearly didn't like what he found because the interpreter informed me: 'The doctor says he must operate immediately.'

The doc led me to a basic operating room with a bed and various bits of surgical equipment littered around, and then vanished. As I sat on the bed, a middle-aged nurse appeared and washed some of the gear in a sink, which would have been very hygienic and laudable were it not for the fag hanging off her bottom lip.

So I was in a second-choice hospital in a close-on third world country, a nurse was smoking in the surgical room and a doctor who didn't speak my language was about to operate on my badly burned eye. What could possibly go wrong?

If I thought things couldn't get any worse, I soon learned that I was mistaken, as the doctor returned and it became evident that he was to perform the operation without anything as tiresome as an anaesthetic. Grasping a giant scalpel that looked to me more like a broadsword, he began to scrape and dig about in my eye.

It hurt, a lot, but after a few minutes of apparently productive excavation, the doctor nodded with satisfaction and smiled, at which point the nurse put out her fag to administer the stitches with what looked like the kind of rope you would use to tie up a fishing boat. I thanked them, but as I drove back to my hotel, my eye ached like crazy.

The next morning it was just as sore, not to mention extremely red and swollen, and filming was clearly out of the question for me for a few days. The director suggested that I took a week off and went home to have it checked out so the next morning I boarded a plane to London.

As I have learned, bad news travels fast in media circles and I was met at Heathrow by scores of Fleet Street's finest jostling to get pictures of the wounded pop star. Even some TV news cameras were there, which surprised me as I had no idea how they had gotten wind of my mishap.

The following morning I travelled to Harley Street to see (well, as well as I could) a bow-tied eminent eye specialist named Eric Arnott who had done a lot of work with cataract sufferers in the developing world. I was braced for bad news, but Eric surprised me: 'Whoever did this did a brilliant job,' he said. 'I guarantee when the stitches are out, the scar will be almost invisible.'

Eric explained that the Yugoslav doctor had done the right thing to operate immediately as gunpowder is highly corrosive and would have eaten my eye away in a matter of hours, leaving me blind on that side. I gratefully decided that on my return to Belgrade I would take the doctor a bottle of whisky to thank him – and, of course, a packet of fags for the nurse.

After a week or so I was once again 'Ka-boom!'-ing and 'Whoosh!'-ing on the *Shogun Mayeda* set. As a baddie, Don Pedro was inevitably to meet a sticky end, and eventually the time came to film the climax that involved Sho slicing me in two with a Samurai sword in a fight to the death in fast-moving rapids.

I clearly had some kind of death wish making that film because I decided to do the stunt myself. Wearing a suit of armour, I had to clunk around in a rapidly flowing river, bouncing off rocks as I battled Sho, before being swept away. Thankfully, the special effect splitting me in half would be added later.

The Japanese fight trainers had slung ropes over the riverbanks for me to grab on to and after Sho had finally vanquished me in a flurry of ka-booms and whooshes, I fell backwards like a discarded tin can. The powerful rapids carried me downstream, crashing off the rocks, and I missed a lot of the strategically placed ropes before finally grasping the very last one.

Wet and probably rusting, I was hauled in to land with my heart pounding to be greeted by a round of applause from the smiling Japanese. I am led to believe – as you would hope – that *Shogun Mayeda* was very big in Japan.

Nearer to home, Derek and Mel were normally besieged before each Christmas with requests for me to appear in pantomimes but we had always turned them down. Even two decades on, the memories of lizard-tongued brown bears and Dandini were still painful, and more importantly the vast majority of the scripts that we got sent were cheesy rubbish.

Nevertheless, I have no snobbery towards the art form and I think pantos are very important. Normally they are a child's first initiation into theatre and if the production is not only bright and colourful but also has depth and intelligence, who is to say they won't be hooked and return in later years to see Shakespeare or Chekhov?

Driven by these noble ideals, I decided to write my own panto and to base it around *Robinson Crusoe*. I dutifully read the classic Daniel Defoe novel but have to confess that I found it rather heavy-going and didn't draw too deeply upon it.

It seemed highly ironic to me that after *Mutiny!* I was willingly undertaking another project based around boats and sailing. A psychiatrist may even detect a degree of masochism there, because boats and I have never got on.

Over the years I have suffered a few red-faced sailing-related moments, not least a holiday in Florida when a company let me take out a turbo-charged powerboat, figuring it would be safe as I was a trained helicopter pilot. With Verity and Dan on board, I immediately went the wrong way around a buoy and smashed the propeller on some rocks. We had to call out the US Coastguard to rescue us.

Verity and Dan were also with me on a boat on the Thames when I decided to circumvent the tiresome lock system by sailing around them. It took an astonished fisherman to warn me to turn back before I reached a concrete weir that we would have had no chance of avoiding.

Despite this, I seem destined to tackle nautical subjects and so began work on *The Adventures of Robinson Crusoe*. Together with friend and writer David Joss Buckley and a great director, Robin Midgley, we took fairly large liberties with Defoe's now outdated plot and came up with a storyline full of magic, hexes and that staple panto theme, the battle of good versus evil.

We were also mindful to ensure that Robinson Crusoe's friend and sidekick, Man Friday, was treated in an enlightened and respectful manner. Pantos did not use to be the most PC of productions, and I still cringe at the memory of one *Crusoe* I saw where Man Friday did nothing except jump up and down in a monkey suit.

I approached the show as I would any musical, writing original songs for it and also recycling some of the score from *Mutiny!* We eschewed women dressed as men but had a tremendous pantomime dame, and Robin cast Verity, who was by now a graduate of the Guildhall School of Music and Drama, as my daughter.

We did a run of *The Adventures of Robinson Crusoe* at the Alhambra Theatre in Bradford and to my surprise and delight it broke their box-office records. It was such a special experience for me to act with Verity, especially as it was so obvious from her voice and presence that her casting was down to talent, not nepotism.

At subsequent Christmases, we transferred *Crusoe* to Liverpool, Bournemouth, Southampton, Edinburgh and Cardiff and it was always a great experience. Robin always directed and the main cast members of Micky O'Donoughue, John Labanowski and Bobby Bennett remained largely unchanged, which gave the company a real family feel.

Musically, I have always sweated over my albums, writing long and hard into the wee small hours of the night as I strive to touch that ghost and perfect the orchestration and arrangements. It therefore made a pleasant change in 1993 when I went into the studio with Mike Batt and the Royal Philharmonic Orchestra to record an album of cover versions.

Cover Shot saw me re-interpret songs I had loved over the years by a host of artists, including the Kinks' 'Waterloo Sunset', Cat Stevens' 'The First Cut Is the Deepest', America's 'A Horse With No Name', the Lovin' Spoonful's 'Summer in the City' and a new take on the Rolling Stones' 'Paint It Black' that I was particularly pleased with.

Cover Shot was primarily a labour of love and I had no idea at all what people would make of it, but it must have touched a nerve because it peaked in the album chart at number three – my first Top Ten album in eighteen years.

Meanwhile, the constant flights to Connecticut and back were draining and time-consuming and so I was delighted when Carlotta, Kit and Bill moved over to live with me. Time had flown and the twins were ready to go to school, and we decided to start their education in England. I just loved having the family together again and we moved to St John's Wood, north London.

My TV sitcoms, ninja movies, pantomimes and covers albums of recent years had not necessarily all been to Derek's taste but he could not have been more elated by the next work offer that came my way in 1993. Sir Peter Hall, the Royal Shakespeare Company founder and former director of the National Theatre, asked me to appear in Oliver Goldsmith's comedy of manners *She Stoops to Conquer*.

I almost felt like I owed it to Derek to do it but in truth I was very wary. While I was sure the experience of working with Sir Peter would be invaluable, I had never attempted any of the classics before, the quality of the cast was daunting, and all in all it seemed a little too far out of my comfort zone, even for me.

Even so, I agreed to take on the part of the scheming Tony Lumpkin and rehearsals began in mid-summer '93. The august Sir Donald Sinden played Mr Hardcastle, my stepfather, while national treasure Miriam Margoyles was my mother. Virtually the whole of the rest of the cast were classically trained actors. No pressure, then.

Even after all those years treading the boards, the world of high theatre was new to me and I found the rehearsals nerve-wracking. It was all very thespian and I didn't really care for the play, which seemed to be two hours of gobbledegook. The days dragged, with the high point being the ride home through the warm summer evenings on my Triumph Bonneville.

Donald, Miriam and the rest of the cast were tremendous and very supportive but I still felt like an outsider and Sir Peter's directing style didn't help. He was the first director that I had ever worked with who spent rehearsals with his nose in the text and hardly watched the performances in front of him. It could be frustrating, but I just told myself, 'Look, this is Sir Peter Hall! He knows exactly what he is doing.'

She Stoops to Conquer opened with a week in Leatherhead in Surrey and then embarked on a tour of Britain. The audiences and reviews were good wherever we went, and Sir Donald and Miriam had an excellent understanding and rapport that won them a lot of laughs.

The lovely Miriam is larger-than-life in more ways than one and we had a bit of a mishap at the Festival Theatre in Chichester. One scene required me to hoist her over my shoulder and exit stage left, but I took a tumble and dropped her roughly on to a flight of stairs. Miriam was unhurt, but I tore the ligaments in my ankle.

The accident had happened just before the play transferred to its West End run at the Queen's Theatre, which meant I would have to appear with a walking stick. We also hit a few problems as Sir Peter decided to revamp the production, strip away some of the niceties we had developed in the provinces, and get back to his beloved text in a more purist fashion.

Sir Peter also wanted to rethink my character in a way that I didn't really agree with. He decided to play Tony Lumpkin as more of a country bumpkin, with a lot more 'Ooh aah!' going on, which for me turned my role from two hours of talking gobbledegook into two hours of talking gobbledegook in a funny accent. There was even talk for a while of me wearing a ginger wig and a fat suit. I thankfully persuaded him out of that one but I didn't see the need for all the changes. Was it just panic, and fear of the London critics?

To cap it all, when the London opening night rolled around I got food poisoning. The stage crew thoughtfully positioned buckets at strategic points in the wings but I could hardly get through my performance and in retrospect I certainly shouldn't have gone on. It was an awful night, the reviews were poor and mine were particularly dreadful: again, it seemed, I was the pop star who was refusing to stay in his box, and getting ideas above his station.

The play limped into the New Year, quite literally in my case. Things were better at home, where Carlotta, Kit and Bill were happy in London. My parents were still out in the wilds of deepest Essex, and we began looking at finding them a place closer to us so they could see more of their grandkids. That was before I received a phone call from a hospital in Essex in my dressing room during the matinee of *She Stoops to Conquer* on Wednesday 24 January 1994.

My dad had died.

The world stopped. He had done what? How? Why? I asked to speak to my mum but as she took the phone she was clearly still in a state of shock. She told me that my dad had decided to have a short nap after his lunch. When she went to wake him, he had gone. A heart attack, apparently. It was that simple.

My mind was racing. What should I do? Dash from the theatre to the hospital? Finish the matinee? I tried to think what Dad would have wanted me to do. Surely he would have said that the show must go on? After all, he had never given up on anything in his entire life.

Yes, that was what he would want. I would finish the matinee and play the evening performance. 'I'm going to carry on and do the shows and I'll be round straight after,' I told Mum. 'OK,' she said. I don't think she knew what was going on.

I put the phone down and stared at myself in the dressing-room mirror. Had that call really happened? I turned up the tannoy linking the room to the stage and heard Sir Donald Sinden booming his lines. It was nearly my cue. In a daze, I watched myself walk to the stage and finish the performance.

I didn't tell the rest of the cast because I didn't want sympathy. 'Oh, I'm so sorry…' I couldn't bear that. I was sorry enough. I told the company manager after the matinee and he said I should go home, but I told him I would do the evening performance.

Between the shows I walked through the streets of Soho. I am not sure what I did but I seem to remember buying a coffee and being asked for an autograph and signing it like a man who was not really there. I don't think that I was.

I was back at the Queen's Theatre by the 'half', which is theatre slang for thirty-five minutes before the curtain goes up. As the evening show neared, I felt a power, an energy and a brightness inside of me. I can't begin to explain what happened and I am not going to: I just knew that it was the strongest performance I had ever given. I felt my dad connecting with me. He was telling me I had done the right thing.

After the show I changed quickly and drove to Essex. Heading through the dark streets and country lanes, I was suffused with sadness, but I knew I had to focus on my mum. She had lost the one man in her life: her lover and companion for more than fifty years.

When she opened the door, I hugged her. She looked so girlish and so lost. Dad had died aged seventy-five, which I guess was quite an achievement when his TB had so nearly taken him at twenty-eight. We sat up until the early hours, talking and sharing memories of him. We cried a lot; we laughed a lot, too.

I couldn't bear to leave Mum on her own in the house full of memories of Dad, and the next morning I suggested she pack a bag and come to stay with us for a while. She moved in with us at our new place in Long Ditton, Surrey and I'm glad to say she never moved out again. We behaved like a proper family should.

Few women would welcome the mother-in-law coming to live with them but Carlotta could not have been kinder and it was good for Kit and Bill to have Mum with us. They had reached a lively age, were often fighting, and would ignore me trying to calm them down. When their granny said 'Oi!' they knew she meant business.

All of my dad's surviving family and friends came to his funeral in the East End. I gave an address, but I honestly cannot to this day remember a word that I said. A choir of children from my primary school, Star Lane, sang a hymn as his coffin was carried through the church, and he was laid to rest in the East London Cemetery. I was proud that the day was as dignified as my dad had always been.

22

WAS THAT MY LIFE?

Losing your parents may be one of those rites of passage in life that everybody has to go through but it is not easy. The wounds heal very slowly. The hardest part is the eerie moments when you forget they have gone and suddenly remember the awful truth with a jolt, like aftershocks of the initial seismic shift. I had a lot of those in the months after my dad's death.

Living with me and Carlotta, Mum slowly and bravely began to rebuild her life. She was only sixty-nine but like many of her generation there was no question of her ever meeting anybody else, or even trying to: that was it, for her. But I think being around Bill and Kit's youthful energy certainly helped her to recover.

For my part, I was still labouring through *She Stoops to Conquer* at the Queen's and had a very bizarre experience a few days after my dad's funeral. Pulling into the nearby Soho Square to look for a parking place, I became aware of a spooky silence then saw two men crawling on the pavement in suits and ties.

From nowhere, a man jumped in front of my car, pointed a gun at me and ordered me to get out. I later learned that he had snatched somebody's bag and when the police had cornered him in Soho Square, he had produced a gun. I had blundered into the middle of a standoff.

I was in no mood to surrender my car to him and so pointed it at him and hit the accelerator. I was trying to move him out of the way, not knock him down him, but the wing clipped him on the leg. As I pulled away he fired a shot at the car, and then another. I swerved quickly down a side-road and as I swung around and returned near to the theatre to try to park, I saw my assailant again. This time he was running, with a noticeable limp.

At the interval of that evening's performance I had to go to the stage door to talk to two plain-clothes policemen. I told them all that I knew and played the incident down to the hordes of journalists that were also crowding the stage door, although this didn't stop a rash of POP STAR'S HIJACK DRAMA headlines the next day. The police arrested and charged the gunman a few days later.

She Stoops to Conquer ended its run shortly afterwards and I was not sorry to see it go. It had not been the happiest of times and the drudgery of doing one show for so long made me loath to take on any more long theatre runs. I decided that, for now at least, a few weeks of *The Adventures of Robinson Crusoe* each Christmas would do me fine.

This didn't mean I wasn't still open to new work avenues and experiences, and in the mid-nineties Mel commissioned me to write the music for a Russian ice ballet company production of *Beauty and the Beast* that he was staging at the Royal Albert Hall. The writer, David Wood, had supplied a storyline that I would flesh out with songs and a score.

This venture hadn't got off to the most auspicious start as its launch press conference and photo-shoot had coincided with my spell in the Hospital for Tropical Diseases recovering from the Tick Typhus fever that I had picked up in Malawi. Nevertheless, I had been determined not to let Mel down and had defied doctors' orders to lurch groggily into the limo that turned up at the hospital to pick me up.

The launch was at an ice rink in central London, and I have a vague memory of smiling wanly for photographers and even managing to complete a few circuits of the rink with some Amazonian Russian skaters before the limo returned me to my feverish sickbed. Maybe those doctors had had a point.

The ballet was finally staged in 1995 and Ian Wherry helped me to produce and arrange the soundtrack. This involved lengthy conversations with artistic director and choreographer Tatiana Tarasova, an animated and autocratic Russian who possibly felt a pop musician was a little beneath her.

Tatiana's English was exactly as fluent as our Russian, which meant that our meetings were conducted via a somewhat mousy, browbeaten female interpreter. 'What kind of music would Tatiana like for this scene?' I would ask the interpreter, and after much shouting and gesticulating from Ms Tarasova, an answer would come back: 'She say she want monkey-up-a-rope music.'

My suggestion of appointing a director to give some shape and organisation to the production was overruled, and composing the music was a fraught process as the dance scenes constantly lengthened and shortened at Tatiana's whim. Nevertheless I was proud of the score, which I think features some of my strongest ever songs, and with Olympic gold-medal skaters whizzing around the ice, *Beauty and the Beast* was a gorgeous spectacle.

The night of the Albert Hall grand charity gala opening came round far too quickly, and with our monkey-up-a-rope music still in a state of flux, Ian and I got virtually no sleep in the week leading up to it. On the big night my fatigue battled with nerves, not least because the troublesome portable ice rink had lately developed a habit of melting in rehearsals, nearly submerging the skaters.

Thankfully, the ice remained frozen, the skaters were poetry in motion and the score seemed to go down well. A Russian TV crew even compared it to Tchaikovsky. The reception at the end was tremendous and Tatiana and I were ushered out on a red carpet on the rink to take a bow, which is apparently the normal etiquette in ballet circles.

The deafening applause ran its course and then for no obvious reason rose in intensity again, augmented with whooped cheers, which baffled me. I glanced behind me and was perturbed to see TV host Michael Aspel stepping gingerly over the ice towards me carrying a big red book.

I knew what he was going to say before he said it: 'David Essex – *This Is Your Life*.'

I had always told Derek and Mel that I did not want to be the subject of this programme, in the unlikely event that I was ever asked, but my managers had clearly overruled me and now there was nothing I could do about it. The die was cast. Feeling mildly delirious from sleep deprivation, I was whisked to a waiting car and on to BBC Television Centre, where I was locked in a dressing room.

As midnight passed and I sat secluded in this bare cell, the thought occurred that it was not unlike being taken prisoner. My wait ended after a couple of hours when a make-up lady arrived to hide the lines and bags under my eyes and I was led to the studio.

As I walked into the brightly lit room, the experience was akin to my whole life flashing before my eyes in one shifting mosaic. My family and friends were arranged all around the studio, including some people I had not seen for years. I might have always been sceptical about this programme but clearly this was going to be quite a night.

The first people on were my mum, Verity, Dan and Carlotta, which was how it should be. My old West Ham youth team pal Frank Lampard was one of the next guests up. He recalled our kickabouts under Avondale Court and said that he reckoned I could have made it as a professional footballer had rock 'n' roll not come along. I was far from convinced but it was a lovely compliment.

Michael Aspel slickly led the studio audience through my life and career, with Sir David Puttnam appearing on video to reminisce about *That'll Be the Day* and *Stardust*. I got a goodly selection of knights of the realm, with Sir Andrew Lloyd Webber praising my performance in *Evita*. Even good old Sir Peter Hall put in an appearance.

Yet the night's highlight by far was a surprise piece of film footage. Following in their father's footsteps, Kit and Bill had recently joined the West Ham academy, and the *This Is Your Life* producers had filmed them nutmegging Rio Ferdinand and skinning Frank Lampard Junior before Billy curled the ball around goalie Luděk Mikloško and into the top corner of the net. It was so cool, and I had the world's broadest beam at the end of the show when Kit and Bill appeared in the studio on the shoulders of World Cup-winning former Hammer Geoff Hurst.

There was one major omission from the show. Derek Bowman, the mentor who had shown such faith in me right from the days when I was the wet-behind-the-ears drummer in an East End pub band called the Everons, and who had opened my eyes to the infinite possibilities of show business, was not there.

Derek had been spasmodically ill for quite some time, suffering from high blood pressure and a range of other ailments, and was in hospital, where his dignity counselled against sending *This Is Your Life* a video message from his sickbed. He was not to leave that bed. On 1 June 1995, he died.

Derek and I were alone in his hospital room in the early hours as he passed away. As he left me, I softly sang the words of a song I had written for him many years previously called 'Friends':

Friends, you and I we are friends,
Friends right up to the end
We are friends, friend
Friends, right through the thick and thin
If we are out or in
We are friends, friend
And every road you walk along

I'll be by your side
Every dream you dream
I'll try to materialise the vision in your eyes
A dream, you and I had a dream
But so many dreams we've seen
We've seen fade, fade
But there's someone, he really cares
Someone that's been so true
I love you, friend

I thought of the day he had told me in the Arts Theatre Club in Soho that he thought I could be a solo star, and of the evening he turned up to meet my parents, a contract under his arm. He had given me all he had and my career would not have happened without him. Quite literally, I owed him everything.

I spoke at Derek's burial a few days later and it reminded me again what a selfless man he had been. Having dedicated his life to his mother, his sister and me, there were no descendants, no children or grandchildren gathered in the church; just a snatch of distant relatives such as his cousin, the actor Ron Moody.

It was a hugely upsetting experience and I couldn't get through my eulogy without breaking down. I knew one thing: there had been too many deaths of dearly loved ones around here lately.

23

OLD BIG 'EAD TAKES A REST

I don't know if it was partly an unconscious reaction to my mentor and guiding light Derek passing away, but in the mid-nineties I began for the first time to think about the possibility of retirement, or at least semi-retirement. Certainly I think that losing both my dad and Derek in such a relatively short space of time made me more aware of my own mortality.

For a while it seemed to me that I had done most of the things I had wanted to: films, theatre, albums, huge concert tours. It felt like time to take a break and I was having such a brilliant time hanging out with Carlotta, Bill and Kit, watching my boys play football and being part of their lives 24/7, that I pulled back a bit from the frenzy of showbiz.

In any case, when it came to music it seemed like the decision had been made for me. Ever since the turn of the nineties, radio stations had ignored any recording I had made. This was crystal clear when *Cover Shot* hit number three and I listened to Radio One's album chart rundown. When he reached the top of the chart, the DJ acknowledged my album but never played a track.

I guess Radio One have their job to do and they are all about youth and the shock of the new, which means my generation of artists don't get played. Status Quo and Cliff Richard have made a big fuss about being ignored by Radio One and I see their point but it's not something I have a chip on my shoulder about. It is just the way things are.

Yet it is frustrating as an artist to make records year-in, year-out that nobody hears and it's dispiriting when a well-meaning member of the public asks me 'Have you stopped making music?' After all, the fact that my tours sell out means that people must still be interested. It's a shame, but not worth getting bitter about.

So in the mid-nineties I continued to plug away making albums like *Living in England* and *Missing You* and touring, as well as going on the odd adventure. In 1996 I returned to Africa under the auspices of Comic Relief on a venture that was awarded the less than gracious title of Balls to Africa.

Because of my experience of Africa, I was made the captain of a football team of celebrities that included Frank Skinner, David Baddiel, Nick Hancock, Angus Deayton, Ainsley Harriott, Karl Howman and John Leslie. Our coach was ex-Arsenal manager Terry Neill, whose sole instruction to us was, 'If you see someone in the same coloured shirt, pass to them.' I guess it's all you could expect from a Gooner.

Terry turned up in a full Lawrence of Arabia outfit one night in Burkina Faso when a sandstorm blew up. We were also taken to meet some village elders, who ordered a dance ceremony in our honour. The native dancers' beaded fringes went horizontal as they shimmied before us, leading the reliably irreverent Frank Skinner to turn to me and whisper: 'Ooh, it's a car wash!' It was impossible not to laugh, even in a country where rainfall is a rare and precious commodity.

The football highlight of our trip was a game against the Ghana women's national team, which we managed to shade 4–3. I was reasonably pleased with my performance, despite being woman-marked by a combative opponent not unlike a female take on Alvin Martin.

Back home on the domestic front, Bill and Kit were now settled in school in England and Carlotta and I decided to get married. This entailed Maureen and I finally getting divorced first: as we had been separated for seventeen years by now, it was probably about time. Maureen was also happily settled with her current partner, Jeremy, who has always been great with Verity and Dan.

A natural free spirit, Carlotta was fairly lukewarm about getting married, and in truth so was I. Both of us were perfectly happy as we were, but in some quarters there is still this ridiculous, old-fashioned stigma about having unmarried parents, and we didn't want Bill and Kit to suffer from that.

For the second time in my life, it was a low-key registry office wedding with no reception and no honeymoon. It was a happy day, though, and my best man was Mick the Greek, a security man that I had first met on *Mutiny!* By then he was more like a brother to me, as he still is today.

So the second half of the nineties were very much about family as my music career ticked over in the background. It was hard to believe but 1998 marked the twenty-fifth anniversary of 'Rock On', and Phonogram marked the occasion with a *Best of* collection. As I also released a new album, *Here We Are All Together*, I played not one but two tours that year.

The following year I put out *I Still Believe* – even if Radio One clearly no longer did! – and another fifty-four-date tour climaxed at the Albert Hall. Yet my major news event of 1999 saw me receive a summons from Buckingham Palace.

The New Year Honours List brought the news that I had been awarded an OBE, or made an Officer of the Order of the British Empire, for my music and charity work. This entitled me to use the letters after my name, although my kids soon made it clear that if I did anything so presumptuous, they would be referring to me, Brian Clough-style, as Old Big 'Ead.

You are allowed to take three people to your investiture, which was an incredibly hard decision, but I settled on Mum, Verity and Dan. Incredibly excited, my mum bought a new hat for the auspicious occasion, and it was one of the very few times I had ever seen Danny suited and booted.

We felt on top of the world as we drove into the palace grounds on the big day. They say pride comes before a fall, though, and my elation was temporarily punctured when an attendant took one look at me driving the car and asked if I was there to drop somebody off.

Her Majesty the Queen herself was giving out the gongs that day, rather than the Prince of Wales who sometimes stands in, and before the ceremony I mingled with the other lucky OBE recipients. They were a fascinating and talented bunch, from senior medics who had cured fatal diseases to architects who had designed life-saving third world dams, and to me their achievements all seemed so much more worthy than mine.

When the time came we filed into a large state room and I waited nervously to renew my acquaintance with HRH. As my name was called, I stepped forward and bowed my head before the Queen.

She took my hand, shook it and at the same time pushed it away, which apparently she has to do as often people are so awestruck to meet her that their brain freezes and they cling on to her hand for ages, gawping and pumping her arm furiously.

'The VSO is a marvellous organisation and you fully deserve this,' she told me as she pinned my OBE on me. Oddly enough, although it had been awarded for my charity work *and* my music, she didn't say a word about the latter. It was almost enough to make you think that she hadn't got any of my albums.

It had been a fantastic day, and for a patriotic man and a royalist like me it had been incredibly special. Mum, Verity, Dan and I posed for family portraits in the Buckingham Palace grounds afterwards and they all looked as proud as I felt.

I might have been moving in the highest of social circles that day but you never forget your roots and when Britain's Gypsy Council asked me to become its patron soon afterwards, I was honoured to accept. The Council is a body that seeks to improve people's understanding of the travelling community, which I think is a very worthy aim. To this end, they made a video in which I met and chatted with some Romany gypsies, sang a few songs with them around a campfire and poked around a traditional caravan.

Even today, when prejudices such as homophobia and racism have largely been eradicated, there is still far too much negative feeling towards gypsies, especially in Eastern Europe, where they suffer terrible persecution. Even here, people will regularly toss 'pikey' and 'tatter' about as casual insults.

I won't pretend I am steeped in gypsy life and lore nowadays but I will always feel closeness with that community. When the Dale Farm furore kicked off last year, the *Daily Mail* called me for 'my reaction'. I didn't give one: it was far too big a topic to be captured in a glib soundbite. I just agree with what my mum always said: 'A land without gypsies is a land without freedom.'

I also furthered the gypsy cause, or maybe set it back, in 2000 when I played a kind-hearted traveller in ITV rural cop drama *Heartbeat*. It was fun, but in truth the main reason that I did it was that it was one of my mum's favourite shows.

Life in the new millennium carried on ticking along. In 2001 I made an album called *Wonderful* and Mel Bush lined up one of his fifty-date tours: it is hugely to Mel's credit that he always thought outside of the usual 'handful of big cities' itineraries. Even more excitingly, along came another of those rite-of-passage moments as one of my children got married.

Verity's big day was held in a castle in the West Country. It was a gorgeous sunny winter's day and special from the outset. Your daughter's wedding day is such a big deal and you want it to be so perfect that inevitably you get nervous, and I sweated long and hard over my father-of-the-bride speech.

Maybe because songs have always come more easily to me than speeches, I also hired a string quartet and sang her a song I had written years ago called 'Verity'. It was actually the B-side of 'A Winter's Tale' and quotes a line of Byron: '*You are the friend to whom the shadows of far years extend.*' Everybody was in tears – including me, trying to sing the bleeding song.

A year later, Verity presented me with my first grandchild. Josef was a beautiful little boy and I learned something very interesting. Becoming a father is a wonderful thing with big responsibilities. Becoming a grandfather is a wonderful thing with much less in the way of responsibility and, whisper it soft, may even be more fun.

Around 2002, Carlotta, the boys, my mum and I moved down to Guildford, in Surrey. It was a nice big old rambling house and Bill and Kit had the top floor, which meant that their teenage fights could start there before carrying on right through the house and into the garden.

My life of semi-retirement continued as I made one album per year: *Forever* in 2002, *Sunset* in 2003 and *It's Gonna Be Alright* in 2004. With Danny producing the albums in my studio down in the basement and me self-releasing them on my Lamplight label then going out on tour, I had effectively turned myself into a small cottage industry.

I had needed a break, and it had been great, but now I felt ready to get back in the game. I began to pay closer attention to the work offers that Mel was fielding and decided to return to the theatre when I was asked to take part in a musical called *Boogie Nights 2* in 2004.

Following on from a production called *Boogie Nights* that had been based around the music of the seventies and had toured for months, *Boogie Nights 2* was what is today termed a jukebox musical featuring hits from the eighties. I quickly formed a close friendship with its very talented writer, Jon Conway.

I played St Peter, the narrator and overseer of proceedings, and we opened in Bromley in August. The play was not a big stretch or too demanding in terms of the acting and singing it required from me, but, to put it in its simplest terms, it felt good to be back.

Another offer came my way and I took two months off in June and July 2005 for a new departure for me: a multi-artist tour. The *Once in a Lifetime* tour of UK arenas featured some fellow artists who had hit big in the seventies in David Cassidy, Bay City Rollers singer Les McKeown and the Osmonds.

When Mel first told me about this nostalgia-fest I was reluctant to be involved and probably a little snobby, but I am glad that I changed my mind because it was a great experience and turned out to be a celebration of a generation. The arenas were packed with forty- to sixty-year-olds every night as each artist played their own set and joyously relived their musical glory days.

I hadn't known any of them first time around but the Osmonds were lovely while Les was also friendly enough. David Cassidy seemed to have a few issues, however. He was always courteous to me, but became a little vexed when I declined to swap places on the bill.

David was following me and going on last. Theoretically this should have been the best slot but he was not so keen, and while I hate to be immodest, it might have been because I was going down well and proving a hard act to follow. I didn't want to swap for a very practical reason: as the penultimate artist, I could get home earlier.

Things came to a head in Belfast, a city that has always loved me because I was one of the few artists to tour there regularly during the Troubles of the seventies. I went down great, and after a short interval, a hacked-off David arrived to woo the audience with a killer opening remark: 'Here we go for another night in a godforsaken city!' What a charmer.

After *Once in a Lifetime*, I was back on the road with *Boogie Nights 2*, finishing up with a three-month season in the north's party capital of Blackpool. That was great fun, particularly when I rented a house in the slightly more genteel Lytham St Annes just up the road.

On the music front, a guy called Bob Stanley from a band named St Etienne got in touch to ask me to be part of a concept album they were putting together called *Tales from Turnpike House*. I liked the central idea of the songs depicting different characters all living in a London block of flats and did a lovely spoken-word piece called 'Bedfordshire' with one of their kids.

In 2006 *EastEnders* briefly entered my life for the first time. My mum religiously watched the soap's Sunday omnibus edition in Guildford every weekend, and when I told her that I had provisionally agreed to do a three-week stint playing Jack Edwards, the father of Holly, she was the most excited she had been since I went on *Heartbeat*.

When I met the *EastEnders* producers, however, it became clear that they would need me for far longer than the three weeks I could spare, and also the character didn't particularly grab me, so I politely dropped out. I guess sometimes in life things just don't happen until they're ready.

Instead, I returned to the West End stage doing four months in a musical version of the *Footloose* movie and also made another album with Danny down in the basement studio, *Beautiful Day*. Mel must have been losing his touch when he booked me the tour for that one: I only did forty-eight dates.

We all needed a family holiday to recharge our batteries and we headed to Cuba so I could re-indulge my fascination with Latin America. As I was walking along the beach my phone rang. It was Sir Andrew Lloyd Webber.

'I'd like you to play George in *Aspects of Love*,' he told me.

Flattered to be asked I promised him I would read the script as soon as I returned to England. It seemed a little straight for my tastes, but when I met with director Nikolai Foster I warmed to him straight away and agreed to be involved.

My semi-retirement was clearly over, and as 2007 dawned I felt that my career was getting back on track and everything was reasonably rosy in my garden. However, something was about to happen that would absolutely knock me sideways.

24

THE TINKER COMES TO TOWN

Dolly had always been in rude health. My mother might have been eighty-two in early 2007 but she was still sprightly, active and never needed to see a doctor. So when Carlotta called me while I was on tour to say Mum had gone into hospital for a minor operation on a badly swollen knee, initially I wasn't worried.

I spoke to her at the Royal Surrey County Hospital in Guildford, where she sounded fine, and arranged to go and see her the next day. Arriving at the Royal Surrey, I made my way to her ward, but when I scanned the room, I couldn't see her anywhere.

'Where is Mrs Cook?' I asked a nurse.

'Oh, she has got MRSA,' I was told.

'That's bad, isn't it?' I asked, shocked.

'Well, we have antibiotics for it.'

Having gone in for a routine knee operation that should have seen her discharged the following day, Mum had picked up one of the deadly MRSA bugs that haunt hospitals, which always strikes me as bitterly ironic as they are the places that people go to in order to get better. She had been quarantined in her own room, and when I saw her I was shocked by how ill she looked.

Mum had always been a fighter, just like Dad, and managed to beat the MRSA, but then she contracted another awful strain of hospital-related infection. When she was still there after two weeks and getting no better, I confronted one of her consultants.

'This is terrible,' I told him. 'This lady has never taken as much as a Lemsip in her life. She came in here for a simple operation and basically you are killing her.'

'Mr Essex, hospitals are *very* dangerous places,' the consultant informed me, in an unpleasantly patronising and supercilious manner. I am not a violent man, but it took all of my control not to knock him out.

I became a regular at the Royal Surrey County Hospital over the ensuing days, during which time Mum steadily became worse and worse. She was transferred to a hospital in Sutton and after two further months of ineffective treatment she was put on a kidney machine. By this point she could hardly communicate. She died on 10 May 2007.

It is hard enough to bear the loss of a beloved parent without also knowing that it should never have happened. Apart from a couple of minor falls, my mum had been in great shape when she was admitted to hospital. I think the NHS is one of Britain's great institutions but it badly let my mum down. In fact, if I am being brutally honest, it killed her.

The burial service was as moving as saying goodbye to your wonderful mum who should still be with you could be, and she was buried next to my dad in East London Cemetery, reunited in death with the man who had been her life. I wondered about taking action against the NHS but in the end decided there was nothing I could do. It was best to draw a line under the tragedy.

Carlotta was hugely supportive as I grieved for my mum, which says so much about her as a person because we had recently decided to split.

The two of us had now been together for more than twenty years and while we were still incredibly close, the spark of romance had died. With a sense of sadness but knowing it was the right thing to do, we began divorce proceedings and Carlotta returned to America. Kit went with her; Bill stayed in the UK.

With such intense upheaval in my personal life, it was a relief to have *Aspects of Love* to throw myself into. As he had at our initial meeting, Nikolai Foster hugely impressed me. Precise, imaginative and hugely dedicated, he was one of the best directors I had ever worked with.

Aspects of Love is quite risqué by Andrew Lloyd Webber standards, with everybody making love to everybody else. My character, George, was married and also had a mistress, but what I liked most about the production was playing somebody my age and being the drama's elderly statesman figure rather than running around still trying to be a juvenile lead like mutton dressed as lamb. It was something new for me and as we toured the length of Britain for more than six months, I enjoyed it.

As the run came to an end, I realised that *Boogie Nights 2* and *Aspects* had whetted my appetite for musical theatre again. Now, though, I wanted to do something with depth that had more meaning for me personally.

There are certain themes that have reappeared throughout my career and the singular allure of fairgrounds, with their juxtaposition of fun and imminent violence, is one of them. An idea took root: why not write a musical using my own songs that was rooted in this fertile ground?

After all, I already had a perfectly good title: *All the Fun of the Fair*. It had been ideal for my concept album back in 1975 and it worked just as well now. Gripped by the heady excitement of a compelling, self-generated new project, I set to work.

Boogie Nights writer Jon Conway shared my enthusiasm for the idea and quickly came on board as my co-writer. As we plotted out a storyline, I realised how adroitly my songs could weave into the narrative, and a script came together remarkably quickly.

I knew that *All the Fun of the Fair* would stand or fall on the strength of this script. I was fairly confident that people would relate to the songs, as they had done previously when they had made them hits, but we needed a strong backdrop and a good reason to sing them.

It was also important that the storyline was not horribly corny. I knew the pitfalls of the musical genre and how awful they can be when not done well. Abba's *Mamma Mia!* has run forever in the West End and you can't argue with success but the script is just a way of getting from hit to hit. We wanted to integrate the songs and story into one coherent, dramatic whole.

I decided to play the musical's patriarch, a strong but stubborn fairground owner and widower whose wife had died in tragic circumstances. His tight-knit family of workers include his own headstrong son and a sexy fortune-telling gypsy, and while I will not spoil *All the Fun of the Fair* for anyone who still wants to see it, let's just say it does not take the easy, fairytale-ending option. There is something dark at its core.

The first travelling man who had ever seized my imagination was my mum's Uncle Levi, the twinkling-eyed gypsy and romantic philosopher who had transfixed me as a boy picking hops in Kent. I named my character Levi Lee in his honour.

Alan Darlow, a very good friend for nearly twenty years, agreed to be the producer and proved incredibly understanding. I had only one director in mind and once Jon and I were happy with the script, I showed it to Nikolai Foster. He loved it, and my *All the Fun of the Fair* dream team was in place. Now it was time to cast it.

Jon and I sat in on the auditions, although Nikolai made the final decisions. The wonderful Louise English blew us all away and was clearly perfect for the hot-blooded, Tarot-reading Gypsy Rosa. After beginning her career as a member of Pan's People on *Top of the Pops*, Louise had since become a very renowned and respected West End leading lady.

I also took note of a very attractive Welsh actress called Susan Hallam-Wright who auditioned well and ended up playing the part of Sally.

Under Nikolai's strong tutelage, the production came together quickly and excitingly, on a great dynamic fairground set that featured dodgem cars and even a wall of death. The dramatic plot worked, and Jon and I were relieved that the songs seemed to merge into the storyline naturally and organically.

We opened in September 2008 with a week at the Churchill Theatre in Bromley. The first-night nerves were jangling, as they should be, but the audience were hugely appreciative and I felt proud to see my conceptual vision become reality.

Queen guitarist Brian May came to the first night and was very complimentary afterwards. I was grateful, especially as I had seen their band musical, *We Will Rock You*, and while the music was unquestionably wonderful, I'd found the story a bit daft. There again, it has now been running for ten years, so what do I know?

We took *All the Fun of the Fair* out on tour and as we rolled through Darlington, Brighton and Manchester, the reviews were great everywhere we went as critics appreciated we were trying to do something different with the often-corny musical format.

Susan and I started as a friendship and fairly quickly became something more. I found Susan a caring and loving person who shares my opinion on the importance of friends and family in life. We hung out more and more and very soon became inseparable.

Of course, there is a big age difference between us – but that didn't bother us, and never has. Age really is just a number and luckily Susan is wise and mature beyond her years. On most issues, I generally find she has an older head on her shoulders than I do.

Being together made touring *All the Fun of the Fair* even more enjoyable and we rolled on into summer 2009. I must have got a taste for life on the road again, because after it finished I went almost straight into a series of rock shows that we called *The Secret Tour*.

This led up to Christmas, which had even greater cause for celebration than usual as Susan and I got engaged. It's true what they say: when you know, you know.

Spring 2010 saw the start of a six-month run of *All the Fun of the Fair* at the Garrick Theatre in the West End. With Nikolai Foster unavailable, a new director took over in David Gilmore, and the cast also underwent a bit of a reshuffle.

Susan auditioned before David for a bigger role in the production. I stayed well out of it because it was his decision and not really my business, but even so I was delighted and very proud when she got the part of Mary, the lovelorn daughter of Louise English's fiery Gypsy Rosa.

The notoriously hard-to-please London theatre critics are often very hard on musicals as a genre, but their pens left *All the Fun of the Fair* relatively unscathed, with the *Daily Telegraph*'s write-up being typical:

> *The show has that essential but often elusive quality for any musical – heart ... it becomes genuinely touching, and it is a pleasure to watch a West End production that puts its faith in its performers rather than hi-tech special effects.*

There is often a sense of anti-climax when a major show comes to an end but there was no danger of that when we reached the end of our Garrick run. I had plenty to look forward to. On 20 September 2010, Susan and I got married.

We did so in style and it was an absolutely wonderful day. We went up to Susan's home area and held the wedding in a nineteenth-century Church of Wales church called St Cross in the tiny village of Tal-y-bont near Bangor. Susan's *Taid* (grandfather) was once the Archdeacon of Bangor.

We had an evening reception at a hotel on Anglesey and while the setting was impressive, the event certainly wasn't stuffy: our first dance as a married couple was a Hokey-Cokey. My best man and best friend Mick the Greek's wedding speech was hilarious. Occasionally, it was even funny when he meant it to be.

Our honeymoon in the Seychelles was everything we could have hoped for and as 2011 dawned we seemed set fair for a nicely enjoyable and undemanding year. I felt there was scope to make *All the Fun of the Fair* better still and decided to take it out on another regional tour, with Nikolai Foster back in the director's chair. And work-wise, that would be pretty much all that the year held for me. I could take it easy.

Or so I thought.

25

YOU CAN PUT THE BOY
INTO THE EAST END...

Nothing goes on for ever and in 2011 one of my longest working relationships came to an end as Mel Bush and I went our separate ways. It had been thirty-seven years since he had promoted my first live tour but things had changed and I simply felt that I didn't need a manager any more. It was purely a business decision: I still love Mel like a brother, and always will.

I also hired a new agent, a lovely woman named Maxine Hoffman at Curtis Brown, who soon called me with an intriguing proposition. The producers of *EastEnders* had been in touch: would I be interested in discussing a hefty new role?

One of my first thoughts was that Derek would have certainly advised me against it. He would have regarded a soap as very lowest-common-denominator TV, but I watched *EastEnders* every now and then and it appeared to me these days to be an extremely viable and credible continuing drama with a terrific pool of actors.

In any case, what harm could a meeting do? I warily agreed to an exploratory chat.

I went into the meeting with a completely open mind. It was obviously flattering to be considered for such a major series that plays such a big role in so many people's lives but also I knew there would be a price to pay. I would be going into a main role in an incredibly high-profile show, with all that that entailed. In all honesty, I was happy with my life of semi-anonymity and my comfortable existence. It would take a lot for me to agree to jolt myself out of it.

The *EastEnders* producers came up with a lot. As we settled down to the first of a string of meetings, they told me their ideas for the character of Eddie Moon, the father figure of one of those extended East End families that tend to populate Albert Square. The uncle of Walford mainstay Alfie Moon, played by Shane Richie, Eddie would arrive in the square and cause emotional mayhem.

Eddie would have complex relationships with his three sons, Michael, Tyler and Anthony, and an alluring dark past. Over the ensuing weeks it would be revealed that his first wife, Maggie, had killed herself in mysterious circumstances. The eldest son, Michael, has always blamed Eddie for this death and refused to forgive him.

I liked the sound of Eddie from the start and we began to flesh out possibilities. Rather than presenting me with a fully formed character as a *fait accompli*, the producers and writers were very receptive to my ideas and willing to let me shape his story. This was starting to sound like an offer I couldn't refuse.

I sat in a big room with the writers and we sketched out ideas. Eddie was to arrive in the square as an antiques dealer. One of his sons, Tyler, was to be a boxer, and the producers wanted Eddie to hate boxing, but I demurred: 'No! He's an

East Ender, and if that is what his lad wants to do, he will support him.'

As the plotlines developed I was getting more and more hooked on Eddie, and the idea of his ex-wife's suicide being slowly and poignantly revealed as the weeks went by seemed to have huge dramatic potential. It took me about three weeks to decide, but eventually I took the plunge. OK. I was on board.

Also playing around my mind was the thought of how much my mum would have loved me doing *EastEnders*. I remembered the Sundays in Guildford when I would hear the door to her room open as regular as clockwork at two in the afternoon as she came out to watch the omnibus edition. I would have given anything for her to still be around to see me in it.

We agreed on a five-month contract. The producers would have liked me for longer but it seemed a decent commitment to me, and a lot can happen in a TV series in five months. We set a provisional date of me arriving on screen on 3 June, meaning I would begin rehearsals a few weeks earlier.

The character of Eddie Moon was a bit of a slow burner and so the first scripts that began arriving through the post were not too onerous. They were easing me in gently, so I felt relatively prepared when I turned up for my first day of rehearsals at Elstree.

That didn't mean that it wasn't intimidating. *EastEnders* is a big show to walk into and on my first day I realised how much the cast is one big tightly knit family. Making the programme is clearly a very intense and pressurised experience that brings everyone close together, and they all look out for each other.

So I was nervous, and they were probably just as apprehensive about me. I was joining the cast as a sort-of big name known for a lot of other things besides acting, and I am sure they wondered just what they would get and how committed I would be. They needed to know I could walk and talk at the same time: as in everything, respect had to be earned.

For the first few days, my main problem was getting people's names right. I had obviously been watching *EastEnders* closely to bone up but this meant that I now automatically thought of everyone by their character's names. I hate to think how many times in my first week I said, 'Hello, Jack! Er, I mean Scott…'

Everyone made me very welcome but initially I was pretty naïve about how everything worked. In my first week, I worked with two different directors. Finding one a little easier than the other, I went to see the producer and told him: 'I'll do all my scenes with the first director, please.'

He looked at me blankly, uncomprehendingly and possibly rather pityingly, and the penny dropped. That really is not how it works. *EastEnders* is such a fast and furious process that each episode features not just different cast members, but a different crew and director. Whoever is there, you just get on with it.

The intensity was unlike anything I had ever worked on before and it took me two or three weeks to get used to the show's rhythms. But everyone in *EastEnders* had been the new boy once and knew what it was like, so they helped me through, and before long I found I was enjoying it.

The punishing hours were difficult. The routine was that I had to be out of bed at 5 a.m. to be on set in Borehamwood by

7.30. I may not have had to clock in like I did at Plessey's, but there were similarities. Some days certainly felt like piecework. The shoots would go on until they were done. When you were not shooting, you were in your dressing room, cramming lines.

The BBC did a good job of building up Eddie's arrival, showing short teasers between other programmes, so by the time of my on-screen debut there was a nice sense of anticipation. There was certainly a buzz when I came to film the moment that I came out of Walford station, collared a passing postie and asked him the way to Albert Square.

After my first scene had aired, I immediately became aware of the power of *EastEnders* and the place that it occupies in the national psyche. For the first time in years, I was turning heads in the street again. I probably signed more autographs in two weeks than I had in two years. Eddie Moon was clearly going to be as big as I had suspected, and more so.

Luckily, most people seemed to like Eddie. The main reaction I attracted seemed to be a lot like the one Shane Richie gets, where everyone just wants to shake your hand and talk to you like their best mate. It's different if you play a bit of a villain, like Steve McFadden playing Phil Mitchell: I think generally people are scared to go anywhere near him.

As I was eased in and became used to the show's dementedly demanding schedules, the writers started to up my workload. Eddie started to get some seriously heavy storylines. There was love interest, first with Lindsey Coulson as Carol and then with Zöe Lucker as Vanessa; his valuable antiques stock was burned to a crisp in mysterious circumstances.

Yet mostly Eddie Moon is all about his tortured and torturous relationships with his sons and his cryptic, mysterious past. As the weeks went by, the scriptwriters mercilessly ratcheted up the tension, particularly between Eddie and his twisted eldest son Michael, a man possessed of an Oedipal wish to destroy his father.

Steve John Shepherd, who plays Michael, and I hit it off great from the outset and it was just as well, because we had to spend an insane amount of time together. On a film set, if you get through two or three pages of dialogue in a day, you generally consider it a good day. Before one shoot of *EastEnders*, Steve and I were confronted with thirty-eight pages.

It was heavyweight stuff, as well. We weren't just popping into the Queen Vic for a pint. The plot was that having discovered his mother's body after her suicide as a boy, Michael had always blamed his absentee father Eddie for her death. Now my son was to embark on an evil Machiavellian plot to destroy me. This was *King Lear* or *Macbeth* relocated to Walford.

In scenes brilliantly devised in inspired script meetings, Michael arranged for his aspiring-boxer half-brother, Tyler, to fight a psychopath that he knew would maim him, or worse; attempted to fool the credulous youngest brother, Anthony, into betting and losing all of Eddie's money on the bout; and blackmailed Vanessa into sabotaging Eddie's relationship with Carol. He needed to break his dad's heart as he felt Eddie had broken his.

These were powerful, overwhelming scripts to read, let alone to act, and inevitably I became close not only to Steve but also to Tony Discipline as Tyler and Matt Lapinskas as Anthony. When we filmed the unlicensed boxing match where Tyler's opponent leaves him in a coma and Eddie's world begins to fall apart, you could cut the atmosphere on set with a knife.

Yet there was more to come. *EastEnders* executive producer Brian Kirkwood had asked when I joined the series if I would be OK with a storyline that gave Eddie a secret Downs Syndrome son, Craig. Obviously I was, which enabled the Moon family tragedy to take another unexpected twist.

In a tremendous pair of episodes, Eddie first finally convinced Michael that he was not directly to blame for his mother's death, and then introduced him to Craig, played by the excellent actor Elliott Rosen. As Michael realised that his dad was flawed but essentially a decent man, the warring father and son reconciled emotionally.

But this is *EastEnders*. Things are never that simple. Eddie was soon to learn the full horror of Michael's plan, and realise that his malign son would have been willing to let Tyler die to gain revenge over his father. Thus enlightened, Eddie resolves that there is only one outcome to this situation: he must destroy the son who strove to destroy him.

My final episode of *EastEnders* contained some of the hardest and most demanding scenes I have ever had to film. Steve, Tony, Matt and I were fully caught up in the dark psychodrama that was unfolding. It was electric. Even Derek would surely have admitted that the scene where the other Moons disowned the broken, sobbing Michael would not have been out of place on the stage of the National Theatre or Shakespeare's Globe.

We were all in tears. When Eddie uttered the fateful words to Michael, 'Don't call me dad – because you're not my son anymore!', my problem wasn't making myself cry, as the script required; it was trying to stop.

The scriptwriters did at least manage to magic some kind of happy ending out of this human horror show as my final scene saw Eddie collect Craig from his carers and leave with his no-longer-secret son to begin a new life in Spain. With a farewell wave, Eddie Moon drove out of Walford never to return – or will he?

It's a very good question. If I had to answer it now, as I write, I would say 'No'. *EastEnders* was a fantastic adventure for me and I feel privileged to have had it. The public reaction to me was very warm, for which I am grateful, and the producers seem keen for me to go back. So why am I reluctant?

I guess there are two reasons. Firstly, after the seismic events that exploded around Eddie before he left, I don't see where the character would go next. I love how Eddie appeared in the show, grabbed it by the neck, shook it and vanished off into the sunset. How do you follow that?

Secondly, and just as importantly, I don't want to get typecast and become synonymous with one character. I did five months on the biggest TV show in Britain, it was brilliant, and at the end of it I am still David Essex – just about – in a lot of people's eyes. Even now, though, as I walk down the street, I still get the odd person saying, 'Hello, Eddie – I thought you were in Spain!'

Indeed, I have had some very funny encounters lately. Just before Christmas 2011, I was back in my old stamping ground of the East End, in Mile End. I had just got out of my car when a young kid aged about thirteen on a mountain bike rode past me. He half-clocked me, did a cartoon double-take, and swerved back for another look.

''Ere, aren't you Eddie Moon?' he inquired.

'I am, yes,' I assured him.

'Ah, Eddie Moon, man!' he exploded with delight. 'You're wicked! I think you're the best actor. You know what you should be doing, don't you?'

'What's that?' I asked.

'You should be doing films with that Robert De Niro, yeah? Because you're f****** great, man!'

I thanked him kindly, returned his broad beam and we shared a little chitchat as he attempted to pump me for information on my character's intentions and future plans.

'When are you going back, man? I ain't seen you in it for a while. When you going back?'

I lowered my voice and told him conspiratorially that I'm not sure and I'm not allowed to say anyway and he nodded, satisfied with my answer, and held up his hand for a high-five.

'Nice to meet you, Eddie!' he yelled over his shoulder as he pedalled off. 'Safe!'

I love meetings like that and it's great to be appreciated but I guess if I went back to *EastEnders*, I would fully turn into Eddie Moon. There are worse things to be – but I don't think it's me.

So after Eddie exited stage left and the dust settled, Susan and I returned to the road late in 2011 with *All the Fun of the*

Fair. With Nikolai Foster back in the director's chair, we have re-proved the old showbiz adage that a musical is not written, it is re-written by improving the script and honing the story until I think what we have now is close to a definitive version.

Late last year we did a week at the Theatre Royal in Bath. I caught a nasty viral infection and for the first time in my career – after almost fifty years – I had to admit defeat and miss a gig. As the tannoy announced that my very capable understudy, David Burrows, would play Levi Lee, some of the audience groaned and booed.

My mind went back forty-two years to the London Palladium and an identical audience reaction to the news that Tommy Steele was unwell and they would be forced to watch a young unknown named David Essex as Dick Whittington. I felt for poor David but he rose to the occasion, just as I had done in 1969. It is what we actors do.

In Bath I sat in the audience and watched *All the Fun of the Fair* unfold, for once not part of the proceedings, and I was proud of it. This was my idea, I told myself quietly, I made it happen, and now people enjoy it up and down the land. Even though I felt horribly ill, I relished the moment.

That is rare for me. Throughout a career that's had many highs – and some lows as well – I have never properly appreciated my successes. Even when I have had record-breaking stage shows, or box-office hit films, or been number one on the pop chart, I've always been focused on the next thing and impatient to move on to a new project. I've always tried to live tomorrow today.

Well, I don't have so many tomorrows left now, so it might be time for a change of attitude. It might be time to take more pleasure in my success and in the moment. I have got a very charmed life right now and a lot to appreciate.

My four children are all doing great and doing what they want to in this world. Verity is a wonderful mum to eight-year-old Josef and two-year-old Daisy and works with my son Danny's wife as my two new personal assistants.

Danny is a music producer, his business partner Dave Needham is a member of my live band, and they produce both my albums and those of other artists. Kit is in the States, writing songs and doing some recordings.

Bill is a gifted actor and has just completed his first feature film, *Gajengi Boy*: it's a gypsy phrase for 'half-breed'. I have a small cameo role in the movie and am writing the score, and while I was on the set, the director of photography, Mikolaj Jaroszewicz, a man with an Oscar nomination to his name, told me that Billy has an amazing presence and may be the future of British film. That was a proud moment.

Between them, my kids have given me four brilliant grandkids in Josef, Daisy, George and David, and spending time with them is the most natural and precious pleasure in the world. And I am lucky that in my lovely wife, Susan, I have somebody bighearted and wonderful enough to enjoy them as much as I do.

None of this means I am going to start taking things easy. As I write, I am considering offers to turn *All the Fun of the Fair* into a film. I'm writing *Che*, a musical based around the life of Che Guevara. I've dreamt up a one-person play called *Tramp* about a man who has lived hard and well. I've started writing poetry (yes, really!) and I still can't imagine a time when I'm not making records and touring.

So, who knows what twists and turns lie ahead? Maybe I will return to *EastEnders* at some point after all. As the old saying goes: never say never. But for now, I think I am probably Over the Moon.

INDEX

in *The Adventures of Robinson
Crusoe* 261–2
Cooper, Ray 119, 145
Coulson, Lindsey 297
Covington, Julie 101, 108, 111, 126,
172, 176
Cox, Harvey 101
Crane, Richard 221
Cuba 284
Cukor, George 180
Cumberland Road 25–6
Curtis Brown 293

Daily Mail (newspaper) 79, 280
Daily Mirror (newspaper) 79
Daily Telegraph (newspaper) 291
Daisy (David's granddaughter) 303
Darlow, Alan 289
Davey, Colin 129, 154
Davey Jones and the Locker 72
Deayton, Angus 276
Defoe, Daniel 260, 261
Delfont, Bernard 88
Delhi 232–3
Des Longchamps, Ines 141–2, 144
DeSouza, Barry 119
Diana, Princess of Wales 196
Dick, John 22
Diddley, Bo 215
Dietrich, Marlene 166
Digance, Richard 210
Discipline, Tony 299
Dockland Settlement nursery school
9, 11
Dolby, Thomas 210
Driscoll, Julie 73
Dubrovnik 256
Dudley, William 225–6
Duncan, Peter 137
Dunlop, Frank 203–4
Dylan, Bob 147, 179

East Ham Odeon 148–51
Edmunds, Dave 137
Eel Pie Island 72
Eileen (David's Cousin) 42
El Grotto club 71, 73, 87

El Morocco club 85
Elizabeth II 241–2, 278–9
Ellen, Aunt 5, 6
English, Louise 289, 291
Equity 68
Essex, David
acting career
All Coppers Are (film) 89
All the Fun of the Fair (musical)
288–92, 301–3
American success 131–2
Aspects of Love (musical) 284,
287
Assault (film) 89, 224
Boogie Nights 2 (musical)
281–2, 283, 287
Carry On Henry (film) 2, 89,
116
Childe Byron (play) 202–5
Cinderella (pantomime) 93, 95,
96, 97
Dick Whittington (pantomime)
90–3, 167, 302
EastEnders (TV soap) 1, 2,
283, 293–301, 304
Evita (as Che Guevara) 2,
176–81, 242, 256, 272
Footloose (musical) 283
Godspell (as Jesus) (musical) 1,
99–114, 116, 118, 121–8,
177, 247
Heartbeat (TV drama) 280, 283
Mutiny! (musical) 221–32,
260–1, 277
Oh, Kay! (musical) 81–2
She Stoops to Conquer (play)
263–6, 268–9
Shogun Mayeda (film) 255–60
Silver Dream Racer (film) 182,
183–5, 187–8
Smashing Time (film) 88
Stardust (film) 2, 128, 135–43,
145–7, 149, 165, 182, 272
That'll Be the Day (film) 2,
113–18, 121–2, 126, 128–30,
134–6, 139, 142–3, 147, 160,
182, 272

307